Bible Translating as a Loyal Activity

"This is a profound book, a must read for anyone who is interested in Bible translation, whether that interest be directing them to translate or to support translation projects. Sadly, many translation projects are earnestly designed, engaged in, and supported without sufficient background knowledge. The tragic result is that all too many translations end up either sitting on shelves or are ignored, simply because they are not understandable or are alien sounding. Dr. Houston unpacks for the uninitiated how translations can avoid this tragic demise and actively demonstrate loyalty and faithfulness to the Lord, to the Scripture, and to the target audience, whom the Lord dearly loves and for whom he died."

—PATRICK KRAYER, affiliate assistant professor,
Fuller Theological Seminary

"In this volume Tobias Houston advocates for an approach to Bible translation that moves beyond the traditional 'form versus function' debate to that of Skopos theory, whose goal is to achieve the purpose (*skopos*) set out in a translation brief between the translator and the receptor community. Houston's innovative and ambitious work will be useful both for those interested in the challenges of translation theory as well as those doing the practical work of Bible translation in diverse majority world cultures."

—MARK L. STRAUSS, university professor of New Testament,
Bethel University

"Bible translation is a complex act of communication that engages at least two, often very different, languages, cultures, times, and places. How can translators remain 'loyal' to all the factors involved? In this captivating book, Tobias Houston explores the salient issues and challenges from several interwoven perspectives. These include modern translation practice (e.g., 'Skopos theory'), an ancient guiding Mozambican metaphor ('beaded necklace'), and the foundational biblical notion of 'covenant loyalty' (*chesed*), which ensures bidirectional contextual fidelity as God's word is conveyed in oral and written form to another expectant people group."

—ERNST R. WENDLAND, ancient studies department,
Stellenbosch University

"While reading this book in a Samo village in Papua New Guinea, I am mindful of my fifty-plus years of translation engagement. Houston clearly lays out the theoretical and practical considerations that have thankfully changed. Remaining loyal to both, the focus must ethically reflect the entire translation context. May we ultimately be loyal to the intent of our God and the socio-linguistic needs of the people for whom the translation makes a difference in the way they live."

—R. Daniel Shaw, senior anthropology consultant, SIL International

Bible Translating as a Loyal Activity

A Model for Bible Translation
in the Majority World

↓

TOBIAS J. HOUSTON

FOREWORD BY
Andy Warren-Rothlin

WIPF & STOCK · Eugene, Oregon

BIBLE TRANSLATING AS A LOYAL ACTIVITY
A Model for Bible Translation in the Majority World

Copyright © 2025 Tobias J. Houston. All rights reserved. Except for brief quotations in critical publications or reviews, no part of this book may be reproduced in any manner without prior written permission from the publisher. Write: Permissions, Wipf and Stock Publishers, 199 W. 8th Ave., Suite 3, Eugene, OR 97401.

Wipf & Stock
An Imprint of Wipf and Stock Publishers
199 W. 8th Ave., Suite 3
Eugene, OR 97401

www.wipfandstock.com

PAPERBACK ISBN: 978-1-6667-7344-6
HARDCOVER ISBN: 978-1-6667-7345-3
EBOOK ISBN: 978-1-6667-7346-0

Scripture quotations marked (ESV) are from The ESV® Bible (The Holy Bible, English Standard Version®) © 2001 by Crossway, a publishing ministry of Good News Publishers. Used by permission. All rights reserved.

Scripture quotations marked (GNT) are from the Good News Translation in Today's English Version—Second Edition Copyright © 1992 by American Bible Society. Used by Permission.

Quotations designated (NET) are from the NET Bible® copyright ©1996, 2019 by Biblical Studies Press, L.L.C. http://netbible.com All rights reserved. Scripture quoted by permission.

Scripture quotations marked (NIV) are taken from the Holy Bible, New International Version,® NIV.® Copyright © 1973, 1978, 1984, 2011 by Biblica, Inc.® Used by permission of Zondervan. All rights reserved worldwide. www.zondervan.com The "NIV" and "New International Version" are trademarks registered in the United States Patent and Trademark Office by Biblica, Inc.®

Scripture quotations marked (NLT) are taken from the Holy Bible, New Living Translation, copyright ©1996, 2004, 2015 by Tyndale House Foundation. Used by permission of Tyndale House Publishers, Carol Stream, Illinois 60188. All rights reserved.

Scripture quotations marked (NRSV) are from New Revised Standard Version Bible, copyright © 1989 National Council of the Churches of Christ in the United States of America. Used by permission. All rights reserved worldwide.

Scripture quotations marked (REB) are taken from the Revised English Bible, copyright © Cambridge University Press and Oxford University Press 1989. All rights reserved.

To my beloved Hezzy. The way your name sounds a bit like *ḥesed* is not lost on me. Thanks for your unwavering loyalty.

I will sing of loyalty and of justice; to you, O Lord, I will sing.
—Ps 101:1 (NRSV)

Contents

List of Maps and Illustrations ix
Foreword by Andy Warren-Rothlin xi
Acknowledgments xv
List of Abbreviations xvi

Introduction 1

1. **Bible Translating as a Purposeful Activity: Theoretical Foundations** 7
   Skopos Theory: A Functionalist Approach to Translation 9
   Criticisms of Functionalist Translation and Bringing in Loyalty 19
   Bible Translation Is Complex but Narrative Framing Helps 26

2. **Loyal Bible Translation as a Model for the Majority World** 34
   The Hebrew Word חֶסֶד (*Ḥesed*) in the Bible 41
   Ḥesed for Loyal Bible Translation 46
   Loyalty to the Source Text (Author) 54
   Loyalty to the Receptors (Audience) 65
   Bible Translation Among Muslims 70
   Loyal Bible Translation Is Radical 74
   Moving Forward with Loyal Bible Translation 80

3. **The Beaded Necklace Model for Loyal Bible Translation** 86
   Explaining the Beaded Necklace Model 88
   Introducing the Mozambican Yawo Beaded Necklace 95
   The Intended Function Is Clear When the "Beads" Are Known 97

x CONTENTS

    The Sociolinguistic "Bead" on the Necklace 99
    The Religious "Beads" 104
        The Yawo as Muslims 105
        The Yawo and African Traditional Religion 109
        Loyalty in Light of the Religious "Beads" 118
    The Historical "Bead" 121
        Setting the Scene: Early Christian Mission Among the Yawo 121
        The Historical Background to Ciyawo Bible Translations 127
        Loyalty in Light of the Historical "Bead" 133
    The Orality "Bead" 134
        Loyalty in Light of the Orality "Bead" 139
            A Literary-Based Approach: Pros and Cons 139
            An Orality-Based Approach: Pros and Cons 142
        Loyalty in Light of Both Islam and Orality 145
    The Organizational "Bead" 148

4. Loyal Bible Translation in Action and the Translation Covenant 156
    Examples from Loyally Translating Genesis 166
    Examples from Loyally Translating Exodus 170
    Examples from Loyally Translating Matthew 171
    Examples from Loyally Translating Psalms 174

Postscript 175

Bibliography 179

List of Maps and Illustrations

Figure 1: The Beaded Necklace Model   89

Figure 2: Map of Yawo Territory   96

Figure 3: Map of Survey Reference Points   101

Figure 4: Book Cover of Mozambican Ciyawo Genesis   165

Foreword

THIS CENTURY HAS SEEN a massive expansion in Bible translation practice. There is increased funding, a much more inclusive and diverse workforce, higher levels of technical expertise, and a much wider range of products in various media and engagement strategies. *Bible translation methodologies* now include working in clusters, secondary adaptations, oral Bible translation, sign language translation, and even the use of secular translation service providers. *Artificial intelligence* is also now being used in exegesis, secondary drafting, back translation, and quality assurance. *Bible translation principles*, too, have become more diverse, with the influence of secular translation studies, postcolonial values (affecting questions of ownership, use of foreign loanwords, etc.), theological and missiological considerations, and controversies, including questions of Muslim-idiom translation (MIT), divine familial terms (DFT), and Insider Movements (IMs). And all of this is set within the tension between missionaries' and funders' frequent preference for what is *faster* and *cheaper*, and churches' and consultants' concern for what is *better*.

This book brings together many of these issues in a fresh vision for Bible translation in our time. It brings together translation theory and practice, European literary translation studies, Mozambican Bible translation projects, general functional equivalence, and, more specifically, Muslim idiom translation, along with missional vision and accountability to local churches. It nicely expresses the encyclopedic approach to knowledge that is needed for this very interdisciplinary task! And it brings these various elements together in a distinctive way, expressing translation theory through two key concepts.

The concept around the Hebrew word *ḥesed*, "covenant loyalty," comes from the biblical source text. It is used here to re-express the principle of loyalty as known in functional translation studies. This may enable those of us working in Bible translation to see more clearly the spiritual dimension of a technical principle, and it allows the author to present a translation brief as something deeper and more relational—a translation *"covenant."*

The concept of a beaded necklace is used to express the frames of reference involved in articulating a translation's *skopos*. Particular "beads" are discussed here in detail—those most relevant to the situation of the Muslim-majority Yawo people in Mozambique. Readers are here encouraged to think of their own situations, with perhaps very different "beads" needing attention, such as different types of demographics, media, neurotype, disability, cultural influence, etc.

My friend Tobias is well qualified to perform this task, with his years of experience working with the Yawo people in Mozambique, his scholarly background in translation research in South Africa, his several publications, and his membership in the mission arm of the Baptist church in Australia. He has spent years developing his thinking in the context of practice, and here distils all of that into a guidebook for others treading similar paths. Noticeable at many points throughout the book is his special concern for Muslim readers of the Bible, reflecting his years of close engagement with the TAZI community hosted by the United Bible Societies.

As all the pieces of the puzzle come together, what strikes me most about this vision for Bible translation work is its *relationality*. Others may emphasize abstract notions of quality applied to physical Bible products (a sterile agenda that could surely be achieved by a machine!). But Tobias describes loyalty to a range of stakeholders, especially to the cultural owners of the receptor language, to their processes and people, their places and concepts of time, their culture and orature—loyalty to the context this new Bible translation will enter as a beneficent cultural product, as "good news." His vision for translation, grounded of course in loyalty to the source text and its own stakeholders (from the Prophets and Apostles to today's churches!) honors the various "beads" that make up the identity of a translation's recipients. Others may regrettably still, in their zealous loyalty to (their own cultural reading of) the source text, weaponize Bible translation in the service of a cultural Christendom, subjugating people's words, idioms, literary forms, and cultural concepts to strange imports from European languages and cultures. But Loyal Bible Translation does the opposite, engaging with communities and their own vision for the place that their Bible translation should have in the history of their people. Only in this way can our work do justice both to our hearers, for whom Christ died, and to the message, made flesh in Christ himself.

As you read this book, I trust you will find many things that are new, as well as many things that are just newly expressed. But most importantly, I think we can find a fresh global vision for what Bible translation can be and how it can be articulated—to supporters and funders, to practitioners (translators, exegetes, consultants), and most importantly to the communities (both Christian and non-Christian) that Bible translations serve.

Andy Warren-Rothlin
Global Translation Consultant, United Bible Societies
Professor of Hebrew, Theological College of Northern Nigeria

Acknowledgments

WRITING THE ACKNOWLEDGMENTS WOULDN'T be complete without a first nod to my family. They're the ones who've had to put up with this book the most. Disappearing into my cave of an office felt like stepping through the wardrobe into Narnia, with time losing all sense of normality (but without Mr. Tumnus and Aslan). I would go in to write and then, before I knew it, I'd emerge bleary-eyed in a brain fog to see that I'd missed lunch or that night had already come. So, thank you to my wife, Heather, and to my wonderful children, Elijah, Rachel, and Lydia—thank you for your patience with me as I've written this book.

I also would like to thank a range of different people who have been part of forming who I am today. Thanks to my high-school English teacher for not believing in me—you unwittingly motivated me to do better; thanks to Dr. Jim Harrison, formerly of Wesley Institute and now with Sydney College of Divinity, who did believe in me and gave me a chance I might not have deserved; thanks to our fantastic supporters who make it possible for me and my family to be in Mozambique working in Bible translation; thanks to my Mozambican colleagues for showing me so much about who you are; thanks to Dr. Andy Warren-Rothlin and Dr. Sameh Hanna for your constructive criticism on drafts of this book—I may not have taken all of your excellent suggestions on board, and so for that failing, the responsibility for any remaining errors and deficiencies remains entirely on me; thanks to my dear friends Agatha, Athena, and Beatrix for your kind faithfulness; and thanks to Mum and Dad for the most loyal support I could hope for.

List of Abbreviations

ATR—African Traditional Religion
BPT— A BÍBLIA para Todos ("The Bible for Everyone")
CEV—Contemporary English Version
CSB—Christian Standard Bible
DFT—Divine Familial Terms
ESV—English Standard Version
Eth. eud.—*Eudemian Ethics*
GNT—Good News Translation
KJV—King James Version
IM—Insider Movements
NASB—New American Standard Bible
NET—NET Bible
NIV—New International Version
NJB—New Jerusalem Bible
NLT—New Living Translation
NRSV—New Revised Standard Version
OBT—Oral Bible Translation
Opt. gen.—*De optimo genere oratorum*
Od.—*Odyssey*
PROMOTYPAD—*Projecto Moçambicano de Tradução Yaawo da Palavra de Deus* (Mozambican Project of the Yawo Translation of the Word of God)
REB—Revised English Bible
Resp.—*Republic*
UMCA—Universities' Mission to Central Africa

Introduction

It's like knowing your way through the forest. You don't keep the whole forest in your mind, but wherever you are, you know where to go next.
—Ken Follett, *The Pillars of the Earth*, 1989

"We've got money to spend! We're going to launch a Bible translation project in the X language for churches in the area!" These words were spoken to me a few years ago by the country director of a prominent Bible translation organization. He continued, "But, tell me, this language does need a translation, right? The money has already been given and allocated to this language group." Although the way I chose to respond to such questioning would not change whether the organization embarked on a new Bible translation project—needed or not—I did begin to feel somewhat disturbed by the question. There was clearly something very wrong, to me at least, with being uncertain of a Bible translation need while the money was already available and burning a hole in the pocket of an initiating organization. Even when I was asked about the need, moves to start the project were already underway. The translators had been selected and negotiations to rent an office space were in process. I felt disturbed by all this because it made me wonder about how many Bible translation projects are underway simply because money is available and needs spending as soon as possible to show donors that the organization is operating productively. How many language communities of the Majority World with genuine needs are missing out? Is money really being put into projects organized by people who haven't actually understood the needs of the community? The reality of the situation above was that a Bible translation was indeed needed for the X language, but the way they went about it meant that they isolated themselves from the very people the new project was meant to serve. They didn't understand the context or ask anyone about it before it was already happening.

In another context, I observed a Bible translation project that similarly didn't seem to pay any real attention to the intended audience. Despite operating among people who identified with a major religious faith other than Christianity, the translation did not seek to utilize the common language of those people but instead borrowed much terminology from another language already steeped in "Christianese." I'd like to think that even that approach was intentional, but the reality was actually far more mundane. It was simply that the translators' first language was not the same as the target language of the people. Hence, they naturally borrowed terms from their own language community, much of which was Christianized language unfamiliar to the recipients. It seems that no one actually sat down and decided how to approach the translation in that context. Although a major Bible translation organization also funded this project, this laxity resulted in translators' work that was insufficiently checked with the actual audience. It was ultimately inadequate because that audience could not own it—let alone fully understand it.

Both cases above are, to me, examples of how to go about Bible translation in a way that seems lazy and ill conceived. Resources for Bible translation globally are stretched thin, and there aren't enough translation consultants for all the existing projects. Although well-intentioned initiators sometimes simply don't know any better, the reality is that we can improve. My book addresses these troubling issues by showing a way forward that does pay attention to the context at hand. Bible translating is a purposeful activity that should be deeply rooted in both the Bible and the environment in which translation occurs. Far from being a mechanical process of rendering words from one language to another, Bible translation is a complex process shaped by social, cultural, religious, and other dynamics. This book aims to explore an approach to Bible translation that honors both the source text and its target audience, emphasizing loyalty to both. This approach is particularly significant in regions of the Majority World where the cultural and religious contexts demand careful and thoughtful engagement during Bible translation project undertakings. For example, this might be in areas where other faiths, such as Islam and Hinduism, dominate.

The concept of Loyal Bible Translation that I introduce in this book intertwines with modern translation studies, particularly in my adapted use of Skopos theory, which advocates for translations guided by their intended purpose and function.[1] This functionalist approach brings more intentionality to Bible translation but has also faced criticisms for its potential neglect of fidelity to the source text. Addressing these concerns, I offer a nuanced model in this book that builds on the concept of loyalty—not only to the original text and author—but also to the audience receiving it.

The Beaded Necklace Model serves as a guiding framework for my Loyal Bible Translation approach, where the interplay of various narrative frames come into view. These frames include, but are not limited to, historical, cultural, religious, and linguistic dynamics. By likening the translation process to a beaded necklace, this model emphasizes the importance of understanding and integrating each contextual "bead"—whether linguistic, sociocultural, religious, or historical frames—to ensure that a Bible translation is loyal to both the source and target audience. The following chapters will build upon the foundational themes, delve into the specific challenges faced in a Majority World situation (in Mozambique), and provide examples of Loyal Bible Translation in action.

Specifically, the book begins by exploring the theoretical foundations. Translation as a practice has evolved significantly over the last half century or more, particularly beginning from the development of Eugene Nida's functional equivalence paradigm through to the relevance theory of Ernst-August Gutt and other modern theories like functionalism—including Skopos theory. Chapter 1, therefore, outlines how Skopos theory sets the foundation of what is to come before discussing criticisms of the theory and bringing in loyalty as a safeguard against going too far with it. The complexity of Bible translation is also acknowledged, and I bring in narrative framing as a tool to help navigate the complexities.

Chapter 2 builds on the loyalty concept by linking it analogously to the notion of *ḥesed*. In biblical Hebrew, *ḥesed* is often translated as "loving-kindness" or "steadfast love." This word encapsulates covenant loyalty between God and his people, as well as the loyalty shown between people in a relationship with one another. I use this Hebrew term, therefore, to strengthen the idea of loyalty in translation studies and to create the new Loyal Bible Translation model. This model is about showing loyalty to

---

1. Readers familiar with academia surrounding Bible translation may have realized that my book title alludes (intentionally) to the title of Christiane Nord's book on Skopos theory and functionalist translation, *Translating as a Purposeful Activity: Functionalist Approaches Explained*. I see myself as continuing on from Nord's ideas, especially in relation to loyalty.

both the source text and the target audience. In Loyal Bible Translation, showing such loyalty means paying attention to the actual context of the audience by carefully considering their religious, cultural, linguistic, and other realities. Loyalty is a relational concept, so this model emphasizes the need to maintain relationships of integrity with the source text and its author, as well as with the target audience.

Chapter 3 explains the Beaded Necklace Model as a tool for Loyal Bible Translation. This model helps decision makers and the communities themselves understand and integrate the various elements relevant to a Bible translation situation, just as beads on a necklace come together to form a cohesive whole. The model recognizes that each bead represents an essential component—whether linguistic, religious, historical, or other—and creates an environment where translation can produce more holistic and loyal renderings of Scripture. This model is expressed practically by highlighting some of the beads of the Mozambican Yawo people's context. In particular, this chapter walks us through the "sociolinguistic" bead, the "religious" bead—which highlights the Yawo's adherence to both African Traditional Religion and Islam—the "historical" bead, and the "orality" bead, which highlights the Yawo's reliance on oral communication. Understanding the significance of each "bead" within the context allows Bible translators to maintain loyalty to the source while also crafting a translation loyal to the target audience.

The book's final chapter provides practical examples of Loyal Bible Translation in action. Although the examples are certainly not exhaustive, I draw on specific biblical texts from translations of Genesis, Exodus, Matthew, and Psalms to demonstrate how loyalty to both the source text and the audience can be realized. I kept the examples brief because Loyal Bible Translation is not just about copying examples but responding loyally to a given context. You'll have to think about how it applies to the specifics of your situation.

Historically speaking, many Majority World Bible translations have been initiated by outsiders. Logistically and economically, this may have been required for pioneering contexts. Indeed, in some situations, it probably remains somewhat necessary. For example, an outsider may have to be the catalyst for a Bible translation in a Muslim context. Despite this necessity or, rather, regardless of the need, this does not mean that outsiders should come in willy-nilly and carelessly initiate projects without appreciating the situation (or without asking what the people themselves think). For this reason, I wrote this book—to avoid the kinds of situations I mentioned at the beginning and to encourage both insiders and outsiders to grasp the situation into which they are translating as best they can. This isn't a book about different translation strategies, such as formal or functional equivalence. It is up to you to decide which strategy might be the best option in the context. This book is about loyalty to the biblical source text and its audience in the real world. It is a book about an ethos. It concerns an ethical approach to Bible translation that treats all the relevant parties with love and respect. By using the Beaded Necklace Model, I hope that the global church is better equipped to work with communities to produce adequate Loyal Bible Translations that fully function in their respective contexts.

1

Bible Translating as a Purposeful Activity

Theoretical Foundations

We naturally like what we have been accustomed to, and are attracted towards it.... The same is the case with those opinions of man to which he has been accustomed from his youth; he likes them, defends them, and shuns the opposite views. This is likewise one of the causes which prevent men from finding truth, and which make them cling to their habitual opinions.
—Moses Maimonides, *Guide for the Perplexed*, ca. 1190 CE

OVER THE PAST TWENTY or so years, the impact of functionalist translation on the global church's efforts to translate the Bible into the world's languages has been substantial. Several Bible translation projects in Majority World contexts have benefited from its use, whether consciously aware of this or not. At its core, functionalist translation refers to translation approaches that focus on upholding the function that the translation is to have, whether or not that aligns with the intentions of the original text being translated. For this reason, some in the Bible translation community don't like it, seeing it as somehow unfaithful to God. Although functionalist approaches to translation, and Skopos theory in particular, arose initially from the secular academic discipline of translation studies in its application to the field of professional secular translation,[1] its potential benefits for Bible translation are apparent. Those who felt that purely linguistic translation theories were inadequate to meet the Bible

---

1. For a general introduction to translation studies, see Jeremy Munday's *Introducing Translation Studies: Theories and Applications*, now into its fifth edition.

translation needs of the church in the Majority World have made use of functionalism. This is most obvious in Bible translation organizations talking about and using "translation briefs." These briefs define the parameters for a translation project (ideally prepared as a collaborative effort by all the stakeholders). Others see Skopos theory as something dangerous and too secular to be of use by Christians—this is a shame.

Discussions about Skopos theory concerning Bible translation tend to take place in the journals and books of specialists. Often there is little direct interaction between the academy and the field of Majority World Bible translators—other than through the influence of such specialists as translation consultants who might know something about Skopos theory. In this chapter, I hope to bring Skopos theory to the fore for Bible translation in Majority World contexts to set the foundation upon which I am building the rest of this book. We will come to the Beaded Necklace Model and Loyal Bible Translation in subsequent chapters,[2] but for now, let's put ourselves at the beginning—at the place where we might make certain assumptions about what Bible translation is and what it looks like to consider it through the lens of Skopos theory as applied to the Majority World.

I begin this chapter by explaining what Skopos theory is and what it tries to do. I will then consider "loyalty" as an addition to the standard expression of Skopos theory before moving into "complexity theory" and narrative framing as ways to manage the complex situations in which Majority World Bible translators find themselves. In summary, even though each of those domains (Skopos theory, complexity theory, and narrative framing) are theories in their own right, I am uniting them in this book in a complementary manner. That is, Skopos theory guides purpose in Bible translation, whereas complexity theory validates the reality of complex contexts by resisting the temptation to reduce complexities to simple patterns or to compartmentalize them until they no longer interact with one another. Narrative frame theory assists by making the situation more manageable by categorizing distinct elements (contextual frames) but not reducing them to mere boxes to be ticked on a questionnaire. With these theories complementing one another in this way and leading us to Loyal Bible Translation and the Beaded Necklace Model, authentic engagement

---

2. I initially developed the Beaded Necklace Model to apply to assessing needs for a Bible translation project in a given context. However, I am expanding its use in this book to apply to Bible translation more generally. See Houston, "'What You Ask For.'"

with the Bible can be made possible for new Bible translations in the Majority World.

SKOPOS THEORY: A FUNCTIONALIST APPROACH TO TRANSLATION

Skopos theory, as stated by Munday,[3] is a general translation theory applicable to all types of texts. It is not limited to the world of Bible translation. In fact, its origins lie in action theory and other theories related to intercultural communication.[4] The formulation of Skopos theory emerged primarily from the foundational works of Hans Vermeer,[5] and complemented by other scholars like Katharina Reiss.[6] Reiss collaborated with Vermeer and played a significant role in the discourse on text typologies within Skopos theory.

Continuing the legacy, another German translation scholar, Christiane Nord, a professional translator and trainer, made notable advancements in the study of Skopos theory and functional approaches to translation.[7] Vermeer's initial version of the theory proposed that translation should be perceived as a part of a speech act, a purposeful endeavor referred to as "translational action ... based on a source text."[8] Reiss and Vermeer emphasized the movement of information from the source text to the target text, describing it as an "offer of information."[9]

The term *skopos* is borrowed from ancient Greek (σκοπός) and encompasses the meaning of "purpose" or "aim."[10] In its ancient con-

---

3. Munday, *Introducing Translation Studies*, 127.

4. Nord, "Functional Translatology?," 26.

5. Vermeer, "Allgemeine Translationstheorie"; Vermeer, "'Richtigen' Übersetzen"; Vermeer, "Skopos and Commission" (1989); Vermeer, "Skopos and Commission" (2004).

6. Reiss and Vermeer, *Allgemeinen Translationstheorie*; Reiss and Vermeer, *Towards a General Theory*.

7. Nord, "Translational Conventions"; Nord, *Purposeful Activity* (1997); Nord, "Defining Translation Functions"; Nord, "Loyalty Revisited"; Nord, "Manipulation and Loyalty"; Nord, "Making Otherness Accessible"; Nord, "Functionalist Approaches"; Nord, "Functional Translatology?"; Nord, "Function and Loyalty"; Nord, "Skopos and (Un)Certainty"; Nord, "Function and Loyalty"; Nord, *Purposeful Activity* (2018).

8. Vermeer, "Skopos and Commission" (2004), 227.

9. Reiss and Vermeer, *Towards a General Theory*, 33.

10. Nord, *Purposeful Activity* (1997), 27; Reiss and Vermeer, *Towards a General Theory*, 86.

text, *skopos* was used in both physical and abstract senses. For example, Homer used the term in the physical context of archery, where an archer's *skopos* is the target they aim to hit.[11] Aristotle, on the other hand, used *skopos* abstractly when discussing the ultimate *aim* or objective in human life.[12] Plato used the term to refer to the *aim* or *purpose* that virtuous people have in life.[13] In the Bible, the term is used once in the New Testament (Phil 3:14) and thrice in the Septuagint (Job 16:12, Lam 3:12, and Wis 5:12) with the sense of a "target" or "goal." Although the ancient and biblical uses of *skopos* realistically have little to do with the present use of the term as used in translation studies, readers may be interested to know where it was used prior to its adoption as a technical term. We can also still affirm that the meaning of the term inspired the present translation theory. Consequently, Skopos theory is classified as a "functionalist" approach since the primary focus and criterion for successful translation lies in the aim/purpose/goal/*function* of the translated target text.

Skopos theory, as a general theory of translation, is different from any specific translation strategy. In many pioneering Bible translation contexts in the Majority World, the preferred translation approach is often assumed to be "functional equivalence" / "dynamic equivalence" translation.[14] These approaches are considered necessary to convey the *meaning* of God's word to language communities that have never had access to the Bible in their own language or to those who are left bemused by "formal equivalence" translations of previous generations. These formally equivalent translations, sometimes also called "word-for-word" or "literal" translations, may have already existed in their language and may have added to any confusion that arose from exposure to the Bible via a more widely used language like English. Whether mother-tongue translators in Majority World contexts who base their translations on Bibles from languages of wider communication are successfully producing their own "dynamic" equivalents in their language or are just translating "literal" translations of other translations is an issue that I am not addressing here. Although all Bible translation should, ideally, be done from the

---

11. Homer, *Od.* 22.6.
12. Aristotle, *Eth. eud.* 2.11.3–4.
13. Plato, *Resp.* 7.519.C.
14. At times, I will favor Eugene Nida's earlier term "dynamic equivalence," as opposed to the later "functional equivalence," in order to avoid confusion with the distinct approach to translation called "functionalist translation" or "functionalism."

biblical languages, it is essential to acknowledge that this is not always possible for many, if not most, projects in the Majority World.[15]

To avoid any confusion, it is important to clarify the distinction between Skopos theory as a functionalist approach to translation and the concept of "functional equivalence" previously mentioned. Functional equivalence, in the context of translation, refers to a linguistic measure in which the translator aims to replicate the impact of the source text on its original audience in the target audience. In simpler terms, it is often referred to as meaning-based translation, where the focus is on transferring the underlying kernels of meaning from the source language to the target language, thus reproducing the effect of the original text.[16]

On the other hand, formal equivalence stands in apposition, rather than opposition, to functional equivalence. This translation strategy seeks to maintain, as much as possible, the form of the original biblical Hebrew, Aramaic, and Greek languages in the target text. However, achieving total formal equivalence across different languages is an unrealistic goal. It is simply not feasible to replicate vocabulary, syntax, and grammar one-to-one between languages, especially when aiming for comprehension in the translated text. It turns out that translation requires a bit more than simply finding lexical matches for words in the source language. So while I generally acknowledge both formal and functional equivalence as suitable strategies for Bible translation in this book, their appropriateness depends on the specific context at hand. It is crucial to recognize that claiming a universal "must" or "ought to" translation approach is not a viable solution to the complex realities of the Majority World, where each situation presents unique differences and needs.[17]

For example, among various English translations, some exhibit greater formal equivalence than others—even if total formal equivalence is unattainable.[18] However, all mainstream translations such as the

---

15. A useful and engaging tool for learning the biblical languages, that anyone from any language background can use, is the "Aleph with Beth" video lessons available on YouTube at https://www.youtube.com/c/AlephwithBeth. Since its initial launch, an equivalent Greek tool has also been launched as "Alpha with Angela" at https://www.youtube.com/c/AlphawithAngela.

16. Nida, *Science of Translating*, 66.

17. Nord, "Scopos and Translational Conventions," 92.

18. Ubaldo Stecconi even goes so far as to suggest the following: "I consider the idea of absolute equivalence as the original sin of Western translation theory. . . . I believe a strict notion of equivalence is, in fact, a sin of pride or vanity because it rests on a semiotically unsustainable belief in the powers of translation. All sign-action—including

English Standard Version (ESV), Christian Standard Bible (CSB), New Revised Standard Version (NRSV), New International Version (NIV), New American Standard Bible (NASB), Good News Translation (GNT; formerly Today's English Version or Good News Bible), New Living Translation (NLT), Contemporary English Version (CEV), and New Jerusalem Bible (NJB) are valuable when used correctly and their underlying translation strategies are known. The preface of each translation usually provides insight into its chosen strategy. While there may be debates about whether each translation consistently adheres to its stated strategy and achieves its intended purpose, all these translations should be appreciated as commendable renditions of the Bible into English. There are many more good Bible translations and revisions in English out there, but there's little point in my naming them here.[19]

In the case of mainstream English translations mentioned earlier, the NASB overall exemplifies the strategy of formal equivalence—its intended *skopos* from the beginning. It pursued this aim and should be judged based on how well it adheres to its stated objectives. Conversely, if the NASB translators intended for it to be exclusively meaning based, then we can deem it relatively unsuccessful in relation to its design. Similarly, if the dynamically equivalent NLT aims to replicate the syntax and grammar of the original biblical languages, it is largely unsuccessful in that regard.

Still, it is worthwhile to consider the historical predominance of equivalence strategies, particularly in the realm of Bible translation. As Nord puts it, these strategies have long served as the measuring rod or "yardstick" for assessing translation quality.[20] A translation's success was traditionally determined by how closely it replicated the source text in either form or meaning. Even today, debates about the merits of formal versus dynamic equivalence continue to animate discussions in churches and among students and scholars of the Bible. Sadly, critics tend to be stuck in this equivalence paradigm and blind to the important discussions

---

translating—is incompatible with equivalent relations between its elements; at most we can speak of similarity relations." Stecconi, "Semiotics for Translation Studies," 21. Perhaps Stecconi is here rather melodramatic in his criticism of equivalence, but the point remains: full equivalence in translation is an illusion. See Newmark, *About Translation*, 101.

19. The number of English Bible translations produced since Tyndale's version in 1526 amounts to many hundreds. Some are of more questionable quality than others. The mainstream modern translations are certainly very good in general.

20. Nord, "Functionalist Approaches," 121.

happening about translation beyond it. I would rather not name names, but it is peculiar that the noisiest criticism comes from North American monolingual evangelicals and not from people using the translations they criticize. Unfortunately, many in the field of Bible translation remain unaware of translation studies as a discipline and thus miss out on the insights that Skopos theory and related concepts can provide. Recognizing what each equivalence strategy aims to achieve can be incredibly valuable in bringing greater clarity and understanding to these debates.

To reiterate, the formal equivalence strategy aims to recreate the grammatical and syntactical form of the source text in the target text. Another example of a contemporary English Bible translation that uses formal equivalence is the English Standard Version (ESV). According to its preface, the ESV "seeks as far as possible to capture the precise wording of the original text and the personal style of each Bible writer. As such, its emphasis is on 'word-for-word' correspondence."[21] On the other hand, the well-known meaning-based approach, commonly referred to as "dynamic" or "functional equivalence," became popularized by Eugene Nida in the 1960s.[22] This approach focuses on transferring "kernel" structures of meaning from the source text to equivalent structures of meaning in the target text,[23] even if this means changing the form of the source text. Despite both formal and dynamic equivalence models using the source text as the basis for translation, their intended outcomes differ. Nevertheless, proponents of each type of equivalence tend to argue that their strategy is superior to the other and should be applied in all Bible translations. Both would claim to offer accurate translations.[24]

The book *Translating Truth: The Case for Essentially Literal Bible Translation* is a clear example of an accessible-to-most study that aims to defend the "essentially literal" equivalence strategy against the perceived weaknesses of other strategies. In contrast, *How to Choose a Translation for All Its Worth* by Gordon Fee and Mark Strauss serves as a useful guide for understanding the differences between translation strategies

---

21. ESV, vii.
22. Nida, *Science of Translating*; Nida and Taber, *Theory and Practice*.
23. Nida, *Science of Translating*, 66.
24. Beyond just "formal" and "functional" equivalence, Mona Baker has chapters in her book *In Other Words: A Coursebook on Translation* on equivalence at word level (lexical and semantic), equivalence above word level (collocations and idioms), grammatical equivalence, textual equivalence (thematic and information structures, cohesion), and pragmatic equivalence (coherence).

commonly used in mainstream Bible translations.²⁵ That book provides an explanation of how functional equivalence works and highlights that a purely "literal" translation is simply not feasible.²⁶ Anyone who speaks more than one language intuitively knows this. Despite the ongoing debates regarding which translation philosophy is more faithful to the original text of Scripture, I am planting my flag and saying that *both* formal and dynamic equivalences are useful for the church and can justifiably claim faithfulness to the source texts. The introduction to the second edition of the New Living Translation (NLT) summarizes the challenges associated with Bible translation:

> All translations contain a mixture of these two philosophies. A purely formal-equivalence translation would be unintelligible in English, and a purely dynamic-equivalence translation would risk being unfaithful to the original. That is why translations shaped by dynamic-equivalence theory are usually quite literal when the original text is relatively clear, and the translations shaped by formal-equivalence theory are sometimes quite dynamic when the original text is obscure.²⁷

The discussion will now revisit Skopos theory, in order to provide a more detailed explanation of its fundamental principles and how it diverges from other linguistic approaches to translation, including equivalence. As previously noted, Skopos is a Greek word that connotes "purpose," "aim," "intention," or "function," although scholars such as Nord occasionally interpret each of these English terms with subtle distinctions.²⁸ Within Skopos theory, the operative function pertains to the role that the translated text performs in the target situation, rather than in the source-text function (which is frequently indeterminate, if not unknowable). The so-called Skopos rule attributed to the theory's originator, Hans Vermeer, posits that the target text should "function in the situation in which it is used and with the people who want to use it."²⁹

---

25. See also Mark Strauss's recent contribution to the 40 Questions series, providing helpful answers to Bible translation-related questions for lay audiences: Strauss, *40 Questions About Bible Translation*.

26. See also Strauss, "Myth of 'Literal Accuracy.'"

27. NLT, A45–A46.

28. See Loba-Mkole, "Intercultural Translations," 165–66.

29. Nord, *Purposeful Activity* (1997), 29. Nord is here citing and translating a quotation by Vermeer in German.

According to Skopos theory, then, a translation should "work for target-culture receivers."[30] This means that the translated text must be tailored to the needs and expectations of the target audience, ensuring that it resonates with them. In other words, "the translation should be understood by target readers based on their educational culture and make sense in the target language culture and communicative environment."[31] The theory, therefore, recognizes that different *skopoi* (translation purposes) may lead to applying particular strategies in various situations. When evaluating translations, such as *The Message*, critics should consider the intended goals of the translator (in that case, Eugene Peterson), rather than applying predetermined linguistic criteria that may not be suitable for assessing such a unique product. Comparing apples with oranges is usually a bad idea—better to judge an apple on how good an apple it is and an orange on how good an orange it is. Even worse to compare apples with oranges when what the situation really needs is a banana.

The "translation brief" is a key element of Skopos theory, serving as a practical hallmark of the approach. This document provides instructions for the translation task, including the intended function of the final product. While Vermeer preferred to use the term "commission," other scholars have referred to it as an "assignment" or as "translating instructions." Janet Fraser is credited with introducing the term "brief" in her translation of the German word *Übersetzungsauftrag*.[32] Today, "translation brief" is the most widely used term in English academic literature on Skopos theory and in Bible translation circles. The translation brief can be compared to the instructions that barristers receive in legal cases or to the design briefs that artists use in creative projects. Later in this book, I will begin to call the translation brief a "translation covenant" to better reflect the relational nature of the dynamics involved in Bible translation.

Although the translation brief generally does not prescribe specific translation strategies or word choices, it does define the function of the text. In team translation projects, the translation brief may need to specify more detailed instructions to ensure consistency among translators. This is often the case in Bible translation efforts in Majority World contexts, where teams of mother-tongue translators work together on different portions of the text. Even individual translators working on their own sections may collaborate with others and rely on the translation

---

30. Nord, "Loyalty Revisited," 195.
31. Wang, "Euphemism Translation," 1175.
32. Nord, *Purposeful Activity* (2018), 29.

brief for a consistent approach to key terms, even if the brief itself does not individually define them ahead of actually encountering the terms in translation.

The prefaces of mainstream Bible translations can offer insights into the skopos and translation brief of the text, making them useful for evaluating the accuracy and faithfulness of a translation. As I mentioned earlier, the preface can be one of the fairest criteria for evaluating a Bible translation because it allows readers to judge it based on what it promised to accomplish.

It might seem that it is new or all a bit technical, but the concept of a translation brief is not a novel idea. It seeks to make explicit something that has always existed—namely that translators work with a specific purpose in mind—whether they are aware of it or not.[33] Hans Vermeer elaborates on this notion when he states that "one does not translate a source text in a void, as it were, but always according to a given skopos or commission."[34] Therefore, the translation brief identifies that purpose and acts as a crucial guide for translators in their endeavor to remain true to the skopos and accountable to the instructions. This purpose is related to the target audience's wants and intentions for the translated text, as well as the relevant context of the target audience's situation. In other words, "the receiver, or rather the addressee, is the main factor determining the target-text Skopos."[35]

It is then up to the translator to interpret the source text and decide the extent to which a change in form is necessary while creating the translated text. Essentially, "functionalist translation theory emphasizes the role of the target text receiver in setting the *skopos* for the translation."[36] If the intended function of the new text varies from that of the source text, Skopos theory permits a change in form to enable the successful fulfillment of the translated text's purpose. For instance, translations between similar "text types"[37] or translations that disclose the structure of the source text may have little formal distinction between the source and translated text. A classic example of such a function would be an interlinear English translation of a biblical language original. However, translations like the NLT and GNT may change the forms of the source

33. Vermeer, "Skopos and Commission" (2004), 236.
34. Vermeer, "Skopos and Commission" (2004), 238.
35. Nord, *Purposeful Activity* (1997), 29.
36. Connelly et al., "Translating Research," 7.
37. Reiss and Vermeer, *Towards a General Theory*, 182.

texts to convey what they see as more critical—the underlying meaning of the biblical text. This approach is arguably more in keeping with the original author's intentions in that they surely intended their work to be meaningful.

Thus, functionalist approaches to translation should not be seen as replacements for linguistic translation theories like formal or dynamic equivalence but rather as complementary to them. Skopos theory, as I discuss it in this book, does not dismiss the relevance of other specific translation approaches; instead, it aims to determine which type of translation will best fulfill the desired function of the translated text.[38] The focus of Skopos theory is not on individual translation choices but on providing a framework to determine the appropriate translation strategy for a given situation. In light of this, I don't advocate exclusively for one specific approach, such as foreignization (keeping foreign elements unexplained or opaque in the translation) or domestication (making it easier to comprehend the foreign elements by bringing them closer to the audience's understanding), or formal or dynamic equivalence. Each of these strategies may be suitable depending on the context. It is crucial for churches in the Majority World and Western churches alike to recognize the validity of both types of translations and understand their differences, knowing when to apply each one effectively.

In succinct fashion, Christiane Nord helpfully defines functionalist approaches as essentially "the idea of choosing translation strategies according to translation purposes."[39] Notably, although the skopos could, I suppose, theoretically apply to the underlying purpose of the translator (such as earning a living), "the term *Skopos* usually refers to the purpose of the target text."[40] I am assuming here that the *skopos* refers to the purpose of the translated text—that is, the purpose of the translation product itself.

As mentioned, Skopos theory has gained prominence in translation studies over the last few decades for addressing the challenges encountered by professional translators. Although Skopos theory is relatively new, this does not mean that it poses a direct threat to the various equivalence strategies if it is carefully considered. Indeed, some critics seem to perpetuate a misconception that Skopos theory is "mainly a theory of adaptation" whereas it actually "accounts for all sorts of both source- and

---

38. Nord, *Purposeful Activity* (1997), 30.
39. Nord, "Functionalist Approaches," 120.
40. Nord, *Purposeful Activity* (1997), 28.

target-oriented forms of translation."[41] So, rather than replacing equivalence theories or any other translation strategy, Skopos theory serves as a tool for demonstrating that there is a valid place for specific translation strategies, including both formal and dynamic equivalence. Translators can take a step back from the debate about which translation strategy is always correct regardless of the situation by utilizing Skopos theory as a helpful guide.[42] No one translation can do it all. For instance, "in a missionary framework where the translation is a pioneer translation, conveying the literary and rhetorical aspects of the source texts has lower priority than communicating, as clearly as possible, the basic messages of the source texts."[43] Instead, Skopos theory sees that certain translation strategies will be appropriate in different situations according to the skopos, the purpose of the translated end product and the "intended purpose of the intercultural communication."[44] That is, "discussions over translation strategies are removed from their imagined vacuum and morph into debates over which strategies are most suitable for which purposes."[45] Equivalence alone is, therefore, no longer the supreme measuring rod for a good translation since it is only one "criterion to assess translation quality"[46] out of many possibilities in a given situation.[47] Thus, the broader notion of adequacy moves us away from the classic measuring rod of equivalence.

Adequacy, as it relates to Skopos theory, concerns the extent to which a translation successfully completes the objectives outlined in the translation brief. Even more succinctly than this, Katharina Reiss claims that adequacy is "simple appropriateness"[48] in relation to the purpose of what is being done. John Barton succinctly states that "the adequacy of a translation cannot be judged unless we know what it is *for*."[49] An adequate translation is, therefore, not necessarily one that is the most formally or meaningfully equivalent to the source text—unless such equivalence is the approach most suited to successfully fulfilling the brief's instructions.

41. Nord, "Functionalism and Bible Translation," 460.
42. Downie, "End of an Era?," 3.
43. Vries, "Bible Translations," 308.
44. Naudé, "On the Threshold," 5.
45. Downie, "End of an Era?," 5.
46. Naudé, "Equivalence," 415.
47. Nord, *Purposeful Activity* (1997), 36.
48. Reiss, "Adequacy and Equivalence," 301.
49. Barton, *Word*, 278.

As the South African scholar Jacobus Naudé clearly states, instead of striving simply toward equivalence,

> translation consists of a series of decisions made by the translator in considering the conflicting requirements of the source text and source culture on the one hand and those of the target language and target culture on the other in the light of the purpose of the intercultural communication.[50]

Bible translation involves intercultural communication because it is necessary to bridge the gaps between contemporary cultures and those of the biblical world. Different strategies for Bible translation are required for each context. Even then, there will not be one correct version for all times—it all depends on the purpose within the context, as even nonspecialist scholars thinking about Bible translation, such as John Barton, can recognize.[51] This is because adequacy is both context and time bound.[52] While formal equivalence may be desirable in some situations to communicate the forms of the original languages,[53] this is not always the case. In Majority World contexts involving new Christians or in evangelism situations, such as Hindu or Muslim contexts, dynamic equivalence is often more useful. Skopos theory has become influential in these contexts because it allows each situation to be properly understood and catered to by translations that function appropriately in the context. However, this does not mean that anything goes for Majority World Bible translations, and there are important limits to keep in mind. The next section will look at criticisms of Skopos theory and introduce the concept of "loyalty" as a safeguard.

CRITICISMS OF FUNCTIONALIST TRANSLATION AND BRINGING IN LOYALTY

In Skopos theory, an inadequate translation or translation errors are defined as failures "to carry out the instructions implied [or explicitly

---

50. Naudé, "Religious Translation," 286.
51. Barton, *Word*, 283.
52. Barton, *Word*, 284.
53. See, for example, Barton, *Word*, 45: "The purpose may be to give the reader a detailed sense of the words of the source text, and in that case a good deal of literalness is needed."

stated] in the translation brief."[54] This, of course, assumes that the translation brief itself is adequate and appropriate in the first place. Indeed, a significant criticism of Skopos theory is that the theory allows translators to produce what Esala calls (despite himself advocating for Skopos theory) "radical or utilitarian" texts,[55] according to whatever intended function is desirable, regardless of the intentions of the source text. Some even suggest that the aim of Skopos theory[56] is to "dethrone" the source text.[57] Jabir downplays the theory itself when he claims that it "is not an original theory in that since functionalism is based on something as obvious as the fact that human actions are guided by their purposes, it cannot claim to be an original theory."[58] He also suggests that translation may not even have purposes. Jabir's particular criticisms do not seem to carry much weight considering that it is still possible to analyze one's purposes and intentions, even if they are "obvious." For example, just because the theory of gravity is widely held to be a valid explanation as to why things fall to earth, this does not negate studying the theory because it is "obvious."

At this point, it is probably clear that, for Bible translators especially, Skopos theory runs the risk of straying too far from the biblical text. The ends seem to justify the means. Although scholars like Vermeer hint at some kind of relationship between source and target in his idea of there being an "offer of information" taking place between the two and that there should be some kind of coherence between them, the truth of the matter is that, unchecked, Skopos theory could theoretically lead translators to produce "radical," "sectarian and unorthodox,"[59] or downright bizarre translations of the Bible. It appears Skopos theory allows for situations where the end justifies the means[60]—that the translation process can be whatever one wants it to be, so long as the target text fulfils its purpose. Critics such as Peter Newmark have long identified this problem.[61] More recently, academic criticism of Skopos theory has filtered down to popular-level treatments by some, such as Seth Vitrano-Wilson who uses

---

54. Esala, "Measuring the Adequacy," 312.
55. Esala, "Implementing Skopostheorie," 303.
56. Yes, I am offering a not-so-subtle nod to the link here between *aim* and *skopos*.
57. Jabir, "Skopos Theory," 37.
58. Jabir, "Skopos Theory," 43.
59. Downie, "End of an Era?," 3.
60. Nord, "Manipulation and Loyalty," 35.
61. Newmark, "Curse of Dogma," 106; Newmark, "Deficiencies of Skopos."

words like "dangerous" about functionalist translation on the polemical *Journal of Biblical Missiology* website.[62] For those who believe in the inspired nature of what they consider God's word, this is clearly a very significant and disturbing problem. If a translator is free to manipulate their translation to suit whatever purpose or function they like, then the possibility (and perhaps likelihood) of dodgy translations is endless—there is no ethical constraint on what a translator can do in the name of "translation." However, I must add a caveat, as there is both a response to and a solution for this issue.

To address the problem of Skopos theory's tendency towards universalism, Christiane Nord introduced a critical element to the theory: *loyalty*. According to Christiane Nord, loyalty mainly involves the "responsibility translators have toward their partners in translational action."[63] So, in her "function *plus* loyalty"[64] version of the functionalist approach, it is the combination of both the *function* of the translated text and *loyalty*[65] that is important. Specifically, loyalty in Nord's thinking "refers to the interpersonal relationship between the translator, the source-text sender, the target-text addressees and the initiator. Loyalty limits the range of justifiable target-text functions for one particular source text."[66]

As Skopos theory is a general theory operating above individual translation choices and strategies, loyalty must be understood as something other than "fidelity" or "faithfulness" to the source text. Indeed, Nord tells us that loyalty "is not the old 'fidelity' or 'faithfulness' in new clothes, which referred to formal linguistic or stylistic similarities between the two texts, but a trusting relationship between persons that will help to strengthen the translator's image as a responsible partner."[67]

This relationship between people should be regarded as the relationship that the translator has with both the source-text author and target-text receivers—it is a bidirectional loyalty.[68] To be loyal to the source-text

---

62. Vitrano-Wilson, "Functionalism."

63. Nord, *Purposeful Activity* (1997), 125.

64. Nord, *Purposeful Activity* (1997), 126.

65. Nord, *Text Analysis in Translation*, 32.

66. Nord, *Purposeful Activity* (1997), 126.

67. Nord, "Function and Loyalty," 571. Nord has a similar line in another article: "Loyalty is not the old 'fidelity' in new clothes, because fidelity usually refers to an intertextual relationship between the source and target *texts* as linguistic entities. Loyalty is an interpersonal category referring to a social relationship between people" (Nord, "Manipulation and Loyalty," 36.)

68. Esala, "Implementing Skopostheorie," 307; Nord, "Scopos and Translational Conventions," 94.

author, Nord emphasizes the need for "an elaborate analysis of the source text before translation proper."[69] She emphasizes that even though the actual human author is lost to us, there is nonetheless still an implied sender.[70] With the help of professional biblical scholars and secondary sources, we can still "cite the consensus of professional biblical scholars or a historical reading from ancient church fathers."[71] That is, the traditional skills of exegesis and techniques for hermeneutics are invaluable at this point, albeit while preferably avoiding ethnocentric and myopic Western-only approaches.[72]

Maintaining loyalty to all parties involved in the translation process is a profound responsibility and must be taken very seriously. Critics of Skopos theory, such as Peter Newmark, who said that loyalty is just an add-on,[73] do not give enough consideration to its benefits. Although Newmark may have considered loyalty as an afterthought, it is a suitable and appropriate one. Therefore, instead of dismissing the addition of loyalty because it arrived late to the Skopos theory party, we should appreciate how it really does limit the possibility of wacky and inappropriate translations. This is because careful consideration of the theory (the one that includes loyalty to the source text) reveals that the deviation from the source text in the fashion critics fear is not inevitable. This deviation only comes to the fore if the skopos *itself* explicitly dictates a departure from the source text. However, this is not the fault of Skopos theory *plus* loyalty. It is the fault of those who would likely depart from the source-text author's communicative intentions regardless. In fact, Nord claims that the principle of loyalty turns Skopos theory into "an anti-universalist model"[74] because it respects the "sender" and their original intentions of the communication.

Skopos theory does not prescribe an "anything goes" approach to the translation task as some scholars seem to fear, and it is indeed enhanced by the loyalty concept as the moral responsibility of "the translator to respect the sender's individual communicative intentions, as far

---

69. Oyali, "Critique of Functionalist Approaches," 58.

70. Nord, *Text Analysis in Translation*, 48.

71. Esala, "Implementing Skopostheorie," 304.

72. See, for example, Elizabeth Mburu's *African Hermeneutics* for an African perspective on and model for interpreting the Bible.

73. Newmark, "Deficiencies of Skopos," 259.

74. Nord, "Manipulation and Loyalty," 36.

as they can be elicited."[75] This notion of loyalty is vital to an appropriate functionalist Bible translation in Majority World contexts because it defends Skopos theory from the criticisms of the "anything goes" attitude toward Bible translation. It is even worth stating that such an attitude is very rare indeed among those practicing Bible translation in the Majority World; it is more of a straw man argument to say that those working on Bible translation have an "anything goes" attitude to their work and that there is a great risk of horrifying translations because of it. Contrary to the suggestion that some do have an "anything goes" approach, most people working in Bible translation in the Majority World, including those criticized for "Muslim-idiom translations" and similar approaches, have the best intentions[76] and are very much trying to do the right thing before God. It is also worth pointing out that so-called Muslim-idiom translation is not some malicious attempt to Islamize the Bible. Rather, it should be seen as a case of *just using the normal language that people use everyday* to express the translatable message in language that people understand.[77] English Bibles are no different in their use of contextualization to express truth to English-speaking audiences. We use the natural idiom of the people as indeed most translators strive for. It just so happens that some people might be Muslim and/or impacted by the Arabic language. With this in mind, perhaps it is unhelpful to keep referring to "Muslim-idiom translations," as though it is some kind of unique approach to translation, but rather to say something like "majority-language translations" or "translations that use the everyday language of the people who happen to be Muslim and influenced by the Arabic language." This would be the same for every other context; in English-speaking contexts, for example, we might say something like "translation that uses the everyday language of the people who happen to be influenced by myriad cultural and religious factors and the French, German, Anglo-Saxon, and Latin languages." The early church was sensitive to the reality of using the language of their context. The New Testament was written in Greek, which inevitably introduced new terms and categories. Although the first believers were Jewish and thought about Jesus using Jewish categories like messiah, this "meant nothing to Greeks, and needed endless explanation. They had to translate, to find a term that told something about Jesus and yet meant

---

75. Nord, "Functionalist Approaches," 126.
76. Brown et al., "Muslim-Idiom Translations," 91.
77. Brown et al., "Muslim-Idiom Translations," 88.

something to a Greek pagan. They chose the word *Kyrios*, 'Lord,' the title that Greek pagans used for their cult divinities (Acts 11:19–21)."[78]

In other words, they had no other language to use than that of the Greek polytheistic culture. Even preceding this Greek transmission of the message concerning Jesus, the Hebrew Bible also made use of its surrounding context. For instance, the Hebrew term usually given as "God" in English, *'ĕlōhîm* (Hebrew, אֱלֹהִים), was borrowed from its use among other Semitic peoples who spoke of *'ēl* (Hebrew, אֵל) as their supreme deity.[79] If the Bible itself in its original languages exhibits the use of language from other socioreligious contexts, it is difficult to see why this would be a problem now.[80] Indeed, this approach was not avoided in English either with the adoption of the pre-Christian word "God." So, if we are honest with ourselves as English-speaking users of the mainstream English Bibles, those Bible translations are just as syncretistic as the so-called Muslim-idiom translations that some worry about. This is not a problem per se because all translation is a product of its cultural and linguistic environment.[81]

Given, then, that adequacy concerns the extent to which a translation product successfully follows the instructions of the translation brief, it is vital to assess the viability of the brief itself. A suitable formulation of the translation brief comes down to the essential need to understand the situation and context of the intended translation's target audience before anything else. A translation cannot be loyal to the source-text author and intended function without understanding both the original context and the target audience's context. Christiane Nord is emphatic in this assertion, writing that "in order to produce an adequate target text, the translator needs as much information as possible about the situation for which the translation is needed (including the addressed audience)."[82] In Majority World Bible translation situations, the contexts of the end users and the readers themselves must be the determining factor as to what

---

78. Walls, *Cross-Cultural Process*, 79.

79. Cross, "אֵל," 242.

80. In the Hebrew Bible, *'ĕlōhîm* is also used of other deities and is not just exclusively used in reference to the God of Israel. In the Decalogue, for example, Exod 20:2–3 uses the term twice but for two different referents (the one true God and other gods): "I am the Lord your *God*, who brought you out of Egypt, out of the land of slavery. You shall have no other *gods* before me" (NIV, emphasis added).

81. See Saleem's article, for example, concerning how the notion that there is such a thing as a theologically neutral term is a myth (Saleem, "Myth of 'Neutral' Terms").

82. Nord, "Functionalist Approaches," 122.

is considered an adequate translation and what is not. Ideally, translation involves importing the original message into the culture of the end users in a way that is well understood, given that the culture one understands best is one's own. Therefore, the stakeholders in such situations must understand the context and clearly understand what function the target audience expects the translated Bible to have within that context. Translational action essentially involves taking an "offer of information" from a source text and then somehow offering that information in a new context.[83] Therefore, it is imperative to understand both the source and target contexts when the stakeholders determine the function of a new Bible translation and offer this information to the target audience.

Indeed, "without any doubt, the needs of target readers are crucial to determine the extent at which the translation is acceptable, optimal and accessible."[84] Even if we think about which strategy to use for a translation, we must recognize the reality that "it is impossible to represent the features of the source text at once, and so some choices must be cautiously made."[85] These features could be those of the meaning or form of the source text—but not necessarily both at once. Even then, texts or even individual words in the same text may be polysemous in meaning and require different treatments anyway. Because of this, "seeking an a priori definition of equivalence between source and target texts is ultimately unworkable."[86]

With the two pillars of functionalism and loyalty established, in line with Nord's version of Skopos theory, we can see how what I am calling Loyal Bible Translation might begin to take shape. So long as loyalty is maintained, translators in new Bible translation contexts (usually those that tend to be situated in the Majority World) can consider what a Bible translation might look like. That is, "once the purpose of translation as well as the culture within which the source text is presented has been determined, the translator will have the ability to proceed with the process. The translator would then choose the relevant translation strategy or approach that would be functional to express the determined purpose of the translation."[87]

---

83. Reiss and Vermeer, *Towards a General Theory*, 33–84.
84. Mohatlane, "Sesotho Translation," 157.
85. Mohatlane, "Sesotho Translation," 158.
86. Connelly et al., "Translating Research," 6.
87. Mohatlane, "Sesotho Translation," 154.

Therefore, Skopos theory that includes loyalty is the underlying and assumed theory at play in this book. But I plan to take it further because, in actual practice in the Majority World and pioneering situations, what does this all mean when moving forward with new Bible translations (often in contexts that have never had one)? To move us forward, then, let us look at how we need to accept and embrace that Bible translation is a complex affair and not one to dive into without acknowledging such complexity. Tools such as narrative or contextual framing can help us as we think about new Bible translations in inevitably complex environments. Once we have established those basics of Bible translation as a complex affair yet manageable through narrative framing and linked them with the underlying theoretical assumptions of Skopos theory plus loyalty in Bible translation, we will look at strengthening the concept of loyalty from a biblical standpoint in chapter 2. Then, with everything relevant firmly established, we can finally introduce and discuss the Beaded Necklace Model for Loyal Bible Translation in chapter 3. After that, examples in practice will follow in chapter 4 to show how these models are useful and relevant to Bible translation.

BIBLE TRANSLATION IS COMPLEX BUT NARRATIVE FRAMING HELPS

Bible translation is complex and we need help to bring all the interlocking factors under control. This is where insights from complexity theory come in. My purpose in utilizing complexity theory in this book is not to engage in "reductionism"[88] but to acknowledge the reality that Bible translation in any context is intricate, with various interdependent factors. As Warrick Farah indicates, "We should realize that people in their contexts are much more complex and quite different from the simplistic way modernist anthropology often describes them."[89] Indeed, reducing a people or context in this way is an unfortunate syndrome of a lot of Western missionary anthropology that objectifies others in overly simplistic ways. This is something that these Westerners would surely not tolerate being done to themselves, in a seeming affront to Jesus's command to "Do to others what you would have them do to you" (Luke 6:31 NRSV).

---

88. Marais and Meylaerts, *Complexity Thinking*, 1.
89. Farah, "Adaptive Missiological Engagement," 110–11.

Hence, this notion of complexity is a crucial premise on which I am establishing this book. Majority World settings may present even more complexities since both insiders and outsiders are often involved in the process. Utilizing narrative frame theory to reduce the context into manageable units is not a way to simplify the complexity of the situation but to define some of the complexities and balance the tension in an organized manner. The concept of emergence in complexity thinking is a way to prevent taking the reductionist concept too far. Emergence emphasizes that "parts are related in unique ways to give rise to unique wholes."[90] Therefore, in regard to Majority World Bible translation situations, I am guided by emergence in this book, not by attempting to reduce individual parts' interaction but by combining them to create a coherent, yet distinct overall picture. Bible translation situations globally are not just the sum of all their parts, but a unique whole made up of the interaction between those elements. Edgar Morin supports this claim by asserting that a system is "both *more* and *less* than the sum of its parts,"[91] even suggesting that this observation goes back as far as the ancient Greek philosopher Aristotle.

Furthering Morin's observations about the ancient roots of such thinking, Jean-Pierre Vernant claims that the attempt at subjecting "the social world . . . to number and measure"[92] in the face of obvious complexity was a characteristic development in Greek philosophical thought. Therefore, Bible translation as a religious activity in this context is a nonlinear phenomenon characterized by the "complex webs of interaction between numerous emergent, complex adaptive systems."[93] These complexities include not only religious communities and their relationships with the Bible as a sacred text but also the ongoing interactions between cultural, historical, social, economic, and linguistic realities. The relevance of these kinds of interactions is highlighted further by Morin, who claims that "not only is the part inside the whole but the whole is inside the part"[94] and by Hans-Georg Gadamer when he affirms that every person belongs to a malleable and changeable system.[95]

---

90. Marais, "Translation Complex," 55.
91. Morin, "Complex Thinking," 15.
92. Vernant, *Origins of Greek Thought*, 132.
93. Naudé and Miller-Naudé, "Sacred Writings and Translations," 183.
94. Morin, "Complex Thinking," 17.
95. Gadamer, *Truth and Method*, 209.

Complexity theory is generally referred to under a broad label and is not yet commonly recognized as a cohesive discipline in its own right but is rather an interdisciplinary one. Kobus Marais similarly suggests that complexity thinking is not a "homogeneous field" but rather a "transdisciplinary" one.[96] Considering the emerging application of complexity theory to translation studies, I am seeking here to leverage complexity theory to highlight the intricate and multifaceted nature of translation, particularly in the context of Bible translation in Majority World settings. I do acknowledge that this process involves a complex interplay of numerous factors, including cultural nuances, linguistic diversity, sociopolitical dynamics, and theological considerations. By embracing the principles of complexity theory, I aim to provide a more comprehensive understanding of the challenges and intricacies involved in translating the Bible for diverse communities around the world. Narrative theory helps us here in looking at this interplay. Sue-Ann Harding wonders whether "narratives might be the 'visible' or traceable aspect of complex systems"[97] and that "complexity is a way of conceptualizing the workings of narratives, yet, in turn, narratives may be a way for us to observe and describe complex systems."[98] In a sense then, I am employing both narrative theory and complexity theory in a broad sense to address the complexity of entire contexts surrounding certain Bible translation situations in the Majority World. For example, these various contexts might require dealing with (at least) national or country-level concerns; the language in question as a linguistic and sociolinguistic phenomenon; the speakers of the language as a people; the Bible and its context, languages, culture(s), and history; and of course with translation itself as an inherently "complex phenomenon caused by factors too complex to compute."[99] Indeed, Marais also claims that "it is impossible for human beings to focus their attention on everything around them. This attentional constraint determines that it makes good sense to study things an aspect at a time."[100] Due to this inability of humans to fully multitask and hold everything together at once, we look to theories like complexity theory and narrative framing to help us.

---

96. Marais, *Translation Theory*, 19–20.
97. Harding, "Resonances," 45.
98. Harding, "Resonances," 35.
99. Marais, *Translation Theory*, 10.
100. Marais, "Translation Complex," 47.

In the foreword to Ernst Wendland's *Contextual Frames of Reference*, Lourens de Vries hints at the complexity of Bible translation in suggesting that Wendland's book, and by inference the notion of contextual frames overall, "shows both the daunting complexity of Bible translation and ways to deal with it, to reduce complexity and make it manageable."[101] Given the clarifications in the previous paragraphs on complexity thinking and emergence within complex systems, the focus in many Majority World situations is not on eliminating complexity but on making it manageable. Thus, while complexity remains an inevitable feature of Bible translation, contextual or narrative frames can assist in simplifying individual elements, allowing them to merge and form a distinct and cohesive whole. Even then, these contextual or narrative frames themselves can be rather complex and indeed may be broken down even further to other frames because what may seem "simple is replaced by complexity."[102] For example, Mona Baker suggests that

> because narratives are dynamic, they cannot be streamlined into a set of stable stories from which people simply choose. Narrative theory recognizes that at any moment in time we can be located within a variety of divergent, criss-crossing, often vacillating narratives, thus acknowledging the complexity and fluidity of our positioning in relation to other participants in interaction.[103]

Mona Baker has played a significant role in the development of narrative frame theory within the field of translation studies.[104] Additionally, Jacobus Naudé has employed this theory to analyze the 1933 Afrikaans translation of the Bible, showcasing its applicability in the study of Bible translations.[105] Although precise and workable definitions of complexity theory are challenging to pinpoint due to its inherently multifaceted and interdisciplinary nature, let's adopt Mona Baker's concise description of narratives as "the stories we tell ourselves and others about the world(s) in which we live. These stories provide our main interface with the world."[106] In other words, we can view "narratives" essentially as the

---

101. Vries, foreword to *Contextual Frames of Reference*, xiii.
102. Detienne, *Masters of Truth*, 35.
103. Baker, *Translation and Conflict*, 3.
104. Baker, *Translation and Conflict*; Baker, "Narratives of Terrorism."
105. Naudé, "Narrative Frame Analysis," 11.
106. Baker, "Narratives of Terrorism," 350.

ever-changing personal and corporate experiences of humanity within a given context and situation. Narratives are important because they not only represent reality, they actually constitute it.[107] By embracing these definitions, I am seeking to explore how narratives function within the realm of Bible translation, particularly in Majority World contexts, where diverse cultural, linguistic, and social factors intersect. This approach allows for a deeper examination of how translation is not merely a technical linguistic exercise but a complex process of meaning making that reflects and influences the dynamic narratives of communities engaged with the Bible.

In congruence with the earlier narrative typologies of Margaret Somers[108] and Gloria Gibson and Somers together,[109] Mona Baker distinguishes between different types of narratives, suggesting the following four types: personal (ontological), public, conceptual (disciplinary), and meta-narratives.[110] Personal narratives usually relate to the centrality of an individual's life history and experiences. They can cover the narratives associated with famous individual figures, such as Nelson Mandela, and how one might relate to these,[111] and the narratives of other individuals within one's own experience, and how they relate to one another. Public narratives are broader than any one individual and include such aspects as religious and educational institutions. Disciplinary narratives refer broadly to an object of inquiry in an academic field,[112] and so ironically, one might consider the study of narrative theory itself as a narrative. Meta-narratives are "particularly potent public narratives that persist over long periods of time and influence the lives of people across a wide range of settings."[113] Other scholars go beyond Baker and hypothesize that there are distinctions between personal narratives and "shared or collective narratives,"[114] with Boéri also proposing "professional narratives" as a category.[115] Baker also mentions that scholarly disciplines themselves

---

107. Harding, "Narratives and Contextual Frames," 106.
108. Somers, "Narrativity"; Somers, "Deconstructing and Reconstructing."
109. Gibson and Somers, "Reclaiming the 'Other.'"
110. Baker, *Translation and Conflict*, 28; Baker, "Narratives of Terrorism," 350.
111. Baker, "Narratives of Terrorism," 350.
112. Baker, "Narratives of Terrorism," 351.
113. Baker, "Narratives of Terrorism," 351.
114. Harding, "Narratives and Contextual Frames," 106.
115. Boéri, "Emerging Narratives," 63.

have their own narratives within them.[116] In a sense, narrative theory is vague because theoreticians are virtually free to conceptualize narrative boundaries in any way they please. In fact, Baker suggests that "ultimately, narrative theory acknowledges that where we choose to draw any boundaries, including boundaries between theoretical categories, is part of the narrative world we are constantly engaged in constructing for ourselves and others."[117] Given its adaptable nature, narrative frame theory lends itself well to contextualized application. Therefore, I embrace and acknowledge the flexibility inherent in the theory in this book, exercising the freedom to draw the boundaries necessary for comprehending the specific contexts that people are in and in which Bible translation takes place in the Majority World.

An additional characteristic of narratives is that they entwine themselves intrinsically in "temporality"—that is, the meaning derived from those narratives is characterized by embeddedness in time and space within the "temporal moment and physical site of the narration."[118] Given the temporal nature of narratives, emerging or evolving narratives can challenge the existing stories that individuals and societies tell themselves. This characteristic is especially relevant in the context of Bible translation, as those who initiate translation projects often seek to create projects that bring about social change and transformation through spiritual conversion and encounter. In addition to existing in this notion of temporality, narratives also exist in "relationality"[119]—meaning narratives are related to one another and intertwined in some way. This relationality is significant because it follows that individual events do not make sense on their own but are understood "insofar as they constitute elements of an overall narrative."[120] In other words, relationality highlights the way in which individual stories are not isolated but are instead part of a broader web of interconnected narratives. These interconnected narratives influence and shape one another, creating a complex tapestry of meaning and understanding. The act of translating the Bible is not merely about rendering words from one language into another; it is about engaging with the interwoven stories, histories, and cultural contexts of both the source and target communities. Each narrative affects and informs the others,

---

116. Baker, *Translation and Conflict*, 39.
117. Baker, "Narratives of Terrorism," 351–52.
118. Baker, "Narratives of Terrorism," 352.
119. Baker, "Narratives of Terrorism," 356.
120. Baker, "Narratives of Terrorism," 353.

whether it be the original biblical text and the author's intentions (as far as they are knowable), the translator's own perspective, or the cultural backdrop of the target audience.

The ideas of "narrative" and "contextual frames of reference" as articulated by scholars such as Mona Baker,[121] Ernst Wendland,[122] and in volumes such as *Bible Translation: Frames of Reference*[123] are helpful for initiating and operating Bible translation projects in Majority World contexts. But even with the breakdown of contexts into narrative frames, this does not mean that our understanding of a given situation is complete. Rather, as Morin indicates, "the aspiration to complexity carries in it an aspiration to completeness, because we say that everything is interdependent and everything is multidimensional."[124] In practical terms, this means that while narrative frames and contextual frames of reference can significantly enhance our comprehension and approach to Bible translation, they can never fully encapsulate the entirety of a situation. Reality is far more complex than what reductionist approaches allow us to see, and thus, there will always be lacunae in our understanding. This does not rule out, however, striving toward a deeper understanding of the complex systems involved in translating the Bible in Majority World contexts. Instead, it invites a more humble and dynamic approach—one that is continually open to learning, adapting, and refining. Translators must remain sensitive to the evolving narratives and contexts, acknowledging that each new piece of information can alter the larger picture and that the process of understanding is ongoing.

The value of complexity theory and narrative theory as they relate to my attempts to formulate a useful model in this book is that they each help to validate the pursuit of a workable way to deal with any given Bible translation situation. In essence, complexity theory and narrative theory serve as two complementary approaches that offer valuable insights into the complexities inherent in Bible translation, particularly in Majority World contexts. Rather than attempting to reduce the complexities of such situations, these theories provide tools to better understand and navigate them. In this book, I employ complexity theory and narrative theory together to develop a workable model for dealing with Bible translation situations, one that acknowledges the complex interplay of

---

121. Baker, *Translation and Conflict*; Baker, "Narratives of Terrorism."
122. Wendland, *Contextual Frames of Reference*; Wendland, "Framing the Frames."
123. Wilt, *Bible Translation*.
124. Morin, *On Complexity*, 46.

various factors. By drawing on these theories, I am aiming to provide a framework in this book (the Beaded Necklace Model and Loyal Bible Translation) for approaching Bible translation that considers the diverse and dynamic contexts in which it takes place and recognizing the agency and perspectives of those involved in the translation process.[125] And so, the Beaded Necklace Model presented in chapter 3 is all about trying to understand these complex systems and the relevant narrative frames for Loyal Bible Translation.

Hence, when considering Skopos theory in the context of Bible translation in the Majority World, two fundamental principles emerge as the pillars upon which these translations must rest.[126] Firstly, the translation must be functional for the intended receivers, as ultimately the translation exists for their benefit. Secondly, these translations must demonstrate loyalty to all the partners involved in the translation process, including the original source-text author. However, determining what constitutes loyalty poses a potential challenge to this assertion. To address this issue, the next chapter will draw upon concepts from the Bible itself to establish a framework for loyalty that will guide Loyal Bible Translation throughout the rest of this book. Finally, we can affirm the following: Bible translation in the Majority World is a complex activity, Bible translation in the Majority World is to be a purposeful activity, and Bible translation in the Majority World is to be a loyal activity.

---

125. For a valuable introduction to complexity theory in the discipline of translation studies from various perspectives, an important place to begin is Marais and Meylaerts, *Complexity Thinking*.

126. Nord, "Loyalty Revisited," 195.

2

Loyal Bible Translation as a Model for the Majority World

We men and women are all in the same boat, upon a stormy sea. We owe to each other a terrible and tragic loyalty.
—G. K. Chesterton, *All Things Considered*, 1908

IN THE FLUCTUATING FICKLENESS of the corporate world and workplace, the English word "loyalty" tends to conjure up ideas of a subordinate demonstrating "loyalty" to a company or an employer above all else. Bound up in this idea is the expectation that an inferior somehow owes loyalty to their superior and that they should show it, potentially even at great personal cost. Loyalty to the company may mean forsaking the other important realities of life, including relationships with family and friends and physical, emotional, and mental wellbeing. In fact, this kind of loyalty might even be an unspoken rule and "rite of passage" for employees. This idea is very different from Hebrew loyalty as exemplified by ḥesed (חֶסֶד) in the Bible. Indeed, Sakenfeld points out that the biblical idea of loyalty diverges from this common conception: "The powerful is loyal to the weak or needy or dependent."[1] In other words, "loyalty in the biblical sense is not 'company loyalty' in the sense of automatic loyalty to one's superior officer or employer. Rather, loyalty is invoked in terms of the serious need of the recipient, a need that places the recipient in a situation of weakness vis-à-vis the one acting loyally."[2] In this book, I

---

1. Sakenfeld, *Faithfulness in Action*, 2.
2. Sakenfeld, *Faithfulness in Action*, 21.

analogously liken this idea of the powerful acting loyally to those in need to the role of "powerful" Bible translators with the knowledge of the good news of Jesus (including Bible translation organizations, initiators, and maybe even foreign missionaries) who must act loyally to those in need (those without the knowledge) by providing an appropriate and adequate translation for and with them.

Without, as it were, putting the cart before the horse by giving away too much too soon, let me at least be clear that this book is all about Loyal Bible Translation. There is some groundwork to be done in this chapter first, but it is good to be up front about Loyal Bible Translation now to clarify where this chapter is going. Loyal Bible Translation is an approach to Bible translation that takes loyalty beyond what scholars like Christiane Nord have said about the idea. That is, I take loyalty further in this chapter by following how the Bible itself characterizes loyalty and then by applying it to the task of Bible translation. More specifically, Loyal Bible Translation is an approach to Bible translation anchored in the relational posture that translators have toward the source-text author and the receiving audience. We talked about the complexity of Bible translation in the previous chapter, and we will talk about how we might handle such complexity in the next chapter. But for now, in this chapter, we will look at what it means to do Loyal Bible Translation in the Majority World.

In many ways, Loyal Bible Translation is for those new situations where the Bible has not taken root or is entering into a culture for the first time. This reality may be because the Bible or portions of it simply do not exist in the language, or it may be that previous endeavors have been insensitive or inadequate for serving the needs of the people for which they were intended. Perhaps the people have been resistant because those seeking to reach them have refused or been unable to deal with them on their own terms—that is, by using *their* language and *their* modes of expression. Even in a "post-Christian" Western world, Bible translations can also benefit from the insights here to reach new generations and contexts. The West has possibly been plagued with more disloyal Bible translations than any other one context, and so the Loyal Bible Translation model can be helpful in such a rapidly changing setting too.

The first comment to make is that loyalty, as defined by Christiane Nord and discussed in the previous chapter, is already a helpful and healthy addition to Skopos theory. This is true even when we apply it to Bible translation. So, I do not intend to supplant Nord's contribution here. However, with criticism and fear of functionalist Bible translation still prevalent among many Bible translation thinkers and practitioners,[3] this chapter outlines the benefits of redefining loyalty with the assistance of the biblical Hebrew term *ḥesed*. Despite Nord offering function combined with loyalty, I believe we can go further with strengthening loyalty in functionalist Bible translation (actually, all Bible translation is functional if we acknowledge that it is done for a purpose). Indeed, even aside from Bible translation, loyalty as a notion for secular translators can still be enhanced by *ḥesed* and the discussion here. The difference between secular translation and Bible translation for our purposes is that *ḥesed* loyalty applied to Bible translation also takes into account loyalty to the divine author of the Bible above and beyond merely human authorship. Nonetheless, loyalty can apply to both. It is simply a matter of knowing who the author is and being loyal to them.

Loyalty differs profoundly from "fidelity" or "faithfulness" as they are typically conceptualized. Fidelity and faithfulness are usually seen as linguistic categories. Philip Noss hints at the importance of meaning for faithfulness when he says that it is "the accepted meaning of the original text as closely as possible across linguistic and cultural differences."[4] However, it is still a linguistic category, whereas loyalty is a relational and interpersonal category. This is not to say that I dismiss fidelity or faithfulness to a text in Loyal Bible Translation, but rather, it is subsumed in a loyal relationship between the translator and God as the source-text author.[5] It may be that the showing of loyalty in this relationship will result in fidelity to the text itself as the actual work of translation is performed. But loyalty determines the general posture of the translator, that they are to conduct themselves in a manner that is loyal to both the author and the audience. We can imagine the translator not only as an individual translator independent of others, but the whole translation project entity can also be imagined as the "translator" and, therefore, the project as a whole

---

3. I wonder if the fear that is exhibited is linked more to the notion that "what is different is dangerous," than to actual real and present dangers (Hofstede, *Cultures and Organizations*, 109).

4. Noss, "Faithfulness," 434.

5. Speaking of God as the author of the source text does not negate the human agency involved in the composition of the Bible. Although much of the Bible was written by anonymous authors, there are many parts where the author is either identified explicitly or named through long-standing traditions. So, regardless of such apparent human agency, I still affirm divine inspiration of the Bible. I am, therefore, comfortable with simplifying my discussion throughout this book by referring to the author of the Bible as God.

is the one guided by loyalty, not just an individual person doing translation (because, sometimes, individual translators may be indifferent to the author of the source text). Furthermore, fidelity/faithfulness may refer to such things in a formally equivalent or dynamically equivalent way. One may be faithful to the text and yet translate it formally. And one may still be faithful to the text and yet translate it more dynamically. It depends on how one defines what faithfulness to the text is (is it faithful to form or meaning?). Depending on the context, one or the other approach may be more loyal to the target audience (whereas both might be loyal to God). In practice, a faithful-to-the-text formally equivalent translation may be loyal to God yet disloyal to the audience. And vice-versa: a dynamically equivalent faithful-to-the-text translation might also be loyal to God yet disloyal to the audience. Or a formally equivalent translation may be loyal to both. Or a dynamically equivalent translation may also be loyal to both. Or indeed, they could each be *disloyal* to both. But in this book, regardless of the translation strategy employed in a Bible translation, I am saying that the goal is loyalty to both.[6] Which strategy works best depends on the context, but it is essential to remember that a translation that is loyal to God is not necessarily loyal to the audience—resulting in probable rejection by the audience. Indeed, when you think you are being loyal to God by sticking to formal equivalence, you may actually be disloyal because you are inhibiting his desire to be known by his people.[7] The same ideas apply to any other translation strategy, such as foreignization vis-à-vis domestication. I am not saying that one strategy is always better than the other, but that one might be better than the other in a given situation when loyalty to the audience is in mind. As a general principle, I believe that both equivalences, and both domestication and foreignization, are always loyal to God when done within the constraints of how they are meant to be done. It just comes down to whether or not the pairing with loyalty to the target audience is undertaken. Of course,

---

6. For instance, Jesus indicates that loving both is possible: "'Love the Lord your God with all your heart, with all your soul, and with all your mind.' This is the greatest and the most important commandment. The second most important commandment is like it: 'Love your neighbor as you love yourself.' The whole Law of Moses and the teachings of the prophets depend on these two commandments" (Matt 22:37–40 GNT).

7. For example, Is 43:10 (NLT) says, "'But you are my witnesses, O Israel!' says the Lord. 'You are my servant. You have been chosen to know me, believe in me, and understand that I alone am God. There is no other God—there never has been, and there never will be.'" Also, 2 Pet 3:9 (NLT): "The Lord isn't really being slow about his promise, as some people think. No, he is being patient for your sake. He does not want anyone to be destroyed, but wants everyone to repent."

poorly done translation can still happen under any translation strategy. But this is not the fault of those particular strategies in and of themselves. Critics should not be too hasty to judge how "good" or "bad" a translation is based on their own desires for what a translation is "meant" to be like. This haste is like judging an apple negatively because it does not taste or look like a banana.

Even with Skopos theory out of the picture and a narrow view of Bible translation theory employed, some argue that the only faithful English translations of the Bible are formally equivalent ones such as the New American Standard Bible, New Revised Standard Version, and English Standard Version[8]—not to mention the more extreme King James Version-only group of people. Many of these proponents of formal equivalence seem not to realize that fully "literal" translations in English (let alone other languages) are simply impossible. Even before Eugene Nida's landmark book on dynamic equivalence, *Towards a Science of Translating*, Bernard Ramm pointed out the weakness of formal equivalence in *Special Revelation and the Word of God* when he wrote that "languages differ so much in vocabulary, word-formation, word order, verb systems, methods of declension and conjugation, prepositional systems, and idioms in almost endless profusion that a simple word-for-word reproduction as the standard for translation is totally unrealistic and impossible."[9] In fact, going back as far as Sirach around two hundred years before Christ, the grandson's preface admits that "what is said in Hebrew does not have the same force when translated into another tongue" (Sir 0:20 REB). Later, Cicero, the great Roman orator, reflected upon his work translating Greek speeches into Latin during the first century BCE, indicating that "I did not hold it necessary to render word for word, but I preserved the general style and force of the language."[10] After Cicero, in around 395 CE, Jerome the great theologian and Bible translator of the early church wrote that "if I render word for word, the result will sound uncouth, and if compelled by necessity I alter anything in the order or wording, I shall seem to have departed from the function of a translator."[11] The great church reformer Martin Luther also knew this about translation when reflecting on his own work in German: "We mustn't consult the Latin text about how to speak German, as these donkeys [papists] do,

---

8. See, for example, Grudem et al., *Translating Truth*.

9. Ramm, *Special Revelation*, 203.

10. Cicero, *Opt. gen.* 14, quoted in Munday, *Introducing Translation Studies*, 31.

11. Jerome, "Letter LVII," 114; Munday, *Introducing Translation Studies*, 32.

but we must consult the mother at home, children in the street, and the ordinary man in the marketplace, watch them mouth their words, and translate accordingly. That way, they'll understand, and see that they're being spoken to in German."[12] More recent scholarship also echoes these sentiments of those translators of the past. That is, we must concede that it is "often not possible to translate literally and retain natural, idiomatic, clear English [or any other language]."[13] The result in such translations is often "cumbersome, awkward" and "poorly constructed."[14] Indeed, Ramm goes so far as to suggest that "a so-called word-faithful translation may well result in a meaning-faithless translation."[15] This is a genuine fear. If we aim for comprehensible Bible translations in Majority World contexts, we need to understand what this strategy will achieve in such contexts. Charles and Marguerite Kraft give us a caveat about the use of formal equivalence:

> This "faithfulness" centers almost exclusively on the surface-level forms of the linguistic encoding in the source language and their literal transference into corresponding linguistic forms in the receptor language.... However, when the forms are retained from culture to culture and language to language, the meanings are inevitably changed.[16]

With that in mind, we need to understand that the reality is that "the languages of the Bible are subject to the same limitations as any other natural languages."[17] Or, in other words, "as is true of all languages, the Greek and Hebrew vocabulary, idiom, and grammar that we see employed in the Bible participate fully in and have their intended meaning only in terms of their interaction with the culture in which these languages were used."[18]

So, in contradistinction from advocates of formal equivalence, others argue for dynamic equivalence and promote translations such as the New Living Translation or Good News Bible because the importance of meaning comes to the fore. In other words, "the very complexity of language

---

12. Luther, *Open Letter*, F8.
13. Barker, "Bible Translation Philosophies," 52.
14. Barker, "Bible Translation Philosophies," 52.
15. Ramm, *Special Revelation*, 203.
16. Kraft and Kraft, *Christianity in Culture*, 206.
17. Kraft and Kraft, *Christianity in Culture*, 213.
18. Kraft and Kraft, *Christianity in Culture*, 213.

prevents a simple word-for-word literalism and a systematic scheme of substitutions and calls for a search for *the meaning* of Scripture."[19] It is important to remember that, actually, "since cultures and their languages do not correspond exactly with each other, formal-correspondence translations frequently are found to create the misimpression that God requires us to learn a foreign (i.e., Hellenized or Hebraicized) version of English before we can really understand him."[20]

My apparent promotion of dynamic equivalence is not what I am going for in all cases or situations. It is not that I think dynamic equivalence is always better than formal equivalence (even though total "literalness" is an impossibility). It depends on the intended audience and desired function to determine which is better in each situation. Within Skopos theory plus loyalty, either equivalence approach might be valid in a situation, depending on the skopos as defined through an adequate process of determining how to be loyal to both source (God) and target audience.[21] Beyond the talk of equivalence translation theories at "kernel" levels,[22] there are also discussions about strategies such as foreignization vis-à-vis domestication. Such strategies apply to the task of translation as a whole instead of just the linguistic aspects of grammar and word correspondence. Limiting Bible translation strategy discussions to those about the rightness or wrongness of certain equivalences is short-sighted and inadequate for many of the world's remaining Bible translation needs. I do tend to think, though, that in most Majority World situations where pioneering Bible translation is in mind, the better strategy will likely be a domesticating, dynamically equivalent one. So, instead of dismissing Skopos theory plus loyalty as inadequate for appropriate Bible translation in a Christian context, I am attempting to preserve the benefits of Nord's loyalty concept in this chapter by redeeming it through an application of biblical Hebrew ḥesed. But before I can continue to the theme of Loyal Bible Translation as an ethos, it is important to talk more about what *loyalty* is and how ḥesed fits into this discussion.

---

19. Ramm, *Special Revelation*, 203 (emphasis original).
20. Charles H. Kraft and Marguerite G. Kraft, *Christianity in Culture*, 209.
21. Houston, "'What You Ask For,'" 4.
22. Nida and Taber, *Theory and Practice*, 39.

THE HEBREW WORD חֶסֶד (ḤESED) IN THE BIBLE[23]

Studies on the Hebrew lexeme חֶסֶד (hereafter, "ḥesed") are numerous. Dissertations, monographs, dictionary entries, and peer reviewed journal articles all serve as treatments of the ḥesed concept. Some of the most well-known studies on the Hebrew term ḥesed include Nelson Glueck's German classic monograph,[24] Katharine Sakenfeld's *The Meaning of Hesed in the Hebrew Bible*, her subsequent *Faithfulness in Action: Loyalty in Biblical Perspective*, and Gordon Clark's more recent study *The Word Hesed in the Hebrew Bible*. Recent popular level studies of the term include Michael Card's *Inexpressible: Hesed and the Mystery of God's Lovingkindness*. A recent and important monograph on how the New Testament utilizes the ḥesed concept is Karen Nelson's *Ḥesed and the New Testament: An Intertextual Categorization Study*.

The noun ḥesed appears almost 250 times in the Hebrew Bible, with no verbal counterpart represented in the biblical text.[25] Although the related verb is unrepresented, the noun is often coupled with the verb *to do* ḥesed (e.g., Gen 24:12, 14). The distribution of its use amongst the biblical books is varied, with at least one use of the term occurring in every book except for Leviticus, 2 Kings (although in Hebrew, 1 and 2 Kings are a united book), Ezekiel, Song of Songs, Ecclesiastes, and several of the Minor Prophets. Certainly, narrative texts provide plenty of examples of ḥesed, but as far as individual books are concerned, ḥesed appears the greatest number of times in the Psalms, with 127 occurrences. Psalm 136 on its own accounts for twenty-six of those occurrences in the repeated refrain at the end of each verse: "for his *steadfast love* [ḥesed] endures forever" (NRSV, emphasis added).

Some of the possible English glosses for ḥesed that Hebrew lexicons offer include "joint obligation,"[26] "loyalty,"[27] "faithfulness,"[28] "goodness,"[29] and "kindness."[30] In English Bible translations, ḥesed is variously

---

23. This section builds upon an earlier article that looked at loyalty for Bible translation, albeit without developing Loyal Bible Translation as it is here in this book. See Houston, "Towards Redeeming 'Loyalty.'"

24. Glueck, *Wort Hesed*.

25. Sakenfeld, "Love," 376.

26. Köhler and Baumgartner, "II חֶסֶד," 1:336.

27. Clines, "חֶסֶד," 3:277; Köhler and Baumgartner, "II חֶסֶד," 1:336.

28. Clines, "חֶסֶד," 3:277; Köhler and Baumgartner, "II חֶסֶד," 1:337.

29. Köhler and Baumgartner, "II חֶסֶד," 1:337.

30. Brown et al., "חֶסֶד," 338; Clines, "חֶסֶד," 3:277.

translated as "steadfast love" (Ps 136 NRSV); "loyalty" (Deut 7:9; Prov 19:22; Jonah 2:8 NRSV, with fourteen other occurrences in the NRSV); "deal loyally" (1 Kgs 2:7 NRSV); "kindness" (Gen 19:19; Ruth 2:20 ESV; and many other occasions in the ESV); "love" (Prov 21:21 NIV); and "mercy" (Prov 21:21 KJV). Interestingly, for this book's topic, Clines lists *loyalty* as the first English gloss in the *Dictionary of Classical Hebrew*.[31] This list of glosses and examples of translations for ḥesed is not exhaustive. Still, it shows the difficulty of restricting such a polyvalent term and concept to only one word in English.[32] In discussions about ḥesed, it is often described theologically in the context of God's "loving-kindness"—a type of kindness that goes above and beyond the common notion of kindness or good behavior toward another.[33] Indeed, the relational aspect of ḥesed appears central to the concept.[34] Although more recent studies have superseded Glueck's analysis from almost a century ago (1927), he rightly identified this relational aspect when he emphasized ḥesed as exhibiting behavior arising "from a relationship defined by rights and obligations"[35]—even if obligation itself does not adequately describe the fullness of what ḥesed is all about. Nonetheless, this idea of mutual obligation is evident when we observe that many examples of ḥesed involve relationships. That is, ḥesed appears in relationships between spouses (Abraham and Sarah in Gen 20:13), between father and son (Israel and Joseph in Gen 47:29), between hosts and guests (Gen 19:19; 21:23), and between friends (1 Sam 20:8, 14, 15), among others. Sakenfeld's study of ḥesed indicates that the relational aspect of the term is central to it, even if the type of relationship itself varies. For example, Sakenfeld states that "loyalty is not restricted to any *one* kind of relationship, such as covenant, but conceptually it cannot be taken out of *some* context of relationship; it is shown within relationship."[36] That is, loyalty (ḥesed) is always manifest in some kind of relationship—whether that relationship is between God and his people, family members, friends, partners, or others. Sakenfeld goes further when discussing Abraham and Sarah's case: "Loyalty

---

31. Clines, "חֶסֶד," 277.

32. Clark, *Word Hesed*, 267.

33. See also The Bible Project's video "Loyal Love," which gives an excellent overview of the term's use in the Hebrew Bible (https://bibleproject.com/explore/video/loyal-love/).

34. Baer and Gordon, "חֶסֶד," 211.

35. Stoebe, "חֶסֶד," 452.

36. Sakenfeld, *Faithfulness in Action*, 41.

consists in doing what is right by the relationship, preserving alive that relationship even though circumstances present the opportunity to do otherwise with no human reprisal."[37] Even though "doing justice provides one important channel for showing loyalty even beyond one's own circle of acquaintance[,] . . . special concern needs to be shown for the least members of the community."[38] This ḥesed to strangers is still borne out of a person's love of God and the belief that God shows ḥesed to all people. In other words, "loyalty is directed toward God as well as toward other people."[39]

Although many emphasize the theological relevance of ḥesed in terms of its application to God and his ḥesed towards people, the word itself is also commonly used in relationships between people. The examples immediately above attest to this reality. However, when we consider ḥesed applied to YHWH, it seems to be used in such a way that it "indicates an essential part of God's character [and that his] ḥesed is closely associated with his covenant love for Israel."[40] This usage is notwithstanding that ḥesed is essentially anthropomorphic.[41] Indeed, Frederick suggests that ḥesed is definable as "loyal love" and "refers to feelings of loyalty and love that motivate merciful and compassionate behavior toward a person."[42] Importantly, however, this is not just *feelings* of loyalty but "'demonstrated loyalty,' i.e., loyalty that exhibits itself in actions rather than words or sentiments."[43] Sakenfeld also highlights the importance of loyalty as action when she rightly claims that "loyalty is attitude made manifest in concrete action."[44] Loyalty is not just about an ethereal and internal feeling toward others (even though such feelings may be present) but is played out in the real world through action. This is a key point when it comes to enacting Loyal Bible Translation.

The emphasis on *loyalty* is seen most obviously in NRSV English translations of ḥesed, where "loyalty" or "deal loyally" appear over twenty times. For example, in Deut 7:9, the writer explains that YHWH is "the faithful God who maintains covenant *loyalty* [ḥesed] with those who love

37. Sakenfeld, *Faithfulness in Action*, 28.
38. Sakenfeld, *Faithfulness in Action*, 102.
39. Sakenfeld, *Faithfulness in Action*, 107.
40. Frederick, "Mercy and Compassion." See also Clark, *Word Hesed*, 267.
41. Sakenfeld, *Faithfulness in Action*, 3.
42. Frederick, "Mercy and Compassion."
43. Mobley, "Loving-Kindness," 827.
44. Sakenfeld, *Faithfulness in Action*, 131.

him and keep his commandments, to a thousand generations" (NRSV). The eternal nature of YHWH's *ḥesed* is strongly emphasized in Ps 136's twenty-six repeated refrains of "his *steadfast love* [*ḥesed*] endures for*ever*" (emphasis added). In addition to identifying the eternal nature of God's *ḥesed*, we should also note the link between *ḥesed* and covenant. In Deut 7:9 above, *ḥesed* is coupled with *bᵉrît* (Hebrew, בְּרִית, *covenant*) as a hendiadys, expressing the single idea of "covenant loyalty." God's *ḥesed* is conceptually linked to the idea of covenant in this example. The covenant does not mean that God is legally bound to show *ḥesed* or that his human partners are coerced into showing *ḥesed* to God in response (ultimately, both are free acts, even if punishment is promised for breaking the covenant). The covenant is itself brought into being through the willingness of God to show *ḥesed* to people. This connection between God's willing and initiatory establishment of the covenant with Israel and its apparent boundness is a fascinating paradox. Sakenfeld discusses this when she says, "To speak of God as free yet bound, and to insist that God's action toward the people stems as much from the freedom as from the boundness, is a paradox that is basic to biblical faith. For Israel, 'loyalty' was the word that expressed this paradox."[45] Michael Card also discusses *ḥesed* in relation to covenant and suggests that "hesed cannot be the subject of a demand, just as love cannot be coerced because of a covenant. A man and a woman first fall in love and only then enter into the covenant of marriage; their covenant is born from their love."[46] It is the same for God: he established his covenants because he loves his people apart from what they have done. Sakenfeld also discusses the link between love and covenant when she says that "to love is not merely to have a certain emotional attitude; rather, it is to live in such a way as to keep the terms of the covenant"[47] and "the oath [of Joseph to Jacob] heightens the general dimension of moral responsibility which is characteristic of biblical loyalty, for such swearing was done with radical seriousness; it was understood that God would bring judgment on anyone who failed to keep an oath."[48] Indeed, "covenant" is the term most often coupled with *ḥesed* in the Hebrew Bible.[49] The next most frequent coupling is *'ĕmet* (Hebrew, אֱמֶת, *faithfulness*) as in, for example, 2 Sam 2:6—"may the LORD now show

---

45. Sakenfeld, *Faithfulness in Action*, 40.
46. Card, *Inexpressible*, 66.
47. Sakenfeld, *Faithfulness in Action*, 44.
48. Sakenfeld, *Faithfulness in Action*, 29.
49. Nelson, *Ḥesed and the New Testament*, 24.

you kindness [ḥesed] and faithfulness ['ĕmet], and I too will show you the same favor because you have done this" (NIV). The positioning of two terms together like this is an example of Hebrew parallelism at a micro level. Such parallelism is usually more obvious in Hebrew poetic texts between lines, but these examples of bᵉrît with ḥesed and 'ĕmet with ḥesed show that the use of such stylistic features exists within smaller units too.

In 2 Sam 2:5, David blesses the people of Jabesh-Gilead for burying Saul, saying, "May you be blessed by the LORD, because you showed this *loyalty* [ḥesed] to Saul" (NRSV). In Ps 101:1, David sings of "*loyalty* [ḥesed] and of justice; to you, O LORD, I will sing" (NRSV). In Proverbs, loyalty is to be sought after and is crucial for a king to have: "What is desirable in a person is *loyalty* [ḥesed]" (Prov 19:22 NRSV) and "*loyalty* [ḥesed] and faithfulness preserve the king, and his throne is upheld by righteousness" (Prov 20:28 NRSV). The prophet Hosea laments the lack of *loyalty* [ḥesed] and faithfulness in the land (Hos 4:1) and Jonah warns that "those who worship vain idols forsake their true *loyalty* [ḥesed]" (Jonah 2:8 NRSV).

Ḥesed as loyalty in these passages and in others, such as Mic 7:20, refers to an unswerving commitment to another in steadfast love. In Deut 7, YHWH chose Israel not because they were worthy or dominant as a people but because he loved them. Indeed, in the context of loyalty to the Davidic line, "loyalty . . . is not dependent upon the behavior of the recipients."[50] This love of God also manifested itself in the loyalty he showed them at the paradigmatic event for Israel's history when he rescued them from slavery in Egypt. On a more human level, loyalty appears in the context of something one does for another and as something desirable to obtain as a character trait. Being loyal is based on the reality of a relationship—even if the relationship itself is not due to any previous action or worthiness. It is a gracious posture to be loyal to another, whether it is YHWH being loyal to the people he has chosen or the loyalty shown among friends, as in the case of David and Jonathan in 1 Sam 20:8, 14, and 15. In that case, despite the evident friendship that already exists between the two, the notion of ḥesed is still followed through with action and commitment. That is, "the loyalty that David asks of Jonathan is based in a covenant (bᵉrît) relationship. The situation is not merely one between friends, although we must surely understand a deep friendship between the two. Rather, there is a formally established pact, initiated by Jonathan

---

50. Sakenfeld, *Faithfulness in Action*, 56.

(1 Sam 18:1–4)."[51] Even then though, the covenant between David and Jonathan was itself based on their relationship with each other. Sakenfeld tells us that, "in the case of David and Jonathan (1 Samuel 20), however, David (or Jonathan) is pictured as reiterating a general oath of alliance which is understood to be the relational basis for loyalty. Here then the relationship itself is sworn to, rather than any particular action."[52] In this sense, then, covenants, pacts, and oaths should be seen as "an optional strengthening of the request or bond rather than a procedure mandated by certain circumstances."[53] In other words, oaths, pacts, and covenants serve to strengthen a bond that already exists when a *ḥesed* "event" takes place[54]—they do not cheapen the existing loyalty or relationship.

As we close this section, let us reiterate some key points. *Ḥesed* is steadfast love, loving-kindness, and loyalty shown through action. It concerns loyalty between God and humans, between humans and other humans, and between humans in relation to God. *Ḥesed* exists where there is relationship and is often manifest in the Hebrew Bible when a superior, such as God, shows loyalty to his usually undeserving subjects. With the sum of the observations above, we can introduce *ḥesed* loyalty and discuss how it moves towards reinforcing the *loyalty* concept in functionalist, Skopos theory-oriented Bible translation. Or, as I like to call it, Loyal Bible Translation. It should already be clear that relationship is emphasized strongly by the biblical Hebrew *ḥesed* concept—a notion that is important for the idea of Loyal Bible Translation, which assumes a strong relationship between the partners in translational action: the translator(s), the source-text author, and the target audience. I am not saying that loyalty in translation studies as introduced by Christiane Nord and the biblical Hebrew *ḥesed* are the same thing. I am using *ḥesed* analogously to redefine what the loyalty concept can be for Bible translation.

ḤESED FOR LOYAL BIBLE TRANSLATION

For now, we can accept that most Bible translation endeavors in the Majority World these days are fundamentally done in new contexts so

---

51. Sakenfeld, *Faithfulness in Action*, 12.
52. Sakenfeld, *Faithfulness in Action*, 30.
53. Sakenfeld, *Faithfulness in Action*, 30.
54. Nelson, *Ḥesed and the New Testament*, 19.

that people can access God's word for themselves. This idea of vernacular translation is a profoundly Protestant Reformation principle,[55] yet it is not confined only to that time in the church's history. Nor should it be taken for granted. But we can say that the Bible is inherently translatable, and this is part of God's design for it. A former professor at Yale University, from the Gambia, Lamin Sanneh identifies an important truth:

> Christianity, from its origins, identified itself with the need to translate out of Aramaic and Hebrew, and from that position came to exert a dual force in its historical development. ... It seems to be part of the earliest records we possess that the disciples came to a clear and firm position regarding the translatability of the gospel, with a commitment to the pluralist merit of culture within God's universal purpose.[56]

Furthermore, Sanneh also recognizes that "translatability is the source of the success of Christianity across cultures. The religion is the willing adoption of any culture that would receive it, equally at home in all languages and cultures, and among all races and conditions of people."[57]

The quest for vernacular Bible translation was, at times, a perilous one and cost the lives of some of the early Protestant Reformers who believed that the Bible should be accessible to everyone.[58] For example, John Wycliffe was tried for heresy and for directing criticisms against the Catholic Church in 1378, having also "felt the need to provide the Scriptures in a form that the ordinary reader could use."[59] Almost two centuries later, William Tyndale was convicted of heresy and sentenced to execution in 1536. After a failed strangulation meant to reduce the pain inflicted during execution, Tyndale was burnt at the stake,[60] partly because of his radical belief that people should be able to read the Bible in English—the language they could understand. This does not mean there has always been hostility to vernacular translation of the Bible. On the contrary, the Septuagint is a testament to the fact that the Hebrew

---

55. This principle is encapsulated succinctly by Martin Luther in his *Open Letter on Translating* from 1530 that I quoted above.

56. Sanneh, *Translating the Message*, 1.

57. Sanneh, *Translating the Message*, 51.

58. Indeed, translators lived perilous lives in other time periods (and still do, in some parts of the world), with reading the Bible altogether sometimes banned during the Middle Ages, too. See, for example, Freedman, *Murderous History*, 75–76).

59. Metzger, *Bible in Translation*, 57.

60. Freedman, *Murderous History*, 112; Metzger, *Bible in Translation*, 60.

original text was inadequate for the Jews of the Mediterranean world in the period following the conquests of Alexander of Macedon and the subsequent Hellenization of the region. Indeed, even within the time of the Bible being written, Neh 8:8 hints that the Torah was translated for the Aramaic-speaking exiles returned from Babylon. Furthermore, the Old Testament of the Latin Vulgate, translated for the common tongue[61] by Jerome between 385 and around 405 CE,[62] was very much intended as a standardizing translation to suit the changing needs of church communities in the West. Eastern churches also produced translations of the Bible, such as those in Syriac, eventually resulting in the Syriac Peshitta.[63] In the Western tradition of the Roman Catholic Church, it is somewhat ironic in light of the tradition of vernacular Bible translation exemplified by the Vulgate that Latin became the exclusive language of the Catholic Mass until Vatican II in the 1960s.[64] Another curious irony, though, is how some churches in the Anglophone world have developed a similar sense of exclusivity about the use of the King James Version. Sadly, too, in some Majority World church situations, the use of English or other European colonial languages of wider communication have risen to similar exclusive status and authority. So, if a value is indeed for Bible translation done in meaningful and transformative ways, why are peoples' commonly used language and existing religious terminologies avoided in favor of traditional jargon from other languages? Forcing the adoption of traditional terms and "Christianese" is just like the pushing of the use of Latin in Western church liturgy among people who did not speak Latin. I am not here criticizing the beautiful Catholic tradition but

---

61. The name Vulgate derives from Latin *vulgāris*, meaning "common, ordinary." Simpson, "Vulgaris," 649.

62. Wegner, *Journey from Texts*, 254.

63. Wegner, *Journey from Texts*, 245–46.

64. This is the case, notwithstanding evidence of various vernacular translation efforts even from within the Latin-dominated milieu of the Western church. For example, Caedmon in about 670 CE rendered sections of the Bible into Old English poems for memorization, Aldhelm translated the Psalms of the Latin Vulgate into Anglo-Saxon in about 700 CE, and the Venerable Bede seems to have produced translated portions of the Bible as well at around the same time (Wegner, *Journey from Texts*, 275–76). Translation of the Bible into other languages such as Ethiopic (Geʻez) and Arabic also demonstrate the inherent translatability of the Bible and its dissemination into a variety of communities throughout the history of the church as a whole. It is important to remember that the Western tradition is not the only tradition, even if the influence of the Vulgate on modern English and other European translations is still obvious in the use of terms such as justification, salvation, reconciliation, propitiation, and so on.

simply pointing out that if an important value now is access to vernacular Scriptures, then why the hang up on having to use certain terminology? All language is culturally bound, and to pretend otherwise by using an unfamiliar idiom in a Bible translation creates an unnecessary barrier to comprehension and engagement. For example, why not use Arabic terminology in contexts already informed and influenced by Islam and/or the Arabic language? The use of Arabic in and of itself is no bad thing if its use enables the reader or listener in a new situation to engage in the discursive meaning[65] of the Bible more fully. God is the master of all languages. What do we fear? That God is not big enough to handle it? No language is capable of fully capturing the transcendent nature of God in words. It is best to accept that reality and move on, allowing for fuller and richer use of the world's languages in Bible translation because we can understand *enough* in the language that we use to know what is true (1 John 5:20). We might even learn something new about God that was previously opaque to us in our own language when we embrace translation into other tongues. Indeed, that is an alluring reminder of the beauty of the multiplicity and diversity of languages in our world and the wonder of Pentecost.

In the opening chapter of this book about theoretical foundations, we acknowledged that radical Skopos theory seems to allow for the legitimacy of translations that are disloyal to the source text. In a sense, the acceptance of this possibility might be traceable to the widespread postmodern viewpoints prevalent in the university scene during the second half of the twentieth century. So it should not be surprising that such disloyalty might seem possible, or even likely if left unchecked. In his online article, Seth Vitrano-Wilson expressed the deep fear of many Christians that functionalist Bible translation inevitably leads to syncretism.[66] Here is not the time to debate what constitutes syncretism and what does not (or even to what extent syncretism is always a bad thing), and even though Vitrano-Wilson does not define what syncretism is, the insights of Derek Brotherson are worth including here if only to remind

---

65. Some might equate "discursive meaning" with "intended meaning." I have used discursive meaning here because I do not want to imply that there is simply only one correct meaning, if only we could find it. Discursive meaning refers to the wider meaning ascertained from considering the full range of textual, cultural, and contextual dynamics at play in biblical discourse.

66. Vitrano-Wilson, "Functionalism."

the reader that the catch-all term "syncretism" is not necessarily well understood. He writes,

> Missiologists have advanced two different types of approaches for distinguishing contextualization from syncretism: structuralist, on the one hand, and outcome-focused on the other. The approach I am proposing here is outcome-focused. A structuralist approach focuses attention on the nature of the form used. The form itself is assessed, and if it is deemed good, permissible or at least neutral, then using it is characterized as appropriate contextualization. But if the form is deemed bad or impermissible, then using it is considered to be syncretistic. ... In the new covenant era, there is an essential freedom with regard to forms. Forms, simply by virtue of their use by other faiths, are neither permitted nor prohibited outright. Rather, using such forms becomes a problem if it leads to a corruption or distortion of God-given worship. What matters, therefore, is the *outcome* of form-usage, permitting us to conclude that the NT teaching on forms supports an outcome-focused approach, not a structuralist one.[67]

On Skopos theory specifically, even when supplemented by Christiane Nord's loyalty concept, this, according to Vitrano-Wilson, only "solves half the problem" in functionalist Bible translation because "our loyalty cannot be split between two masters." For example, this concept of loyalty might be able to keep us loyal to God, but "we cannot simultaneously maintain equal loyalty to God as author and to the target audience's 'needs and expectations.'"[68] I do not think that this allusion to Matt 6:24 is helpful or that it is inevitable that I must serve two masters. It is possible to serve both God and the target audience simultaneously. This does not mean that one is my master at the expense of another. In Brotherson's terms above, I think that for Bible translation, critics of dynamic equivalence and Muslim-idiom translations, as well as those concerned with divine familial terms (DFT) issues and insider movements,[69] seem

---

67. Brotherson, *Contextualization or Syncretism*, 300.
68. Vitrano-Wilson, "Functionalism."
69. Divine familial terms (DFT) refers to the translation of the familial metaphors in the Bible, and the New Testament in particular. Specifically, it concerns the translation of the terms God the "Father" and Jesus the "Son." Critics accused some translations and translators in Muslim settings of removing these terms. Although not necessarily aligned, insider movements (IM) refers to movements of Jesus followers who may choose to remain in their socioreligious and cultural contexts while still faithfully worshipping Jesus. For an overview of these topics from various perspectives, see Brown et

to be taking a structuralist viewpoint. But from an outcomes approach perspective, what does Loyal Bible Translation do? For me personally, I would like to see it aiming for a response of true worship, ultimately, because true loyalty to God, as the source-text author, is equated with such.[70] Therefore, for divine familial terms questions and the like, our test should be whether translations produce faithful believers and transmit the message behind the forms—assuming that such an outcome fulfils the purpose of the translation. Using natural Arabic in a situation that allows for it, for example, does not mean disloyalty to God, especially when people understand it and can respond to it. God can speak Arabic, after all.

This fear and criticism of functionalist Bible translation appearing amongst nonspecialists (often on the internet), even when supplemented by loyalty, motivates me in this book and especially in this chapter's attempt to redeem loyalty using the Hebrew *ḥesed* concept. The complaints about *radical* Skopos theory leading to disloyal translations are valid for Bible translation. This concern is especially true considering that most of those working in Bible translation are committed followers of Jesus and expect that God's word is faithfully translated. You would be hard-pressed to find a Bible translator who thinks otherwise. I, too, am worried about disloyal Bible translations that betray the author (who I think, ultimately, is God). But, I do not think that all the fears about syncretism or what constitutes going "too far" are necessarily valid. Preemptively judging all efforts that use Skopos theory plus loyalty as syncretistic is like calling the result of a football game before a ball has even been kicked. We need to give the players a chance to perform. Likewise, we need to give translators an opportunity to produce translations that result in the desired outcomes—assuming, as always, that the intended purpose is determined responsibly. The same could be said about criticism directed against Muslim-idiom translation. Many criticize such translations without knowing the context, afraid perhaps of what seems to them to be a capitulation to another religious tradition. Of course, what "faithful" translation means is already up for discussion and is regularly debated at length in the Bible

---

al., "New Look at Translating"; Brown et al., "Brief Analysis of Filial"; Miller-Naudé and Naudé, "Covert Religious Censorship"; Johnson, "Familial Language Debate"; Norris, "Familial Language Debate"; Naylor, "Consequences"; and Talman and Travis, *Understanding Insider Movements*.

70. This, notwithstanding that other purposes may exist as determined by the stakeholders of a given Bible translation situation.

translation community among those who disagree with one another, often at the level of discussions over equivalence translation theories.

I wonder, sometimes, if the negativity toward Skopos theory by some Christians is due simply to the fact that the theory first arose in the secular sphere. This is unfortunate and unfair to Skopos theory, particularly as articulated by scholars such as Christiane Nord, who demonstrated a genuine concern and interest in Skopos theory as it relates to Bible translation. Indeed, along with her late husband Klaus Berger, Christiane Nord translated the New Testament and other early Christian writings into contemporary German using a functionalist approach.[71] A great deal of good happens in our societies that originated in or continues to occur in the "secular" sphere. Sadly, I have observed a generally naïve view on display in online Christian forums and websites by people expressing disdain for Eugene Nida's model of dynamic equivalence, claiming that this also goes too far. Scholars such as Bill Mounce have demonstrated that these concerns are nonsense—there is no such thing as perfect formal equivalence between different languages. Mark Strauss even demonstrates that "while formal equivalent Bible versions function as useful tools for beginning language students for identifying formal features of the Greek and Hebrew text, as a philosophy of translation formal equivalence is fundamentally flawed."[72] I already pointed out that complete formal equivalence is an impossibility and that all translation is meaning-based to some degree.[73] We have to accept that the translator really is a traitor in one way or another.[74] We must be comfortable with a certain level of compromise and betrayal of the source text in translation because it is inevitable. Something will be lost. But surely, in many Majority World Bible translation situations, it is better to lose some form over meaning if one must choose between them. The only alternative would be for all to speak the same language in a reversal of Babel (so that there would be no need for translation at all) and Pentecost (showing that God speaks every language). Reversing these moments, however, seems contrary to God's intentions to see the glory of the different nations in the new creation (see Rev 21:24, 26) and that people "from every tribe and

---

71. See Berger and Nord, *Neue Testament*.

72. Strauss, "Myth of 'Literal Accuracy,'" 189.

73. Mounce, "Formal Equivalent Translations," 486.

74. I am alluding here to the old Italian adage *traduttore, traditore*—"the translator is a traitor."

language and people and nation" (Rev 5:9 NRSV) will be part of the new creation.

So, an undergirding assumption I make here is that all translation is done according to a specific purpose,[75] regardless of whether this is consciously known or explicitly stated by those involved. Even critics of Skopos theory work to a purpose. Considering this reality, consciously utilizing Skopos theory with loyalty becomes valuable because it provides direction through the translation brief. A remaining concern is that loyalty ungrounded in something outside itself is liable to be used according to the whims of the translator. (This is a problem of morality in general: Who gets to define what is morally acceptable and what is not?) Insights gleaned from the biblical Hebrew word *ḥesed* help to keep us on a better track regarding what loyalty might mean for functionalist Bible translation. And so, given that it is *Bible* translation in mind here, it seems appropriate that this discussion around what *loyalty* is in this book comes from the Bible itself.

Therefore, the following two sections will look at ways in which biblical *ḥesed* motivates loyalty in Bible translation by (1) translators maintaining loyalty to the source text (God) as shown in the *humans to God* pattern of *ḥesed* exemplified in the biblical passages mentioned above; and (2) translators maintaining loyalty to the target audience, as in the *humans to humans* cases of *ḥesed* in other examples, also mentioned above. An underlying basis for both directions of *ḥesed* is the *God to human* category. This category connects with the notion that God has already shown loyalty to humans by giving us his word in the first place, thereby establishing *ḥesed* as originating from God himself as a manifestation of his intrinsic character. That is, God's loyalty to his people happens because that's the way he *is*. His people can appeal for help to his very disposition because of his characteristic *ḥesed*.[76] That is the way Bible translators should also be when it comes to showing loyalty to the people served. Going beyond simply saying that *ḥesed* is in the very essence of who God is, for Christian translators of the Bible in particular, we might even suggest that the giving of the *word* in this context of the Bible can ambiguously refer either to the *word* of God as in the Scriptures, or to the *Logos* of John 1:1–18 in the New Testament (or indeed both, at the same time). Sakenfeld suggests that the Old Testament experience of Israel's

---

75. Vermeer, "Skopos and Commission" (2004), 236.
76. Nelson, *Ḥesed and the New Testament*, 129.

loyalty to YHWH is in "response to God's initiative."[77] That is, any ḥesed that Israel showed to God or to its neighbors was because "divine loyalty" preceded it and set the template to follow. Similarly, we show ḥesed in translating the Bible because God first showed ḥesed to us.

LOYALTY TO THE SOURCE TEXT (AUTHOR)

Although Christiane Nord tends to speak of loyalty to the source-text *author* as opposed to the source *text* per se,[78] in this chapter I take loyalty to the source text as essentially the same thing in practice. The words and text we are left with are the result of an author who put them there, and they intended the words and text to say something meaningful. But one needs to understand that I am not saying loyalty to the source-text author and loyalty to the source text are the same thing *if* we take relationship out of the equation. Loyalty is not about the source text on a form level, as though the individual pen strokes on vellum or paper constitute *the* authoritative source text. This view would obviously make the existence of copies of such a manuscript redundant as an authority. Further, textual criticism shows us that this viewpoint would be untenable due to variants that exist between manuscripts (and the nonexistence of *the* original manuscripts/autographs anyway). Given that divergent manuscripts exist, "translators must decide which to follow."[79] For example, for 1 Sam 14, where there is a problem with the Hebrew (in that some of it appears to have been skipped over), most modern translators follow the Septuagint rendering because it makes sense and is more complete.[80] This approach also fits into the idea of loyalty to the source-text author: What was/is

---

77. Sakenfeld, *Faithfulness in Action*, 5.

78. Nord, *Purposeful Activity* (2018), 115.

79. Barton, *Word*, 239.

80. See Barton, *Word*, 246: "The majority who follow the Septuagint [for 1 Sam 14] think that the translator's job is to render what the text originally said, so far as this can be reconstructed, irrespective of the traditional wording. The (more conservative) minority holds that the text is authoritative as it stands, and must be translated without emendation. Not surprisingly, the minority tends also towards formal equivalence, the majority towards functional, though the correlation is not complete." Another issue is with the previous chapter, 1 Sam 13, where the Hebrew makes no sense: "Saul was one year old when he became king, and he reigned for two years over Israel." The Septuagint drops this sentence altogether, so we are left with a mystery. A cursory look between different English translations will show how it has been handled. The NRSV is probably best in leaving it vague: "Saul was . . . years old when he began to reign; and he reigned . . . and two years over Israel."

God saying? What did he mean? It's not about always definitely translating from the Hebrew even when it is clearly deficient. God is who we are to be loyal to, not the text as some infallible object.[81] We might also ask ourselves, If the text itself is inerrant, then why is the Bible not written entirely in "good" Greek and Hebrew when there are clearly parts of it that are badly written? John Barton points this out as well: "The fact that the Bible is not written throughout in the best varieties of its languages, but can even contain bad Hebrew or Greek, is hard to square with claims that it is inerrant or perfect."[82] Indeed, he highlights the issue that "most existing translations are a compromise, following the traditional text unless there is a problem but in that case turning to the ancient versions and to conjectural emendation. The result is a translation of a Hebrew Bible that in a sense does not actually exist. But perhaps we have to live with that."[83]

Instead, loyalty to the source *text* implicitly refers to loyalty to the original *author* and their communicative intentions, whether badly written or not. Peter Enns tells us that "most will quickly acknowledge the benefits of having our interpretations 'anchored' somehow in what the writer himself wanted to say. No effective communication can occur when an author's intention is simply brushed aside."[84] In the same discussion, Enns also reminds us that "the problem, however, is that arriving at a text's original meaning is not a simple task. For one thing, a good number of biblical books are essentially anonymous, so the quest for uncovering an *author's* intention takes on a dimension of difficulty."[85]

On the point about textual criticism, I believe that just because we only have copies of the source text does not lessen the reality that what we have is a preserved authentic message from an original author. For example, just because you as the reader have a physical book in your hands or are reading words on a screen, this does not lessen the fact that you have my authentic words before you (words that I originally wrote by hand on paper—yes, even in this modern age, I write first by hand). Furthermore, the original writers of the New Testament wrote in Greek,

---

81. Of course, this discussion about infallibility gets interesting when we start to think about how Muslims view the Qurʾān as God's verbatim and perfect revelation to Muhammad via the angel Gabriel.

82. Barton, *Word*, 157.

83. Barton, *Word*, 246–47.

84. Enns, *Exodus*, 20.

85. Enns, *Exodus*, 20 (emphasis original). We must also keep in mind that there is not necessarily just *one* original meaning to be found.

while Jesus undoubtedly spoke Aramaic. In this case, we cannot simply claim that the words of Jesus in Greek form are what he *actually* said. We need to consider that the Bible in this instance is more than just some kind of verbatim record of conversations. John Barton further explains, "In the case of the New Testament this goes with a realization that some of the most important words in that collection, namely the sayings of Jesus, are already a translation from Aramaic into Greek anyway. Insistence on the precise wording of these sayings ignores this fairly obvious fact."[86] Therefore, when I speak of loyalty to the source text in this chapter, I mean loyalty to the source-text *author* in the sense of an interpersonal relationship between the translator(s) and the author(s). Of course, one might reasonably ask if this is even possible without access to the living author. Peter Enns makes some good points about this, warning us that

> to acknowledge that the author and the audience cannot be precisely identified is not to say that we can freely mold the text to any shape we desire. Even though we do not have access to the mind of an author, we most certainly have the words he has produced, and it is to these *words* that we are bound. Our starting point for interpreting the text, therefore, is not a private notion of what an author intended. It is the other way around: A correct handling of the words on the page—the only "objective" data we have—allows us in due time to offer some suggestions as to what the author's intention might have been. In other words, understanding an author's intention comes at the end of the interpretive process, not the beginning.[87]

This is where the relationship loyalty comes in—that is, doing the most faithful job possible with tried and tested exegetical processes and tools but from a profoundly relational posture. This relational posture is vital and I cannot stress it enough. Evangelical Christians often talk about their relationship with God. That is the kind of thing I have in mind—getting to know who God is and what he is like and demonstrating that through the act of Holy Spirit guided Bible translation. If we believe that God cares about his Word, then we can trust him to help us, especially when we embrace a relationship with him as key.

For some, Christians should be the only ones doing Bible translation. Indeed, even though he was speaking before there was such thing as a Christian, the biblical prophet Hosea laments that "there is no

---

86. Barton, *Word*, 52.
87. Enns, *Exodus*, 21.

faithfulness or loyalty [*ḥesed*], and no knowledge of God in the land" (Hos 4:1 NRSV). It is true that Bible translation should be conducted under the assumption of loyalty to God. However, it is not critical for a translator to be a Christian to be able to maintain loyalty to God. I have seen more loyalty to God exhibited among Muslim colleagues in their translation work than I have seen among many "Christians" in my context. For many of the world's contexts, it might be an impossibility to have Christian translators. How else are translation projects in such settings meant to operate? Even if an expatriate translator did the bulk of the work, as many did during the nineteenth and twentieth centuries, they would inevitably still require the assistance of non-Christians. Does that mean those translations are invalid and disloyal by definition?

I do also acknowledge that loyalty to God as the author might be easier said than done. Even among Christians, one translator's view of God is undoubtedly different from another translator's view. Again, this is where the relational aspect of loyalty comes to the fore. That is, Bible translators in new situations who have a deep and stable relationship with God themselves will likely produce a more loyal translation of the Bible than a translator who is uninterested.

Further to the issue of identifying the original author, Enns also recognizes that a similar problem exists that "involves the identification of the original audience. The precise identity of the audiences of biblical books is often difficult to determine. To be sure, some general observations can be made with a fair degree of certainty."[88]

Relevant to both the issue of authorship and original audience are Enns's words when he writes that an

> important factor to keep in mind in interpreting the Bible is that the question of biblical authorship is more than simply identifying the *person* who did the writing. All Christians who confess some notion of inspiration believe that the Bible is "authored" by God in some sense. . . . [The] question of authorship of any biblical book—precisely because it is God's Word—*must* go beyond merely the question of human authorship, his historical setting, and the setting of his audience. Scripture ultimately reaches beyond its own time and place, for it is a book that ultimately comes from God. The fact that all Scripture has not only

---

88. Enns, *Exodus*, 21.

> a human author but a divine author is vital to any investigation of a text's meaning.[89]

Following Peter Enns further, he also suggests that

> biblical interpretation is a spiritual matter, taken up by spiritual people, whose object is ultimately the deeper understanding of who God is and what he has done (1 Cor 2:14–16). When we interpret Scripture, we are involved in a spiritual exercise. It is therefore not simply a matter of applying some "neutral" tools and methods to the text. It is both an adventure and a journey.[90]

But even if we assume that all of the Bible is "God-breathed" (2 Tim 3:16 NIV) and that translation is a spiritual task, translators of the Bible who are not Christians can maintain loyalty by conducting themselves ethically toward the source text through responsible exegesis and following the translation brief (assuming, of course, that the translation brief itself was established from a posture of ḥesed loyalty). The Muslim translators I work with acknowledge that their task involves seeking "the deeper understanding of who God is and what he has done" (to quote Enns above). Muslim religious leaders in the community have also stated openly that translating brings to light many truths about God that they did not know. It seems perfectly conceivable for non-Christians to loyally translate the Bible. Those who oversee translation projects might be the ones who need to keep the relationship with God intact as the actual translation task is carried out. In this sense, the values of ḥesed loyalty to the source text in Bible translation can be widened to any translation endeavor that takes the audience seriously. The factor of a loyal relationship is still applicable, but perhaps the relationship is encapsulated in the translation brief. That is, the translation brief can also define what is acceptable and what is not in each situation (so long as the situation is well understood in the first place). Indeed, Christian translators must also conduct themselves responsibly in this way. It may be that we envisage that the project itself is in relationship with God rather than each individual translator. I think though that if Heb 4:12 is true—that "the word of God is alive and active . . . penetrat[ing] even to dividing soul and spirit, joints and marrow" (NIV), then even unbelieving translators can soften to the message they are translating. In most cases, it is likely that translators will already be believers of good standing, but this is not

---

89. Enns, *Exodus*, 21–22.
90. Enns, *Exodus*, 23.

always the case in pioneering contexts such as those dominated by Islam or other religions. For example, despite the good intentions of many, and while it is appropriate to assume that some local expression of the Church participates in Bible translation, "we should not lose sight of the significant remaining contexts around the world where no known or visible witness of some expression of the Church is present."[91] In such cases, working with people outside of the established church will be necessary. This is where a translation brief prepared from a posture of ḥesed loyalty to God and the people we serve comes to the fore.

In Loyal Bible Translation, new Bible translation endeavors in the Majority World require a posture of loyalty and not a posture of legalism or pedantry to form. Jonah warns that "those who worship vain idols forsake their true loyalty [ḥesed]" (Jonah 2:8 NRSV). Although Jonah is referring to the actual worship of idols, translating the Bible in a supposedly faithful way because it is formally equivalent (but rejected by the target audience), for example, may be forsaking true loyalty to both God and the audience (when insisting on such translation approaches). This echoes Ramm's warning about faithless translations that I brought attention to earlier. In the Bible translation task, then, there must be ḥesed toward the source on the part of those doing, and those responsible for, the translation. This ḥesed is relational in that the translators are in a relationship with the source text as a manifestation of the ḥesed of God himself to humanity. Hosea further reminds Israel that YHWH desires "steadfast love [ḥesed] and not sacrifice, the knowledge of God rather than burnt offerings" (Hos 6:6 NRSV). Micah, perhaps even more poignantly, says that God "has shown you, O mortal, what is good. . . . To act justly and to love mercy [ḥesed] and to walk humbly with your God" (Mic 6:8 NIV). Or, as summed up nicely in the words of Mays in a section title to his commentary on Mic 6:6–8: "It's *you*, not something, God wants."[92]

The translation brief could explicitly reflect this posture of the translator to the source text and God. In this way, by taking note of the link between Hebrew ḥesed and bᵉrît (English, *covenant*), the translation brief can be modeled after the idea of a formal covenant in the same way that God's ḥesed is manifest in his covenant with Israel. In fact, in Loyal Bible Translation and in this book, I will begin to call the translation brief the "translation covenant" because it reflects better the nature of a

---

91. Kenmogne, "At Home," 132.
92. Mays, *Micah*, 136 (emphasis added).

relationship by describing not simply the idea of following instructions. With this posture at the forefront, functionalist Bible translation, Skopos theory, and the translation covenant are constrained in their radicalism based on the translator's steadfast and loyal relationship with the source of their translation.

Verifying loyalty is undoubtedly elusive. Who is to say that one translation is loyal and the other disloyal? I'm trying to create a model so that answering this question is not just a matter of opinion. The plethora of Christian traditions and denominations alone testifies to the reality that uniformity is not attainable—indeed, it should not be the goal.[93] However, an indication that Loyal Bible Translation is working is somewhat verifiable in the way the target audience is treated. If it is demonstrable that they have been treated as we would like to be treated, and if the translation works toward making God known, then the translation could well be on the right path. God desires for people to walk humbly with him (Mic 6:8), yes, but he also requires us to act justly and to love mercy (ḥesed). That means it involves others. A Loyal Bible Translation exhibits loyalty to both for it to count as being successful.

In this ḥesed version of loyalty for functionalist Bible translation, the loyalty shown to the target audience and the source-text author are just as important as one another. Although the beginning point is, of course, the source text (because without it there would be nothing to translate), such a sequence does not exclude the need for simultaneous loyalty to the target audience, as some fear about serving two masters. Loyalty to the source text comes first in a sense, but that is not the same as abandoning loyalty to the intended audience. Also, loyalty to the intended audience does not mean abandoning loyalty to the source text. It is not about serving two masters who are at odds with one another. In fact, the Bible shows how much God is committed to people despite their repetitive failures. Perhaps this indicates something about how much we should be committed to people too. Being loyal to the target audience in Bible translation *is* a way of showing loyalty to God. If God is love and we are God's image bearers, then we should show that in the way we treat others.[94] The pattern in the Bible is that loyalty is shown to both God and fellow humans.

---

93. The Bible, rather, tells us that diversity is a component of the new creation: "After this I saw a vast crowd, too great to count, from every nation and tribe and people and language, standing in front of the throne and before the Lamb" (Rev 7:9 NLT).

94. "God is love, and those who live in love live in union with God and God lives in union with them" (1 John 4:16 GNT). See also Gen 1:27 (NLT): "So God created

Sakenfeld highlights Niebuhr's goal of "radical monotheism" as being: "to live a moral life based on a commitment to all others as neighbor, 'as companion in being', just as God manifests loyalty to all creation, not just to a particular subgroup."[95] Jesus himself models such loyalty to people when he dines with the tax collectors and sinners (Matt 9:10); he came to serve the sick and not the well (Matt 9:12).[96] In fact, in Jesus's rebuke of the Pharisees in Matt 9:13, he says to them, "Go and learn what this means, 'I desire mercy, not sacrifice.' For I have come to call not the righteous but sinners." The Greek term for "mercy" here, ἔλεος (*eleos*), is the most common word used by the Septuagint to translate the Hebrew *ḥesed*. Karen Nelson's study demonstrates at length that *eleos* in the New Testament often evokes the idea of *ḥesed*.[97] Indeed, the English translation *mercy* misses the connection between *eleos* and *ḥesed* that exists quite clearly. For example, "intertextual evidence indicates that the relationship between *ḥsd* and *eleos* in the scriptural tradition influences the connotations of at least some of the twenty-seven New Testament occurrences of *eleos*."[98] In the case of a specific instance, "Luke's gospel indicates that the activity of the Samaritan in Jesus's parable is more than an expression of compassion. It is also a demonstration of *ḥsd*."[99] This is clear at the end of the parable when Jesus asks the law expert which of the men was a neighbor to the robbed man, and he responds with "the one who did the *eleos* with him."[100] Furthermore, Jesus rebukes the Pharisees in Matt 9:13, suggesting that they learn what it means that God desires *eleos* and not sacrifice. This is a quotation from Hos 6:6, which uses *ḥesed* in the Hebrew Bible yet *eleos* in the Septuagint. Drawing the analogy from Matt 9 that it is the sick who need a physician, we can apply this to Bible translation in terms of our attitude to those in need of a Bible translation that addresses their needs—unlike the Pharisees who did not recognize that "Jesus does *eleos* (cf. *ḥsd*) to the 'sick' in this scene."[101] That is, the

---

human beings in his own image. In the image of God he created them; male and female he created them."

95. Sakenfeld, *Faithfulness in Action*, 139–40, citing Niebuhr, *Radical Monotheism*, esp. 16–23, 32–35.

96. Sakenfeld, *Faithfulness in Action*, 128.

97. Nelson, *Ḥesed and the New Testament*, 57.

98. Nelson, *Ḥesed and the New Testament*, 175.

99. Nelson, *Ḥesed and the New Testament*, 100.

100. Nelson, *Ḥesed and the New Testament*, 107.

101. Nelson, *Ḥesed and the New Testament*, 71.

"religious leaders prioritize external ritualism and legal minutiae over doing *eleos*."[102] Is this the same attitude some of us have when it comes to Bible translation in the Majority World? Are we more concerned about prioritizing traditionalism and word-for-word minutiae over loyalty to the people the Bible translation is meant to serve?

To use Hill and Hill's assumption in *Translating the Bible into Action*, God's word can exist in all cultures and languages because "the diversity of languages and cultures is compatible with the plan of God. Our unity is based on love, not similarity."[103] Utilizing *ḥesed* as loyalty in Bible translation is not about servitude to masters. It is about the translator's relationship with the source text (God) and the target text (represented by its receptors/audience/the actual *people* who will use it). At the core of this *ḥesed* loyalty is coming to terms with the reality that all translations happen according to a purpose but that the guiding principle of *ḥesed* loyalty will inhibit disloyal *skopoi* and translations. For Christian translators of the Bible, disloyal translations are those that do not show *ḥesed* to the source-text author (ultimately, God). However, equally disloyal translations are those that may pay attention to the source-text author but abandon loyalty to the target text receivers. This is just as inappropriate because the translation is ineffective in reaching the audience in their context. The whole point of doing translation in the first place is lost. God is big enough to handle translations that use such strategies as dynamic equivalence (and this is not a license to do whatever one wants). After all, if God saw fit to give us four different Gospels with their own unique portrait of Jesus according to their own purposes, then why would we think God cannot cope with meaningful and purposeful translations in new contexts? Indeed, the very translatability of the Bible and the gospel message has been core to its global expansion. On this "translatability" of the gospel, Tennent points out that "the word *translatability* reminds us that we must always remain faithful to *both* the apostolic message and the particularities of the target culture."[104]

In cases where it is not possible to utilize devout Christian translators who might seem, at first, more likely to remain faithful to both the message and target culture, the translation covenant can guide the conduct. This might be the reality if the translators are employed by a translation

---

102. Nelson, *Ḥesed and the New Testament*, 72.
103. Hill and Hill, *Translating the Bible*, xv.
104. Tennent, *World Missions*, 352 (emphasis original).

organization but perhaps have no genuine faith relationship themselves or where the translators belong to another faith tradition such as Islam or Hinduism. For example, suppose the approach to a translation project, based on loyalty to the target audience, is that *indigenous terminology will be favored over adopting Christian terms from other languages*. In this case, this should be followed and developed in the translation covenant. This is not because it is just a non-relational rule to follow but based on the very real notion that God desires relationship with the people and that he is perfectly capable and willing to use such terminology to establish and maintain such a relationship. Indeed, Jesus's incarnation is the ultimate condescension of God to speak our language and provides the model on which we should base our attitude.

Being loyal to the source-text author (who is God) does not, in my mind, mean that we must always be loyal to form. The form may have its quirks and uses, and indeed, personally, I am edified by reading the original languages of the Bible without translation. For example, I find it particularly poignant to read poetic texts such as the Psalms in Hebrew. Aside from the more apparent semantic parallelism, I learn so much from the beautiful grammatical and syntactical parallelism behind much of biblical Hebrew poetry. However, for contexts in which I have Loyal Bible Translation in mind, where people cannot read the original languages or even access them, it is often the meaning that must take precedence over form. Again, this does not mean that I do not like formal equivalence. For my own English devotional reading, I actually prefer it. But I have the advantage of experience and training to know what to do with it. Many Majority World translators struggle to have enough food to feed their families without also trying to worry about figuring out the meaning behind stilted and inadequate Bible translations in a context where there is no prior exposure. The people I have engaged with just want to know what the Bible *means*. People live on more than bread alone, but even the spiritual bread that Jesus offers us needs to be digestible. To further elaborate on the centrality of what the Bible *means*, John Barton says,

> It may come as a surprise, therefore, that functional equivalence often goes hand in hand with a high view of the inspiration of the Bible. The logic of this is as follows. The Bible contains an essential message, or gospel—good news for humanity. The essential task in and reason for translating it is to convey this message, not so much the exact words in which it is couched. Especially in versions intended for cultures that are unfamiliar

with the Christian message, functional equivalence is not only permissible but actually imperative if people are to hear the gospel in ways they can assimilate.[105]

In criticism of this kind of approach, and, in particular, of domestication of translations, the "great opponent of fluent or transparent translation in modern times," Lawrence Venuti, "argues passionately that 'domesticating' translations, in which the foreignness of the original is so far as possible concealed, represent what he calls 'ethnocentric violence,' forcing the source text into the language and values of the target language."[106] This seems like a noble criticism, but my mind is drawn to contexts where people simply will not read a foreign text—either because they are unable to or because it is not seen as relevant to them, and so they won't even pick it up to start with. Contrary to Venuti[107] and other writers such as Robert Alter, who also defends formal equivalence while implying the inferiority of meaning-based translations, with Barton,[108] we can claim that "functional equivalence also tries to respect the Bible, but holds that this aim is best served by making it more comprehensible to a modern reader. Equally unwise is the argument that formal equivalence makes for a more 'accurate' reading."[109]

---

105. Barton, *Word*, 53.

106. Barton, *Word*, 59.

107. Lawrence Venuti may have softened in recent years when he advanced a "hermeneutic model" of translation: "Translation is imitative yet transformative. It can and routinely does establish a semantic correspondence and a stylistic approximation to the source text. But these relations can never give back that text intact. Any text is a complex cultural artifact, supporting meanings, values, and functions that are indivisible from its originary language and culture. Translation interprets a source-text process of signification and reception by creating another such process, supporting meanings, values, and functions that are indivisible from the translating language and culture. Change is unavoidable." Venuti, "Theses on Translation," 166.

108. Barton, *Word*, 71–72.

109. One ridiculous idea is that if we were to truly keep the form of the biblical Hebrew, for example, then we should be writing our Latin-script Bible translations from right to left. Barton also hints at the preposterousness of this idea: "In the same way it is not long before the learner of Hebrew starts to be unable to read it from left to right and automatically begins each line at the right without thinking about it. To signal the foreignness of a Hebrew text by writing all the words of the translation backwards would certainly foreignize it, but would surely not be sensible." Barton, *Word*, 101. He further defends against such an approach, writing, "Once one gets inside another language, it stops seeming strange. For example, putting the verb at the end of subordinate clauses is counter-intuitive for English-speakers, but one does not have to get far into learning German for it to start seeming entirely natural. Producing an English version of a German text that deliberately replicates this feature then comes to seem rather perverse, almost a refusal to credit the speakers of another language with common

As I begin to hint at the importance of the target audience, we now turn to a discussion about showing loyalty to the receptors in Loyal Bible Translation.

LOYALTY TO THE RECEPTORS (AUDIENCE)

We established that Bible translation must be loyal to the source text (that is, its author). For Christians, the ultimate author is God himself, so loyalty to the source text as a relationship with God is paramount—albeit, keeping in mind that it is God who is perfect and not the Bible. This is a fact we can easily identify by looking at textual differences in the ancient manuscripts, and so it should be clear that I am really all about loyalty to God and not to the Bible itself as a physical document. However, Bible translators also need to consider the audience for and with which they are translating because loyalty to God is not the same thing as a "literal" translation. Indeed, being "literal" in translation may itself be *disloyal* to God if we accept that God wants to be known by all people and speakers of all languages, dialects, and idioms.

In Gen 47:29, Joseph's father, Israel (Jacob), is dying. He makes Joseph swear to him, if he is to find favor with him, that Joseph must "deal loyally" (*ḥesed*, NRSV) by promising to bury him outside of Egypt in the land of Canaan along with his ancestors. This moment is very relational. Ḥesed manifests as the loving act of a son to grant his father's dying wish. In numerous other instances, *ḥesed* appears in relationships between people—between Abraham and his wife Sarah (Gen 20:13), between Abraham and the king Abimelech (Gen 21:23), and between David and his friend Jonathan (1 Sam 20:8), among others. The key to the point is the fact of relationship with others. Suppose that a Bible translation is a true manifestation of God's initiatory *ḥesed* in sending his word in the first place. In that case, it is vital to show that same loyalty to the target audience in a reciprocal act of *ḥesed* toward God. Such mutuality of *ḥesed* is defended by Robin Routledge, who claims that "*ḥesed* is expected of those to whom *ḥesed* . . . has been shown."[110] Indeed, if Christians translating the Bible are members of God's covenant, then his "covenant community are to show *ḥesed* in their relationships with one another."[111]

---

sense." Barton, *Word*, 101.

110. Routledge, "Ḥesed as Obligation," 181.
111. Routledge, "Ḥesed as Obligation," 195.

However, even though showing *ḥesed* to others is a natural and proper response to God's display of *ḥesed*, loyalty to the target audience's needs is not a license to do whatever a translator wants at the expense of loyalty to God as the source-text author.

A so-called faithful translation may be rejected if the target audience's needs are unmet. These unmet needs may be linguistic, based on an incompatible equivalence strategy in place, or they may be due to other sociocultural or religious issues related to the form of the end product not matching target community expectations. For example, this could be an issue as seemingly innocuous to Western outsiders as a black cover on a printed Bible in a Muslim context. Or it may be as simple as avoiding words like "Bible" or "New Testament" when "God's word" or "Scriptures" would be wholly sufficient and more suitable. Indeed, that is what the Bible itself uses in self-designation.[112] In fact, the word "Bible" does not appear to enter the Christian lexicon in relation to the sixty-six canonical books of all Christians until John Chrysostom may have referred to them as "the books" (Greek, τὰ βιβλία, or *ta biblia*) in the fourth century CE.[113] Indeed, some modern and ancient Christians, such as Catholic and Eastern church traditions, accept more than just the sixty-six books counted by Protestants and embrace other books as canonical. So sometimes, in Majority World communities, speaking of "Bible" translation may be harmful and damaging. It certainly is not necessary. For example, Andrea and Leith Gray point out that

> Muslim readers (or listeners) are more likely to approve of a translation that does not seem to alienate them from their community. Factors that can influence acceptability of a translation are the physical layout, script, and endorsements. Color is very important. Bibles in the Middle East traditionally have had black covers. For Muslims, black is the color of Hell. Green, on the other hand, is the color of Paradise, and has positive connotations for Muslims. ... A decorative frame around the Scripture text, and arabesque designs on the cover rather than a cross, are other features that have enhanced the acceptability of some Bible translations.[114]

On the issue of using certain identity labels, Martin Accad and Jonathan Andrews even point out that "in some societies, when you say that

---

112. Gray and Gray, "Imperishable Seed," 44.
113. Bruce, *Canon of Scripture*, 214; Metzger, *Canon of the New Testament*, 214.
114. Gray and Gray, "Imperishable Seed," 44.

you are a Christian, you are actually making a statement of faith. You are saying that you have a personal commitment and loyalty to Christ and that you belong to a community of faith with Christ at its core. ... In other societies, however, when you say that you are a Christian, you are making a political and sociological statement."[115]

This observation is also accurate in some contexts where the label "Christian" does not mean what we would like it to mean (that is, a genuine follower of Christ). In my context, the term "Christian" in the view of some Muslims has become associated with individuals who are unabashedly intoxicated, as some Christians in this community have developed a reputation for engaging in excessive drinking. Conversely, Muslims within the same community are often viewed as more conservative in their behavior. Religious identity is inseparable from a person's identity, and so assumptions about behavior are often made when labels of identity are used of a person.

Loyalty to the target audience means we must take their needs seriously out of love when formulating the translation covenant and doing the translation work itself. It simply will not do to dismiss the existing context as invalid as a vessel for communicating the biblical text meaningfully. Lamin Sanneh sees "translation as a fundamental concession to the vernacular, and an inevitable weakening of the forces of uniformity and centralization."[116] In other words, all languages, dialects, and idioms are acceptable avenues for transmitting and translating the Bible. Moreover, embracing linguistic diversity underscores the translatability of the Bible. By affirming the legitimacy of all languages, we affirm the inherent value and dignity of every individual and community, regardless of their linguistic background. Sanneh also contended that

> the distinguishing mark of scriptural translation has been the effort to come as close as possible to the speech of the common people. Translators have consequently first devoted much time, effort, and resources to building the basis, with investigations into the culture, history, language, religion, economy, anthropology, and physical environment of the people concerned, before tackling their concrete task. This background work was often indispensable to the task of authentic translation.[117]

---

115. Accad, "Introduction," 2–3.
116. Sanneh, *Translating the Message*, 53.
117. Sanneh, *Translating the Message*, 192.

Furthermore, Sanneh argues that "the effort of scriptural translators to come as close as possible to the speech of ordinary, everyday life is a remarkable example of their confidence that the profoundest spiritual truths are compatible with commonplace words, ideas, and concepts."[118]

The inescapable historical reality is that "Bible translation preserves the essence of Christianity as a religion without a fixed language, culture, or location. . . . [It] enables the advance of what Sanneh calls a 'World Christianity.' By this, he refers to Christianity as a global religion which aims to be at home in every context."[119] Additionally, it is rather exciting that "the advent of Scriptures in the languages and cultures of people for the first time has meant a lot more than the mere availability of new information. It has primarily been viewed as affirmation that their languages qualify as recipients of the revelation of the Creator God."[120]

The original text came to its first audience in a way that was meaningful to them. In fact, for a lot of the Bible, the first time people received it would have been orally. In remaining loyal to the target audience, translators may find themselves compelled to adopt forms and mediums that diverge significantly from the source text's existence now as ancient written manuscripts and codexes. This recognition prompts us to consider how the Bible might have taken on different forms had it been revealed at another time or to a different people. It would likely exist in another form. But it would still be just as translatable. For example, moving to the present time, an oral Bible translation might be used in a context where the target audience cannot engage in written texts. Would such an application of orality in place of a written manuscript be evidence of disloyalty to the source text or God? Some would likely suggest that it is. However, is the message itself not the same? Does it not communicate the coming of Jesus of Nazareth and his mission?

In further defense of orality, it is important to consider the insights offered by biblical performance criticism perspectives. These perspectives shed light on the notion that much of the biblical text appears to be imbued with an underlying orality.[121] By recognizing the oral roots of the biblical tradition, we gain a deeper appreciation for the fluidity and flexibility of biblical interpretation and transmission. Indeed, orality not

---

118. Sanneh, *Translating the Message*, 200.

119. Kenmogne, "At Home in All Languages," 112.

120. Kenmogne, "At Home in All Languages," 116.

121. Rhoads, "Biblical Performance Criticism," 157; Wendland, *Orality and the Scriptures*, 12. See also Acker, *Exegeting Orality*.

only seems to have played a foundational role in the composition and transmission of the biblical text itself but also continues to shape how it is understood and engaged with in contemporary Majority World contexts. Further to this, William Graham points out that "the spoken word of scripture has been overwhelmingly the most important medium through which religious persons and groups throughout history have known and interacted with scriptural texts."[122] In this case, utilizing orality in the present as a medium of translation might be simultaneously *more* loyal to both the source and target. We see this idea encapsulated as a premise in James Maxey's book title *From Orality to Orality*[123]—that is, going from the underlying orality of the original context to the contemporary orality in many (if not all) of today's societies.

Returning to the topic of loyalty, remember that the defining aspect of *ḥesed* in Loyal Bible Translation is relationship. At some point, we must recognize that there will always be disagreement about the "correct" way to do things. This is no different in the Bible translation world in debates over equivalences—without even bringing in the discussion about Loyal Bible Translation that I am initiating here. Therefore, even though disagreements will happen, a clear *skopos* and translation covenant are essential. The Beaded Necklace Model in the next chapter will help us to nail down what narrative frames to consider for a good *skopos*, translation covenant, and eventual and actual translation product. If we have a relationship both with God (source) and people (target), then we should be able to produce faithful and adequate Bible translations that show disloyalty to neither. Loyalty for me in this book is not just an abstract concept but a posture characterized by a genuine relationship between translator and source and between translator and target. It may be that the "translator" is not an individual person. The translation covenant can guide individuals regardless of their personal posture and attitude. Indeed, for the Bible translator (whether an individual or not), it goes even further: it is about mediating a relationship between source and target—between God and those receiving his translated word. The translator must imagine themselves as in dialogue with both parties and show loyalty to each through the translations they produce. Sometimes, these translations will be dynamically equivalent, formally equivalent, domesticating, foreignizing, or otherwise. But all of them should be loyal.

---

122. Graham, *Beyond the Written Word*, 155.
123. Maxey, *From Orality to Orality*.

Such a relational posture should alleviate many of the fears that critics of Skopos theory plus loyalty have. The fear writers such as Vitrano-Wilson have about syncretism[124] and disloyal translations could be alleviated by applying *ḥesed* to the loyalty concept in functionalist Bible translation. Using *ḥesed* to characterize loyalty provides a biblical basis for the idea and preserves the status of the original author—who for me and many others in the case of Bible translation is God himself.

BIBLE TRANSLATION AMONG MUSLIMS

Just like how God shows *ḥesed* to us, I believe that God calls us to show *ḥesed* to others. This is especially the case for those who have not perceived God's *ḥesed* before. For example, if Bible translators truly believe that Muslims should encounter Jesus so as to follow him, then we need not be so self-assured as to force Muslims to accept our terminology. It has not always been the case that translations force people to adopt the jargon of another language group. For example, "in the 19th century, when Western missionaries fostered translations of the Bible into additional languages spoken by Muslims, they often used the terminology that was normal to each language."[125] Speaking briefly of my own sociolinguistic context, this phenomenon of using ordinary language is observable in the earliest Ciyawo Bible translation efforts of that era. For example, in the 1880 publication of the Gospel of Matthew,[126] the translator Chauncy Maples used Islamic terminology throughout the translation, including in the title *Isa Masiya* ("Jesus the Christ")—and this in a translation done by a high-church Anglican clergyman. The story is the same for the earliest Kiswahili translations, such as those by Edward Steere, another Anglican. In his 1876 translation of Matthew,[127] Steere's use of Islamic language is also obvious.[128] Contrary to this approach, "as might be expected, when the Good News is delivered to Muslims in language that shows disrespect

---

124. Vitrano-Wilson, "Functionalism."
125. Brown et al., "Muslim-Idiom Bible Translations," 88.
126. Maples, *Anjili ja Ambuje Wetu*.
127. Steere, *Anjili ya Bwana Wetu*.
128. Indeed, the approach that Chauncy Maples used to translate Matthew into Ciyawo was very likely influenced by the Kiswahili translation by Edward Steere. Both men were members of the Universities' Mission to Central Africa (UMCA) and contemporaries of each other.

for their mother tongue, it gets rejected."[129] This is what happened *after* the initial efforts of 1880 into Ciyawo. Once Bible translations went "Christian," the Muslim Yawo community and Christian Yawo converts developed separate and somewhat static identities. The ratio of Christian to Muslim Yawo people remains more-or-less the same to the present day, with the vast majority identifying as Muslim.

The point of so-called Muslim-idiom translation (would it be better just to call it the language of the people who happen to be Muslim?) is not to "Islamify" the translation of the Bible. On the contrary, "the whole purpose of Muslim-idiom translations is to overcome the linguistic barriers that have hindered interested Muslims from reading the Scriptures. Translations overcome these barriers by showing respect for the language and customs of Muslim readers/hearers, by making the text easy to understand, and by avoiding wordings that are viewed as abhorrent or indecent."[130]

We can certainly find ways that are loyal to God to express who Jesus is to Muslims (and anyone else) and what he has done for humanity. The richness and diversity of salvific metaphors in the Christian tradition offers a multitude of ways to communicate the gospel message. Who can fully grasp all these metaphors in their heads and heart at once? According to various models, God saves us, ransoms us, liberates us, loves us, we are his children, and more. Each of these metaphors encapsulates a different facet of the profound truth of salvation in Christian theology. For our Muslim brothers and sisters, certain metaphors may resonate more deeply than others. It is essential to recognize that our own experiences and understandings are not necessarily normative for everyone else. The journey to faith is often deeply personal and context specific, shaped by individual backgrounds, cultures, and languages. Despite this, critics are often quick to voice their negativity toward practitioners who endeavor to be sensitive to the Islamic context in certain situations. These critics may argue that such sensitivity dilutes the gospel message or compromises theological integrity.[131] However, this perspective overlooks the profound

---

129. Brown et al., "Muslim-Idiom Bible Translations," 88.

130. Brown et al., "Muslim-Idiom Bible Translations," 95.

131. It is often overlooked by critics of Muslim-idiom translations that approaches to Bible translation that pay attention to Islamic contexts by using Islamic terminology and styles are not just a modern phenomenon but inherit practices dating back to at least the ninth century. Such early engagements reflect "the vivid and creative atmosphere that characterized and affected religious communities in the Middle East during late antiquity and medieval times" (Hjälm, "Qur'ānic Intertextuality,"

Christian theological and missional imperative to communicate the gospel in ways that are both faithful and accessible to the "other."[132] Such criticism is no less controversial when discussing "divine familial terms." However, avoiding such terms in translation could actually be *more* loyal to God in Arabic-speaking contexts than using "direct" equivalents of the metaphors ("son," "father"). For example,

> It has been claimed that Muslim-idiom translations seek to communicate the deity of Christ less clearly than more literal translations. This is not true. Muslims do not think that "Son of God" means anything more than "God's offspring," so a literal translation does not communicate the status of Christ. A higher view of Christ is communicated by phrases that describe Jesus' unique role and relationship to God.[133]

It is also important to note that "a common mistake readers make is to assume that the words and phrases used by everyday Jews speaking Aramaic at the time of Jesus had the same meanings as the technical terms defined in fourth century Greek theological discussion."[134] These particular mistakes can be categorized, with Carson, as "semantic anachronism" and "false assumptions about technical meaning."[135]

Further obvious examples of assuming words and phrases have the same meanings across cultures and times "are terms like 'Son of God' and 'Son of Man' that had common usages among Jews that were less technically defined than are the technical uses of these terms in theological discussion that occurred decades or even centuries later."[136] Even for native English speakers, the terms "Son of God" and "Son of Man" are

---

314). Indeed, Andy Warren-Rothlin reminds us that "in historical perspective, MIT practices are not unusual, but demonstrate in some way greater continuity with the history of biblical transmission and translation than modern Christian-idiom translation" (Warren-Rothlin, "Linguistic Equivalence," 355). For other helpful sources on historical perspectives, see Griffith, *Bible in Arabic*; Hjälm, "Changing Face"; Hjälm, "Scriptures beyond Words"; Hjälm, "Qurʾānic Intertextuality"; and Reynolds, *Qurʾān and Its Biblical Subtext*. A clichéd use of Eccl 1:9 also comes to mind when thinking about how Muslim-idiom translations are not a recent development: "There is nothing new under the sun."

132. I am thinking of commands such as the so-called Great Commission in Matt 28:19–20 and other biblical passages that allude to the need for messengers to communicate good news to others, such as Isa 52:7 and Rom 10:14–15.

133. Brown et al., "Muslim-Idiom Bible Translations," 92.

134. Brown et al., "Muslim-Idiom Bible Translations," 101.

135. Carson, *Exegetical Fallacies*, 33, 45.

136. Brown et al., "Muslim-Idiom Bible Translations," 101.

confusing because despite how it might initially seem, "Son of God" is the human title, whereas "Son of Man" is a title that conjures of thoughts of a great heavenly figure.[137] Besides debating the linguistic foibles associated with translating "Son of God" and coming up with a once-and-for-all solution, Warren-Rothlin challenges us with the distinct possibility that "ultimately, in the case of 'Son of God,' the major fault line may not in fact be one of translation philosophy, but between translators' and biblical scholars' awareness of polysemy and meaning shift on the one hand, and evangelical theologians' and missiologists' concern for singular systematic theological orthodoxy on the other."[138]

This basically means that while critics keep insisting on talking in theological terms, the issue with divine familial terms—that writers like Warren-Rothlin above point out—is that it is actually a linguistic problem. This is helpful to keep in mind because it means that critics and proponents alike are generally more closely aligned theologically than critics would make it seem at first. I have yet to encounter someone favorable to Muslim-idiom translation that is also a raging heretic, who denies trinitarian theology, for example.[139]

On a practical and physical level, what is lost when we print a Bible or Bible portions using designs that could be deemed Islamic? Were Bible translations and manuscripts in medieval times not produced with comparable beauty? Take, for example, the physical embellishments in such examples as the cover page from the *Leningrad Codex* in Hebrew (eleventh century CE) or the illuminated manuscripts of the even older *Lindisfarne Gospels* (eighth century CE) and *Book of Kells* in Latin (probably early ninth century CE) from the British Isles. Indeed, other examples probably predate the birth of Muhammad (c. 570 CE), such as the *Rossano Gospels* and *Vienna Genesis* (early to mid-sixth century) in Greek, and

---

137. Warren-Rothlin, "Linguistic Equivalence," 357.

138. Warren-Rothlin, "Linguistic Equivalence," 358.

139. Some critics argue that "Son of God" is an ontological description of Jesus's relationship to the Father. However, the ontology of God is not built upon the words we use to describe it. If that were the case, then no translation could ever be adequate—there would have to be some mystical element to the Koine Greek used in the New Testament when describing Jesus as Son and God as Father. But human language is limited, and the fact that there are different words for "son" and "father" in different languages means that there are different ways of referring to God's essence. If there weren't, there would be a singularity of language for describing God. Our words are not the ontology; we must find words in limited human language to describe something we simply cannot fathom. Hence, supposedly avoiding the use of divine familial terms ultimately comes down to being a linguistic problem, not a theological one.

the even older *Garima Gospels* in Geʻez from Ethiopia (from around 500 CE). Despite the European nomenclature associated with the first two of these examples, the *Rossano Gospels* and *Vienna Genesis* were probably produced in Syria or Palestine, not Europe. There are also examples of illuminated manuscripts of other important texts, such as versions of Virgil's *Aeneid*, as in the case of the fifth-century *Vergilius Romanus* and *Vergilius Vaticanus*, and of Homer's *Iliad*, as in the *Ambrosian Iliad* (also fifth or sixth century CE). These beautiful presentations of the Scriptures and other works, even if they did not necessarily directly inspire the Qurʾān to be presented in a similar fashion, are examples from late antiquity that predate the customs we might now erroneously associate exclusively with Islam. This is not to say that Islamic tradition did not develop its own specificity but just to show that Christians once decorated their Bibles beautifully too. It is not the fault of Muslims that a significant number of Bibles these days are an uninviting and dreary black. The mentions above about illuminated manuscripts from past Christian traditions is a sad reminder that, in general, Bible translation has lost its spark when it comes to presentation. We can also learn a lot from Islam in the way that holy books are respectfully treated. By producing Bible translations that are of good quality and beautiful to look at, we also show honor to the book that we care about so much. By doing *ḥesed* in this way—by showing honor to the Bible ourselves—the new readers and listeners of such a book will know that it is a book worth treasuring and even sharing. Indeed, in many cultures, honor is profoundly important, and so we would do well to pay attention to it.

LOYAL BIBLE TRANSLATION IS RADICAL

Loyal Bible Translation calls for radical *ḥesed* loyalty, even when that might make Christians squeamish. For example, what if, metaphorically, we approached Muslims and Hindus and all "others" in the same way as we are to approach the widows and orphans spoken about by the prophets?[140] What if we extended the same kind of loyal love to Muslims and Hindus as Hosea demonstrated to his prostitute wife? While such a notion might sometimes unsettle us, it is important to remember that God transcends our discomfort and yearns to embrace the "other" as his

---

140. See, for example, Isa 1:23; Jer 7:6, 22:3; Zech 7:10; Mal 3:5.

own. After all, his desire is for none to perish.[141] By persisting in the use of Christianized terminology, are we inadvertently contributing to the continued marginalization and exclusion of the "other"? This does not mean we forsake loyalty to God. But are we—by clinging to traditionalist translations solely because "that's the way it's always been done"—complicit in perpetuating the spiritual estrangement of the "other"? Do we see this as a just thing to do? I rather think that a just Bible translation is one that takes seriously the people who will use the translation.[142] People cannot come to Jesus if they do not understand the words that he is saying. Indeed,

> where other religions are dominant and access is politically constrained and restricted[,] . . . the prevailing strategies that assume the leading role of a local expression of the Church will not necessarily prove effective. . . . Instead, they will require cross-cultural and creative pioneering engagements that allow Bible translation alongside church planting to lay a solid foundation for the ongoing and multigenerational transformation of the communities. . . . Bible translation serves the purpose of evangelism in the regions of the world that are still unchurched or without a Gospel witness. However, where a Church is already established, Bible translation should essentially aim to further spiritual maturity, theological formation, and identity affirmation.[143]

In these contexts that have no church or community of Jesus followers, for example, such as in a predominantly Muslim setting, "loyalty means taking the obligations of all relationships (personal or communal) seriously, even those it would be easy and convenient to ignore, those where the need is great and no repayment is foreseeable. Loyalty means

---

141. See 2 Pet 3:9: "The Lord is not slow in keeping his promise, as some understand slowness. Instead he is patient with you, *not wanting anyone to perish*, but everyone to come to repentance" (NIV, emphasis added).

142. Warren-Rothlin, "Bibel in muslimischer Sprache," 1. Warren-Rothlin draws attention to *Die Bibel in gerechter Sprache*, or *The Bible in Just Language*, a German Bible translation that aims to translate the biblical writings into contemporary German that does justice to women in the Bible. Regardless of any theological debates that may arise and have arisen concerning this translation, I think the term "just" (*gerechter*) in the title is poignant. A good Loyal Bible Translation is undoubtedly one that does *justice* to both the source-text author and the target audience.

143. Kenmogne, "At Home in All Languages," 132–33.

putting another person or group or even the whole world at greater value than oneself."[144]

Sometimes, the situations in which we work do not allow for dialogue with existing church leaders or congregations. However, rather than viewing this as a setback, we can recognize it as an opportune time to enact Loyal Bible Translation because the translator must seek to understand the other and endeavor to show *ḥesed* to them—even when it seems futile. Essentially, the inability to engage in direct dialogue with established church leaders or congregations (in cases where such communities do not exist, for example) should not be viewed as a hindrance but rather as an invitation to embody the principles of Loyal Bible Translation in their purest form. During these moments of apparent futility, the true essence of *ḥesed* as commitment to the other is revealed. Sakenfeld discusses how loyalty (*ḥesed*) is "invoked in terms of the serious need of the recipient, a need that places the recipient in a situation of weakness vis-à-vis the one acting loyally."[145] That is, taking a Muslim or other context and attempting to mold it into a Christianized (Western?) version of oneself is not reflecting true loyalty. True loyalty involves meeting such people where they are, using their own words and cultural idioms. For instance, using terms and concepts familiar within Islamic tradition, like referring to Jesus as *Isa* and emphasizing his role as a prophet, can build a bridge to deeper conversations about his divinity and purpose. It is then up to them how they continue from there. They should not have to learn a new language or adopt unfamiliar jargon to encounter Jesus as described in the Scriptures. Such an encounter does not require the additional burden of cultural assimilation. God already speaks their language.

People have, can, and will argue about what showing loyalty to God looks like. We need only look to the diversity within Christendom to see that loyalty to God is demonstrated in myriad different ways. But perhaps that is the key—it is okay, even desirable, to show loyalty to God in various ways. Certainly, historically, such a notion has not always been possible within the history of the church. When I first drafted this chapter, I had recently read Ken Follett's historical fiction novel *A Column of Fire*. Set in the sixteenth and seventeenth centuries, during a period marked by intense violence between Protestants and Catholics in Europe during the Wars of Religion, it makes for some harrowing reading. One of the

---

144. Sakenfeld, *Faithfulness in Action*, 120.
145. Sakenfeld, *Faithfulness in Action*, 21.

events depicted is the tragic Saint Bartholomew's Day massacre in Paris that unfolded in 1572. This was a profoundly embarrassing moment in the history of Christianity when mostly civilian mobs killed thousands of Huguenots (French Protestants) over the course of a few days.[146] At least some of the perpetrators likely believed they were demonstrating loyalty to God. However, from our current perspective, it is evident that by murdering their friends and neighbors, they were not being loyal to God at all. They failed to demonstrate *ḥesed* (steadfast love and loyalty) to their friends and neighbors, which starkly contrasts the call to treat others as we would like to be treated. Thankfully, the Christian church as a whole has largely moved beyond such animosity and has entered an era of renewed tolerance and even mutual interest in one another's traditions. For example, I greatly admire the Eastern church's *theosis* concept—the process by which people unite with God and participate in the divine nature. I hope that when translating the Bible in contexts where the "other" is present—be they Muslim, Hindu, Shinto, or otherwise—we will approach with tolerance and respect for those who may express truths about God in ways that seem unfamiliar to us. This is about showing them *ḥesed*. But surely their expressions of faith in Jesus can only emerge from their own linguistic and cultural context—the vocabulary, jargon, and language they already know and use. As translators, we must be careful not to place unnecessary stumbling blocks in the paths of those we seek to serve and care for. While we must remain faithful to the realities of who Jesus is as presented in the Bible, we should also strive not to prevent people from encountering him simply because of our reluctance to embrace the other and the words that they use.

The good intentions of many to translate the Bible into the world's languages are highly commendable and necessary. This should be celebrated. However, the problem arises when good intentions blind people to the realities of the communities for whom they would like to translate. Thus, Sakenfeld tells us succinctly that "while good intentions are very important, they are not the ultimate standard for loyalty."[147] In pursuing the commendable task of translating the Bible into all the world's

---

146. See, for example, Holt, *French Wars of Religion*, 95. Holt estimates the total number of Huguenots massacred in Paris and surrounding provinces was around five thousand. I highly recommend a documentary series entitled "For the Love of God: How the Church Is Better and Worse than You Ever Imagined," which deals with the varied and challenging history of Christianity. The docuseries is accompanied by the book Moore et al., *For the Love of God*.

147. Sakenfeld, *Faithfulness in Action*, 26.

languages, remember that it is important to maintain loyalty not only to God as the author but to the receptor audience as well. Language and culture complement one another and separating them is impossible. Or rather, a Bible translation done in a new context should not separate language from culture so that a meaningless translation results. Translations are of course audience-centric—we wouldn't be doing translation if it wasn't for the audience. What is the alternative? Should we give everyone facsimiles of Hebrew, Aramaic, and Greek manuscripts without translation at all, as though the only way God speaks is through languages no one else understands anymore?

Maintaining loyalty to the receptors, according to *ḥesed* loyalty, means doing what is right by the relationship[148] even when the receptors themselves may be behaving badly. That is, "loyalty . . . is not dependent upon the behavior of the recipients."[149] Loyalty to the receptors involves a commitment to them even if the circumstances are difficult.[150] It is not just about an emotional posture but involves action. In the context of Bible translation, this means taking the receptor's context and situation seriously. There is quite a bit at stake here because "how we, Christians, view the 'religious other' affects our attitudes toward them, which will be reflected in how we interact with them, which in turn will affect how they perceive the God whom we worship and seek to serve."[151] How we interact with the "religious other" in our approach to Bible translation will affect how they respond to such translations and ultimately how they respond to the God that Christians believe the Bible reveals.

Ḥesed loyalty calls Bible translation practitioners to people who are not (yet?) "in the fold." That is, *ḥesed* extends just as much to those "in the fold" as it does to those out of it—*ḥesed* embraces the "other," for "God is not only judge of all nations but also One who cares for all nations, not just for Israel."[152] A core component of *ḥesed* is the demonstration of loyalty to others. When we translate the Bible for and with Muslims or Hindus, for instance, this is a crucial point. The story of Jonah provides a striking example of God's call to preach to a people outside "the fold" (the Ninevites); God calls Jonah to do so despite Jonah's fury that God could be so gracious, even to them. We must embody the attitude of God

---

148. Sakenfeld, *Faithfulness in Action*, 28.
149. Sakenfeld, *Faithfulness in Action*, 56.
150. Sakenfeld, *Faithfulness in Action*, 113.
151. Accad and Andrews, preface to *Religious Other*, xv.
152. Sakenfeld, *Faithfulness in Action*, 50.

when we translate the Bible for and with Muslims and "others"—we must be gracious, patient, and loyal to them because God was first gracious, patient, and loyal to us. Indeed, as Sakenfeld suggests, "special concern needs to be shown for the least members of the community."[153] Or, in other words, "we must shun caring only for our own. God taught Jonah to have mercy for the other, to care for the other."[154] In fact, we need to go above and beyond for the sake of the "other," just like God did with the people of Israel when he would have been justified in abandoning the covenant he made with them.

If we in the Bible translation community are unwilling to show *ḥesed* loyalty to communities of Muslims or Hindus or others, how can we reasonably expect them to find the Bible meaningful? This is not to suggest that challenges do not exist—they certainly do—but rather to affirm that "loyalty implies also the free taking on of that obligation to the other, even though the responsibility could easily be shirked."[155] But surely rejections of loyal action are better than rejections for disloyalty by not taking the reality of the other seriously. Sakenfeld also says that "if a person makes every effort to support a friend, for the sake of the friend, and yet is rebuffed, loyalty has still been carried through."[156] Jesus himself was rejected by many of his own peers, but at least he understood the context in which he was speaking. We must ensure that rejection does not occur simply because we refused to present (that is, translate) the message in an appropriate, contextualized, and accessible way.

Sakenfeld makes a powerful assertion about the role of "us" and the importance of demonstrating loyalty to others as an outworking of the loyalty shown to all through Jesus:

> The Creator of all extends loyalty to all peoples of the world through Jesus of Nazareth, thus establishing in a new key the Abrahamic promise of blessing to the nations. The New Testament bears witness to Jesus as expression of God's continuing but transformed loyalty to the Davidic line. At the same time, it testifies to the ongoing role of Israel as a light to the nations, another way for the outpouring of divine loyalty in the world.[157]

---

153. Sakenfeld, *Faithfulness in Action*, 102.
154. Botros, "Jonah," 13.
155. Sakenfeld, *Faithfulness in Action*, 103.
156. Sakenfeld, *Faithfulness in Action*, 138.
157. Sakenfeld, *Faithfulness in Action*, 133.

Again, if we in the Bible translation world can liken the "other" to the outcast, the widow, and the orphan, then it is imperative to show loyalty to them because the Bible calls people faithful to God to have such compassion. It is the responsibility of Jesus followers to do this because this is how Jesus also behaved. For example, "choose any pericope [in the Gospels], and one finds Jesus portrayed as a person freely living out commitment to others, a person especially concerned for the downtrodden and outcast, those overlooked or ignored."[158]

As this section on the importance of the audience concludes, Jay Matenga's words about the attitude one must have towards one another are poignant when pursuing Loyal Bible Translation:

> But Jesus, knowing he was in the very nature God, didn't consider it something to be grasped or used to his own advantage. No. Instead, he enacted a process of "kenosis," a surrender or giving up of his privileges for the benefit of others. Similarly, we have a responsibility to give way or yield to one another. To seek each other's wellbeing. To prioritise the preferences of others over our own. This attitude permeates the New Testament. It is the essence of mutuality and speaks of a community known for highly reciprocal relationships. Where this is difficult to achieve and impossible to sustain in most communities, we have the enabling of the Holy Spirit to make it so in our covenantal communities in-Christ—a witness to the reconciling and transformative power of the Gospel.[159]

MOVING FORWARD WITH LOYAL BIBLE TRANSLATION

As a reminder and caveat, in general, I am assuming that Loyal Bible Translation in the Majority World is aimed at those contexts for which (a) there is no Bible or Bible portions, or (b) where existing Bible translation endeavors are not used or are inadequate for use. In other words, Loyal Bible Translation assumes that the point of doing it is to facilitate a new or renewed communication of God's word that is meaningful and powerful in the new context. I am not necessarily talking about second, third, or fourth translations for communities where God is already powerfully and regularly encountered through the first translation. In such cases,

---

158. Sakenfeld, *Faithfulness in Action*, 134.
159. Matenga, "Centring the Local," 6.

mature Christians may benefit from being able to study different types of translations. In many ways, what I have in mind is finding a way—through Loyal Bible Translation and the Beaded Necklace Model to be presented in the next chapter—to translate the Bible in a way that is truly meaningful and actually comprehensible in new situations. This means meeting people where they are at and using their own language without necessarily importing the baggage that exists behind our "traditional" and "Christianized" terminologies.

At the heart, too, of my model for Loyal Bible Translation, developed from the biblical Hebrew term *ḥesed*, is that loyalty is a commitment. In particular, it is a commitment to relationships. It is a persistent, consistent, and focused process by which a translator (or organization, or church, or other initiator) chooses to commit to "doing" loyalty. Although it is not an *at all costs for the sake of the other* endeavor (because forsaking loyalty to the source author is ultimately also a betrayal of the target audience—that is, giving a false impression of what the original author of the source text wanted to convey is wrong), it is a commitment to show loyalty even when the going gets tough and when radical commitment is required to see it through. This is where the translation covenant steps in, to remind the stakeholders that they are committed to a common goal. Sakenfeld tells us that *ḥesed* "knows no fickleness."[160] For example, in translating the Bible for a Muslim community, we might do well "to live loyally in the midst of human confusion and uncertainty, in the midst of opposition, in the midst of dejection and frustration."[161] I suspect, though, that the main source of frustration in this case might not be detractors from the intended audience but from those in opposition to such endeavors as so-called Muslim-idiom Translation. Based on my experience, those we aim to translate for are likely to be more embracing.

Practically speaking, when showing loyalty to Muslims, Hindus, or "others" when doing Bible translation, we can also think of it in the context of a covenant. Many times, *ḥesed* is manifest in covenantal relationships. Drawing upon this notion, we can apply the concept of covenant when formulating translation briefs, or what I am calling "translation covenants." That is, the translation covenant outlines who we are loyal to and serves as a tangible expression of our commitment to the communities we serve and are in relationship with. By clearly defining who we are

---

160. Sakenfeld, *Faithfulness in Action*, 137.
161. Sakenfeld, *Faithfulness in Action*, 137.

loyal to and articulating our status, the translation covenant becomes the guiding document we adhere to, even in challenging circumstances. So even when times are tough, we still stick to it because that is the bond to which we are committed. As I emphasized earlier in this book, I do not mean that such a document or formal oath forces or coerces loyalty, but rather I mean that it is an "optional strengthening" of the relationship.[162] Again, it does not mean that the relationship or loyalty is illegitimate, but it strengthens the bond that already exists.

As a translation strategy, the core aspects of Loyal Bible Translation are not entirely new in themselves. Loyal Bible Translation is about approaching the Bible translation task as a relationship. This is already encapsulated in Christiane Nord's view, when she said that loyalty is a relational and interpersonal category.[163] The same is true for Loyal Bible Translation's emphasis on a relational posture, but with the added bonus of *ḥesed* to define it. Therefore, in Loyal Bible Translation, having established the relationship in the first place, other translation strategies can come to the fore in actual translation situations. For example, if translators are loyal to both God and to a target audience that comprises Muslims *and* also those unable to read a printed Bible, then a Loyal Bible Translation for them might use a dynamic equivalence and domesticating approach that uses Islamic terminology yet while doing it all orally.

Furthermore, regarding word choices, the best option may be a translation that employs common, everyday language, which may occasionally draw from Arabic or Islamic terminology in a Muslim setting if it provides the clearest understanding or when no suitable "everyday" language equivalent exists. If translating in a context where the people are already Christians and frequently use "Christian" terminology from another language, then it is likely that the loyalty shown to them would maintain the use of such language. I am, therefore, not advocating for the abandonment of traditional Christian terminology altogether, but I am trying to allow for space when dealing with communities that are not Christian and do not have the benefit of centuries steeped in the stories of the Bible and the accompanying "misleading relics of Christian jargon."[164] Sometimes, it is the continued use of "Christian" terms that keeps isolating them. We need to do better than simply expecting them to come over to our "side," as though our side has got it all together (it does not).

162. Sakenfeld, *Faithfulness in Action*, 30.
163. Nord, *Purposeful Activity* (2018), 116.
164. Warren-Rothlin, "Linguistic Equivalence," 355.

Sure, the "other" can learn from "us," but surely, "we," too, can learn from "them" as they discover how to follow Jesus within their own context and experience of language. In keeping with Lamin Sanneh's insights that I mentioned earlier, he again tells us that "Christianity is remarkable for the relative ease with which it enters living cultures. In becoming translatable, it renders itself compatible with all cultures. It may be welcomed or resisted in its Western garb, but it is not itself uncongenial in other garbs."[165]

The reality of the translatability of the Christian message that Sanneh identified connects to the radical and powerful notion that God became flesh and dwelt among us.[166] This is the ultimate expression of ḥesed. The coming of Jesus in the flesh in a great act of condescension is what I think about when applying Loyal Bible Translation to contexts such as those dominated by factors like Islam. Although a full-on incarnational model is out of reach for most on the mission field and, indeed, potentially damaging to physical and psychological health, perhaps we can envisage an incarnational model of Bible translation. That is, in seeking to show loyalty to a target audience, Loyal Bible Translation is an incarnational model because it embeds itself in the linguistic and sociocultural milieu and psyche of a given people. John 1:14 tells us that the Logos, the Word, became flesh and lived among us full of "grace and truth." In fact, this phrase appears to echo the ḥesed we'ĕmet (חֶסֶד וֶאֱמֶת; English, *steadfast love and faithfulness*) formula in the Hebrew Bible somewhat, showing that Jesus's coming itself was an act of ḥesed. So, let us now, in embracing the ethos of Loyal Bible Translation, seek to translate God's word so that it embeds itself, indeed incarnates itself, in communities in which it currently is lacking or is inadequate. Let us allow God's word to dwell among all peoples—including among Hindus, Muslims, and all those who have not yet encountered it in a way that speaks to their experience and in language they can understand.

If loyalty is that which is informed by ḥesed in biblical Hebrew, a steadfast commitment to the other in relationship (often backed up by a covenant)—and I am saying that it is—then we can now look at how it

---

165. Sanneh, *Translating the Message*, 50.

166. "Look! The virgin will conceive a child! She will give birth to a son, and they will call him Immanuel, which means 'God is with us'" (Matt 1:23 NLT; cf. Is 7:14); "The law of Moses was unable to save us because of the weakness of our sinful nature. So God did what the law could not do. He sent his own Son in a body like the bodies we sinners have" (Rom 8:3 NLT).

works in reality when applied to the Beaded Necklace Model. To do this, a succinct definition of Loyal Bible Translation is important to bring this chapter to its conclusion. Therefore, I define Loyal Bible Translation as *a relational posture to Bible translation that values both the source's author and the target audience without forsaking either, mutually formalized by a translation covenant.* It is an approach to Bible translation that may need to go above and beyond what might be normally expected to create a meaningful, transformative, and acceptable translation in a given context. Particularly in the case of translation in new languages or in contexts that have tended to reject translation efforts, it may be necessary to move away from the "traditional" or the "Christianized" or "churchy" influences to create something truly meaningful, yet loyal to the source. One of the problems in our present time is that practitioners who favor more dogmatic approaches in new translation situations (such as formal equivalence or "traditional" language borrowed from other languages) miss the likelihood that their translations will be meaningless to new audiences (and therefore rejected).

The Protestant Reformation championed a now widely held yet poignant idea that everyone should be able to read the Scriptures for themselves in their own language. This was a monumental shift, dismantling barriers and fostering a more personal connection with the Bible. However, a paradox emerges when we cling to "traditional" language in Bible translations in the Majority World. While these influences and forms may hold historical significance, they can become a barrier to understanding for present-day audiences. The power of the Reformation's message lies in accessibility—and that principle can be hamstrung by clinging to language that is no longer readily understood by everyday people. This is especially true in contexts where the audience does not benefit from centuries of Christian history and influence behind them. Indeed, continuing to use traditional forms contradicts the ideal for people to have the Bible in their own languages. Forcing communities to adopt the unfamiliar jargon and language of other translations is a sad state of affairs when the more impactful approach would be to translate the Bible in the jargon and language they actually speak. If God is truly transcendent, as the systematic theologians tell us he is, he is big enough to handle the foibles of human language; perhaps we should be big enough to cope with it too. Surely, God's desire for people as revealed in the Bible outweighs our insistence on rigid adherence to form in the translation of it.

To close this chapter and to echo the sentiments above of Jay Matenga (and to risk upsetting those who may be offended by manipulating a perfectly good Bible translation), I offer you an altered translation of Phil 2:3–8 that gets at the heart of what Loyal Bible Translation is all about (italics added to show where I changed the original text):

> Instead of *translating with* selfish ambition or vanity, each of you *translators and initiators* should, in humility, be moved to treat *the recipients* as more important than yourself. Each of you *translators and initiators* should be concerned not only about your own interests, but about the interests of others as well. *When you translate for and with an audience,* you should have the same attitude toward *the recipients* that Christ Jesus had, who though he existed in the form of God did not regard equality with God as something to be grasped, but emptied himself by taking on the form of a slave, by looking like other men, and by sharing in human nature. He humbled himself, by becoming obedient to the point of death—even death on a cross![167]

---

167. The unaltered text of Phil 2:3–9 reads as follows: "Instead of being motivated by selfish ambition or vanity, each of you should, in humility, be moved to treat one another as more important than yourself. Each of you should be concerned not only about your own interests, but about the interests of others as well. You should have the same attitude toward one another that Christ Jesus had, who though he existed in the form of God did not regard equality with God as something to be grasped, but emptied himself by taking on the form of a slave, by looking like other men, and by sharing in human nature. He humbled himself, by becoming obedient to the point of death—even death on a cross!" (NET).

3

The Beaded Necklace Model for Loyal Bible Translation

The wise man, who deserves praise, is the one who fixes his attention on the realities of things, and adapts his belief to them. Thanks to his wisdom he relies on that which can indeed be relied on and guards against that which must be guarded against. The fool, who is blameworthy, is the one who makes his belief the standard, and decrees that the realities of things must follow his belief. Thanks to his folly he relies on that which should be guarded against, and guards against that which can be relied on.
— Sa'adia ben Yosef Gaon, *The Book of Beliefs and Opinions*, ca. 933 CE

LOYAL BIBLE TRANSLATION RESTS on the premise that one can be loyal to both the source text *and* the target audience. To do that, though, we can benefit from tools and models. The Beaded Necklace Model below gives us a good idea of the "beads" (narrative frames) that we must consider in order to maintain loyalty throughout. But what does being loyal to the beads actually mean? How do we think about those beads? Well, there are, if you like, two complementary models at play here in this book. The overarching model is the conceptualization of what I've called Loyal Bible Translation. The other is the Beaded Necklace Model, based on the metaphor of an everyday object, which is common to many cultures. Another assumed perspective I hold here is that these models build from Skopos theory and use narrative frame theory to deal with the complexities of Bible translation situations. I initially developed the

Beaded Necklace Model for assessing *needs* for Bible translation.[1] That is, it was initially all about establishing what the real-world contexts are in each situation so as to guide planners and practitioners about whether they should undertake a Bible translation project or not, and why. In this book, however, I expand the Beaded Necklace Model to the translation task itself. In pairing with the idea of Loyal Bible Translation, the Beaded Necklace Model helps define the contexts in which Loyal Bible Translation is operating and the relationships that need cultivating to conduct Loyal Bible Translation in a given situation successfully. Each of the two models (the Beaded Necklace and Loyal Bible Translation) is informed by existing theories and thinking. The Beaded Necklace Model borrows the concepts of narrative/contextual framing from established thinkers such as Mona Baker, and the Loyal Bible Translation model assumes a posture of openness to functionalist translation and particularly Skopos theory. That is, all Bible translations are done according to a specific purpose ("function"), whether this is explicitly articulated or not. Therefore, with that assumed, the Loyal Bible Translation model takes Christiane Nord's loyalty-plus-function notion further by anchoring the conceptualization of loyalty in the Bible itself, in the Hebrew idea of *ḥesed* discussed in the previous chapter.

As I further develop and explain the Beaded Necklace Model in this chapter, I will specifically discuss the case of the Yawo people in Mozambique as an example of the kinds of things to be aware of. For example, in the Yawo people's situation, the overarching sociocultural frame includes smaller frames such as identity and culture (who the Yawo are, including where and how they live). The religious frame consists of the realities of the Yawo people being both Muslims and adherents of African Traditional Religion. Additionally, the historical frame encompasses the past efforts at Bible translation in their language of Ciyawo[2] and what has or has not worked to inform future translation efforts. The linguistic frame not only includes sociolinguistic data but also considers the prevalence of orality as a primary means of communication among the Yawo people in Mozambique.[3]

---

1. Houston, "'What You Ask For.'"
2. Houston, "Utenga Wambone."
3. Houston, "Sociolinguistic and Extensibility Survey."

EXPLAINING THE BEADED NECKLACE MODEL

The model I propose here draws upon the symbolic imagery of a beaded necklace to conceptualize the nature and process of Bible translation (see fig. 1 below). The metaphorical necklace comprises three principal elements. The central pendant is at the heart of the necklace, symbolizing the source text. The pendant is the most important of the elements because it is the focus point of the necklace or, in other words, the basis of a translation. Without it, there can be no translation. The second element, surrounding the pendant, is an array of beads. These beads are the narrative frames, and they encompass the sociocultural frame, the religious frame, the historical frame, the linguistic frame, the organizational frame, and more besides.[4] The number and diversity of these beads are contingent upon the specific context and depth of analysis involved in each translation project. Thirdly, the string that threads through the pendant and beads represents the functionalist loyalty notion enhanced by *ḥesed*—the guiding principle that underpins this model. This string symbolizes the inseparable commitment to ensuring that the translation remains loyal to both the source text and the target audience. In the same way that the string on a necklace runs through all the beads on it, so too does loyalty run through everything and everyone it encounters, ensuring that nobody falls by the wayside.

---

4. Wilt and Wendland, *Scripture Frames*, 107. Other frames, aside from including things not explicitly mentioned here, may also include sub-frames within broader frames. For example, later in this book, African Traditional Religion and Islam are discussed as their own frames while also being encompassed by the wider religious frame. This is because each of those "beads" are unique in their own right, despite their categorization within the religious frame.

FIGURE 1

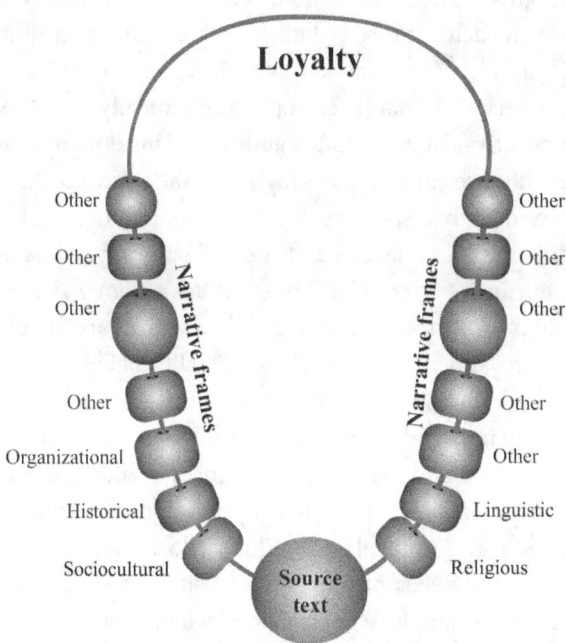

The Beaded Necklace Model

In this Beaded Necklace Model, loyalty as a theoretical concept is entwined not only with the source text, as in Christiane Nord's model of Skopostheorie[5] but also encompasses the other narrative frames that characterize each Bible translation situation. This notion of loyalty holds all the beads and the pendant together in a functional and complete necklace (translation) that can be worn and used. Just as each bead contributes to the overall aesthetic and integrity of the necklace, each narrative frame plays a crucial role in shaping the translation's completeness and relevance. However, the absence of any bead disrupts the balance of the necklace, rendering it crooked and incomplete. Similarly, without the string of loyalty holding everything together, the entire necklace falls apart, rendering it unwearable and ineffective. Thus, loyalty permeates all the beads and the pendant—the narrative frames and the source text—in this model. A Bible translation must be loyal to the source text and the recipients' situation in all its complexity. This commitment to loyalty means that a Bible translation must engage the realities that an investigation into

---

5. Nord, "Function and Loyalty," 93–94; Nord, *Purposeful Activity* (2018), 115.

the narrative frames reveals, such as an Islamic identity, orality dominance, sociolinguistic issues, educational challenges, or whatever else we may encounter in each context. A faithful Bible translation must honor and remain loyal to these narrative frames just as fervently as it does to the source text, ensuring that it resonates authentically with the experiences and perspectives of its intended audience. This does not mean that loyalty to the audience compromises loyalty to the source text.

I acknowledge that showing loyalty is ambiguous and difficult. Sometimes different relationships and "beads" will "put claims of loyalty into competition and even conflict."[6] But, it is not as though such difficulties are without precedence, for the "biblical narratives are full of persons making very hard and ambiguous choices."[7] Ultimately, though, when faced with difficult decisions about such elements as translation choices and key terms, "living loyally before God involves considering the world from God's viewpoint and making choices for the sake of others rather than oneself."[8] This does *not* mean "that any decision is acceptable so long as one's heart is in the right place."[9] What it does mean is that we are to be sensitive to the needs of others even if it makes us, as outsiders, uncomfortable. For example, what is gained when we reject the existing terminologies of a given community in favor of adopting "Christianized" terms from another language? Possibly very little, or even nothing, if the translation is rejected outright because of it. And what is lost? Potentially everything.

Practically speaking, what does the Beaded Necklace Model do? Simply put, it organizes complex contextual realities in concrete terms that stakeholders can utilize in the planning and execution of a new Bible translation (if one is needed) in any situation, including those dominated by Islam or other faith traditions.[10] Initially conceived within the context

---

6. Sakenfeld, *Faithfulness in Action*, 138.
7. Sakenfeld, *Faithfulness in Action*, 138.
8. Sakenfeld, *Faithfulness in Action*, 139.
9. Sakenfeld, *Faithfulness in Action*, 139.
10. Another useful model in Scripture engagement contexts is that of T. Wayne Dye's eight conditions of Scripture engagement and the accompanying "Welser Scale." See Dye, "Eight Conditions." Dye lists eight conditions that need to be satisfied to have adequate engagement with the Bible. The conditions are (1) appropriate language, both dialect and orthography, (2) appropriate translation condition, (3) accessible forms of Scripture, (4) background knowledge of the hearer, (5) availability, (6) spiritual hunger of community members, (7) freedom to commit to Christian faith condition, and (8) partnership between translators and other stakeholders. Yet another helpful resource is the multilingualism assessment tool for Bible translation produced by SIL and

of rapid appraisal sociolinguistic surveys and assessing the needs for Bible translation in Majority World contexts, the model has evolved to encompass the entire task of Bible translation. From the initial stages of project planning to the actual execution of translation tasks, this model offers practical guidance and direction, ensuring that every aspect of the translation endeavor is informed by as comprehensive an understanding as possible of the contextual narrative frames. And so, whether assessing needs for Bible translation or embarking on a project, it is vital that we consider each bead on the necklace (the narrative frames of the situation) because by avoiding them, we compromise the functionality and integrity of the necklace (the translation). Considering all these frames is essential because without the "string" of loyalty running through each, the end translation (necklace) will be disjointed. Indeed, the whole thing can fall apart and become unwearable (unfit for its intended purpose). In practical terms, if planners, organizers, and translators of a Bible translation project forsake the "necklace beads" of their situation, then the translation will likely fail like an imbalanced necklace (not that there needs to be an even number of beads for the metaphor to work). I demonstrated in earlier chapters what it means to consider the narrative frames for producing an adequate translation for communities in the Majority World. According to this model, presenting these frames and incorporating loyalty to them is like putting a necklace together that fulfils its purpose as a wearable item of jewelry.

In order to achieve the goal of a suitable *skopos* and intended appropriate function of a new Bible translation in the Majority World, the initiators and other stakeholders must have a way of dealing with the complexity of the situation. In this book, therefore, I am highlighting narrative/contextual framing as a strategy for grasping the multifaceted and complex nature of Bible translation so that the relevant issues can be understood alongside one another.

When deciding to embark on a new Bible translation project, regardless of the language or cultural context, one should transcend mere sociolinguistic considerations. We must also engage adequately with the complex and multifaceted contextual realities of the people for whom the translation is intended. Undoubtedly, linguistic factors play a crucial role in determining the form and structure of the translation. However, to truly serve the needs of the target audience, translators must delve deeper

---

currently hosted on https://emdc.guide/resources/mat/. This tool also references Dye's eight conditions model.

into the sociocultural, historical, and religious landscape of the community. Essentially, Bible translation is not simply a technical endeavor but a deeply relational and transformative process. By embracing the complexities of context, translators can ensure that the translated Bible speaks to the hearts and minds of the people it seeks to serve, fostering spiritual growth, empowerment, and community flourishing.

Hopefully, the model gets us closer to what Bible translation initiators and stakeholders actually want from Bible translations. I assume that the initiators and stakeholders of a project want a Bible translation and product that is functional and purposeful[11]—that is, a Bible translation that intentionally fulfils a specific purpose as outlined in a carefully prepared translation covenant.

The model proposed here takes seriously the imperative to acknowledge and respond to the complex contextual realities inherent in any Bible translation endeavor. So, rather than relegating sections such as "religious situation," "population," "history," and "culture" to mere introductory remarks within a translation covenant document, each of these elements should be recognized as constituting its own distinct and vitally relevant narrative frame.

Given the paramount importance of context, it becomes imperative to delve deeper into the concept of narrative framing and remind ourselves of some aspects indicated earlier. Scholars often employ various terms interchangeably to describe narrative framing, such as "contextual frames."[12] In essence, narratives encapsulate the dynamic human experience within a specific context and situation, encompassing both individual and collective realms. They serve as the lens through which individuals interpret and navigate the complexities of their surroundings. Far from static, narratives are fluid and ever evolving, reflecting the ongoing interplay between personal experiences, societal norms, and cultural dynamics.

Crucially, narratives play a dual role for humanity because they both represent and constitute reality.[13] Moreover, narratives serve as vehicles for conveying and perpetuating cultural values, beliefs, and ideologies. They transmit collective wisdom, historical memory, and cultural heritage from generation to generation, shaping communities' and societies'

---

11. Nord, *Purposeful Activity* (2018), 26–28.

12. Harding, "Narratives and Contextual Frames," 108; Wendland, *Contextual Frames of Reference*, 1.

13. Harding, "Narratives and Contextual Frames," 106.

collective identity. Understanding the role of narrative framing, therefore, allows us to respond appropriately to the intricate interplays happening in Bible translation situations in the Majority World. By acknowledging this dynamic nature of narratives, we can better grasp the complexities in a more nuanced and meaningful manner and thereby produce better Bible translations.

Writing from a missiological perspective, Timothy Tennent agrees that "the gospel must be communicated within the frame of reference of the target group. This calls for cultural identification, rather than extracting people out of their cultural moorings and insisting that they can discover Christ only on *our* cultural terms."[14] Charles and Marguerite Kraft are similar in their conclusions, but from an anthropological viewpoint: "Human beings live in different contexts or frames of reference. And this causes communication problems, since all the symbols (cultural forms) by means of which people can communicate derive their meanings totally from the frame of reference in which they participate. There are no such symbols with universal meanings."[15] The Krafts continue the theme, suggesting that instead of employing an "extractionist" approach, if "*the communicator adopts the receptor's frame of reference* as that in terms of which the communication takes place, we may label the approach 'identificational' or 'incarnational.' In this approach communicators become familiar with the conceptual framework of the receptor and attempt to fit their communication to the categories and felt needs of that frame of reference."[16]

Again, at the risk of laboring the point, Farah states that, for Christian workers, "adaptive missiology aims to get at the heart of how Jesus and the apostles approached 'the other' in the New Testament. No two evangelistic addresses were identical; they always took the context into account in their witness. . . . They were continually adapting to the challenge of seeing lives and communities transformed by the power of God. . . . As ministers of the gospel, we must adapt to people in the complexity of their contexts."[17]

When it comes to assessing Bible translation needs and embarking on projects, it is crucial, for example, to investigate the socioreligious and

---

14. Tennent, *Invitation to World Missions*, 335.

15. Kraft and Kraft, *Christianity in Culture*, 118; See also Nida, *Message and Mission*, 89–92.

16. Kraft and Kraft, *Christianity in Culture*, 119 (emphasis original).

17. Farah, "Adaptive Missiological Engagement," 117.

communication frames as far as possible. What is meant by this is that the stakeholders should seek to understand the religious and social realities and identities of the people, what communication means the people rely on, how they access religious content, and so on. That is, who do these people say that they are? What narrative do they tell themselves? Are they Christian? Are they Muslim? Are they Hindu? Nonreligious? Something else? This is crucial when stakeholders are aiming for a new Bible translation with a clear and specific function in mind. Without this mental clarity and thorough understanding of the contextual realities, there is a significant risk that the translation will turn into a confusing mess and fail to meet the expectations and needs of any stakeholders involved. A lack of proper contextual understanding can lead to translations that are misaligned with the target audience's cultural, religious, and linguistic nuances, resulting in a final product that feels alien and unrelatable to the very people it aims to serve. This disconnection often contributes to a sad and unfortunate reality in the world of Bible translation: numerous completed translation projects end up gathering dust on shelves, unused and unappreciated. The effort, resources, and hopes invested in these projects go to waste when the translations do not resonate with the target communities. The books remain untouched because the translations do not speak to the hearts and minds of the people. This can mostly be avoided. To avoid this pitfall of irrelevancy, it is crucial for Bible translation projects to adopt a holistic approach that prioritizes contextual understanding at the initiation and implementation stages, as well as throughout the life of the project, when it comes to translation decisions on key terms and so on. For outsiders, this means investing time and effort in learning about the target community's way of life, their values, their modes of communication, and their spiritual landscape. For insiders, this means knowing their own culture and language well so that the Bible's message can be communicated effectively. By weaving these understandings into the fabric of the translation project, the translators and other stakeholders can create a translation of the Bible that not only conveys the original message adequately but also resonates deeply with the local audience.

Clarity and contextual insight on behalf of all those involved are indispensable for producing Bible translations that genuinely serve their intended purpose. Without such a grasp of the realities on the ground, the risk of creating irrelevant and unused translations increases, leading to wasted efforts and missed opportunities for meaningful translations with real engagement. Therefore, a commitment to loyalty to the target audience is essential for the success and longevity of any Bible translation project.

INTRODUCING THE MOZAMBICAN YAWO BEADED NECKLACE

In what ways can we apply this model in the real world? Essentially, we apply it by utilizing insights learned from the context. Specifically, we shall now discuss the Mozambican Yawo situation and show how the Beaded Necklace Model seeks to address the following question: How can one plan, organize, and operate a Bible translation project in Muslim-majority communities in sub-Saharan Africa (or indeed in any other place, including where there is a majority Muslim group embedded in the broader non-Muslim culture)?[18] In seeking to answer this question, the model here begins from Skopos theory, as discussed in chapter 1, by assuming that a functional translation is intended in a given context. That is, the stakeholders desire the translation to fulfil a specific purpose. With this assumption at the forefront, the following discussion shall delve into the model to see how it looks in a particular context. The insights provided, while rooted in the Mozambican Yawo context, are also applicable to similar Majority World contexts in terms of how loyalty affects our attitudes and approaches to such analogous situations.

The Yawo are presently and predominantly located within the three countries of Tanzania, Mozambique, and Malawi in southeastern Africa. However, small communities of Yawo may exist elsewhere in countries such as Zambia, Zimbabwe, and South Africa due to migrations. In Tanzania, the Yawo people are mainly found in the Tunduru District in the southern Ruvuma region. In Mozambique, the Yawo are situated throughout much of Niassa Province, particularly on the western side of the Lugenda River, except for lakeside areas from around Metangula to the Tanzanian border. In particular, the Yawo situate themselves mainly in the Niassa districts of Mecula, Mavago, Muembe, Sanga, Ngauma, Majune, Mandimba, and the vicinities immediately surrounding Lichinga.

---

18. This chapter focuses a lot on the Yawo people, but some of the insights may apply in other contexts. The whole point of this model is to emphasize the importance of each context on its own, even if it can be informed by others. We can learn from one another, but we must not lose sight of the individual situations in which Bible translation happens around the Majority World.

Most Yawo people consider Muembe District to be the traditional home of their ancestors. The Malawian Yawo are primarily located around the Blantyre and Mulanje areas up through Zomba, Machinga, and Mangochi to the lake in the country's south. On the map in figure 2 below, it is possible to see Yawo territory highlighted within a corridor from around the southern end of Lake Malawi up to the Tunduru area of Tanzania.

FIGURE 2

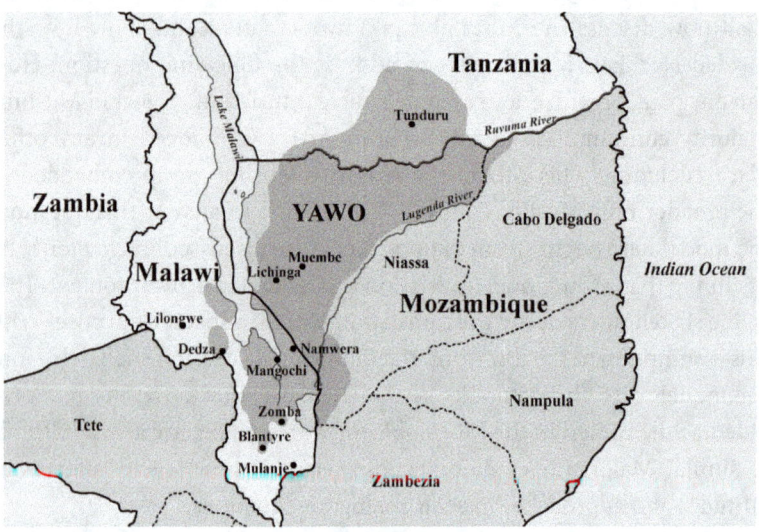

Map of Yawo Territory

Ciyawo is a Bantu language in the Niger-Congo family of languages,[19] indigenously spoken by the Yawo people. In various historical writings concerning the Yawo, they are referred to by such names as *Yao*,[20] *Ajawa*,[21] *Wahiao*,[22] *Waiyau*, and *Waiau*.[23] The term *Yawo* appears to refer specifically to a grassy and treeless area that is considered by many to represent the traditional homeland of Yawo. Ciyawo follows a noun-class

---

19. Eberhard et al., *Ethnologue*.
20. Hetherwick, *Handbook of Yao Language*; Mitchell, *Yao Village*; Sanderson, *Yao Grammar*; Sanderson, *Dictionary of Yao Language*; Steere, *Collections*.
21. Livingstone and Livingstone, *Narrative of an Expedition*, 55.
22. Lacerda, *Journey to Cazembe*, 39.
23. Waller, *Last Journals*, 67.

concordance system common to other Bantu languages.[24] When the *ci* prefix is applied to *Yawo*, it refers to the language spoken by the Yawo people because the noun corresponding to *ci* is *ciŵeceto*, which means "language." More precisely, the term alludes to *something spoken* as it derives from the verb *kuŵeceta*, meaning "to speak." The Ethnologue, the database of the world's languages, classes Ciyawo as a "developing" language.[25] This classification is described as "in vigorous use, with literature in a standardized form being used by some though this is not yet widespread or sustainable"[26] nor widely accessible or available. I will explore the actual vitality of Ciyawo, in northern Mozambique specifically, later in this chapter. The language classification of Bantu languages by Malcolm Guthrie places Ciyawo in P21.[27]

About 2 percent of Mozambique's total population of over thirty million inhabitants[28] are indigenous Ciyawo speakers, numbering approximately 600,000 people. In southern Tanzania, there are also around 600,000 speakers, made up of about 1 percent of the total population of almost sixty million[29] and about 12 percent (2,280,000 speakers) of Malawi's population of nineteen million.[30]

THE INTENDED FUNCTION IS CLEAR WHEN THE "BEADS" ARE KNOWN

Historically, Bible translation in the Yawo context appears to have been conducted with minimal explicit intentionality or clearly articulated functions in mind. Various Christian missionaries have initiated Bible translation projects over the years, often operating with implicit assumptions or occasionally stated intentions. However, these assumptions and intentions rarely result in a consistent, cohesive outcome. One of the significant contributions of Skopos theory to the field of Bible translation is its emphasis on making these implicit intentions explicit. This is

---

24. Dicks and Dollar, *Practical Guide*, 19; Ngunga, "Lexical Phonology," 9; Steere, *Collections for a Handbook*, 6.
25. Eberhard et al., *Ethnologue*.
26. Eberhard et al., *Ethnologue*.
27. Guthrie, *Classification*; Guthrie, *Comparative Bantu*; Maho, *NUGL Online*.
28. Sheldon and Penvenne, "Mozambique."
29. Mascarenhas et al., "Tanzania."
30. Kayambazinthu, "Language in Malawi," 379; Kadzamira et al., "Malawi"; UN Department of Economic and Social Affairs, *World Statistics Pocketbook*, 124.

typically achieved through crafting a translation brief document, which outlines the intended function of a translation project. By documenting the purpose and goals of the translation, Skopos theory helps ensure that all stakeholders are aligned and that the translation efforts are directed towards a coherent and shared objective. But, in this Beaded Necklace Model, we can only determine the intended *skopos* once we appropriately understand the context/people/situation—that is, once we know the beads on the necklace—and the stakeholders have negotiated the purpose together—with loyalty at the forefront, of course. In fact, as I mentioned earlier, the traditional translation brief gets subsumed by my idea of the translation covenant, which is more than just a set of instructions but is a documented relational commitment to one another.

The desired function of a Bible translation project is also influenced by the ideologies and convictions of the stakeholders involved, and so those involved need to be aware of this as the translation covenant develops. After all, as John Barton tells us,

> translation is never neutral. . . . The choice of translation correlates with, or is even driven by, particular convictions about the character of the Bible. Those who have a strong belief that the Bible is always self-consistent will tend to translate so as to make this apparent, in the process skewing, as it will seem to the detached observer, the facts of Hebrew grammar and syntax. Theological stances on the Bible's status and character thus affect, and are registered in, decisions about seemingly specialized, perhaps even trivial, questions of linguistics that will appear to most as purely factual and without bearing on matters of faith. What is at stake, it seems to me, is whether these decisions help to produce the Bible as we would like it to be, rather than as it actually is. . . . The Bible and its faiths are not identical, and translation is one of the primary sites where the difference between Scripture and religious beliefs is negotiated.[31]

The sooner we come to terms with the realities of bias, the better. Yet, we must not despair at this. The translated Bible has "enormous power."[32] After all, it was through the translation of the Bible "that Scripture's dominant ideas achieved currency not only in the two world religions that hold the Bible sacred but in Western culture at large, secular or not."[33]

---

31. Barton, *Word*, 254–55.
32. Barton, *Word*, 285.
33. Barton, *Word*, 285–86. Although translation of the Scriptures certainly helped to

It is also vernacular, translated Scriptures that Lamin Sanneh says are the hallmark of Christianity globally since its inception as a movement.[34] For our purposes here, the lack of neutrality[35] that is a reality in every Bible translation project includes the views of the initiating organization, initiating church, or other stakeholders desiring to get a Bible translation going. The theological beliefs, missiological strategies, and cultural perspectives that these institutions and individuals value also play a crucial role in shaping the translation brief—or rather, translation covenant.

An outline of the narrative frames will feature further below to justify the *skopos* of a Bible translation project in the Mozambican Yawo context. The following section is not intended to be exhaustive on these issues. Rather, it aims to highlight, by way of example, the general approach to dealing with some of the relevant narrative frames within the Yawo context and the intended *skopos* of a Bible translation project among the Mozambican Yawo. Some of the frames discussed in this chapter include the sociolinguistic "bead," the religious "beads," the historical "bead," orality "bead," and organizational "bead." Organizations with different visions and objectives may adopt alternative approaches in their responses to the various narrative frames within the Mozambican Yawo context. Rather than being a question of right or wrong, it is my conviction that the following responses will increase effectiveness for "reaching" the Mozambican Yawo people with the word of God in their own language. Reaching the Yawo does not mean proselytization to a particular Christian tradition but rather means the heart-level conversion to the message about Jesus that the Bible itself communicates.

THE SOCIOLINGUISTIC "BEAD" ON THE NECKLACE

To address the sociolinguistic bead and how to understand the Yawo situation in this regard, I conducted an extensive survey of Ciyawo-speaking

---

"achieve currency" in later Judaism and Christianity, I could also argue that the Scriptures themselves in their original languages also achieved similar currency for the first recipients of them. So it is not the *translation* of the Bible that holds the power, it is the message of the Bible itself, translated or not.

34. Sanneh, *Translating the Message*, 29.

35. For example, "Not even the most literal translation is neutral. All renderings of the Bible inflect the text. Formal equivalence transmits the text's meaning, as all types of translation aspire to, but often conveys in addition a sense that the text is foreign and oddly worded, which is not how it would have appeared to its original readers." Barton, *Word*, 285.

communities in Niassa Province, Mozambique.[36] The survey's primary purpose was to determine whether Bible translation materials from Malawi would be adequate for use in Mozambique. There was little other information available at the time to be able to make an informed judgment on the situation. This led to my survey research and, eventually, writing this book in light of the results and outcomes of that research. I am not suggesting that such extensive research be undertaken in every context—unless the situation calls for it. But, certainly, finding all that can be found out from existing sociolinguistic surveys and ethnographic data in a given context is vitally important.

I strategically selected several locations within each district where Ciyawo is spoken, ensuring representation from at least one village per district (except for Lago, which is predominantly made up of the Nyanja people). Central to Yawo territory and history, I included Chiconono (specifically Ligogolo Village) in Muembe District as a reference point. I chose locations first based on the outer boundaries of Ciyawo-speaking areas and then on their prominence and centrality within those boundaries. In Majune District, Matekuta marked the eastern edge of Yawo territory for the survey. The village of Canika in Mandimba District defines the southern boundary within Mozambique. On the western side, I selected Ntendele in Lichinga District, near the small lakeside town of Meponda. Kapunda Village in Sanga District represents the northern boundary. To the northeast, I chose two villages within Niassa Reserve, Mbamba and Nalama, with Nalama being relatively close to the Tanzanian border. I selected Matondovela in the heart of Niassa Reserve. Finally, I chose Pambuyu Village near Mavago to represent the western edge of the reserve. See figure 3 below for a map of the final selection of reference points, including some locations that I also used for word lists and intelligibility testing.

---

36. Houston, "Sociolinguistic and Extensibility Survey."

FIGURE 3

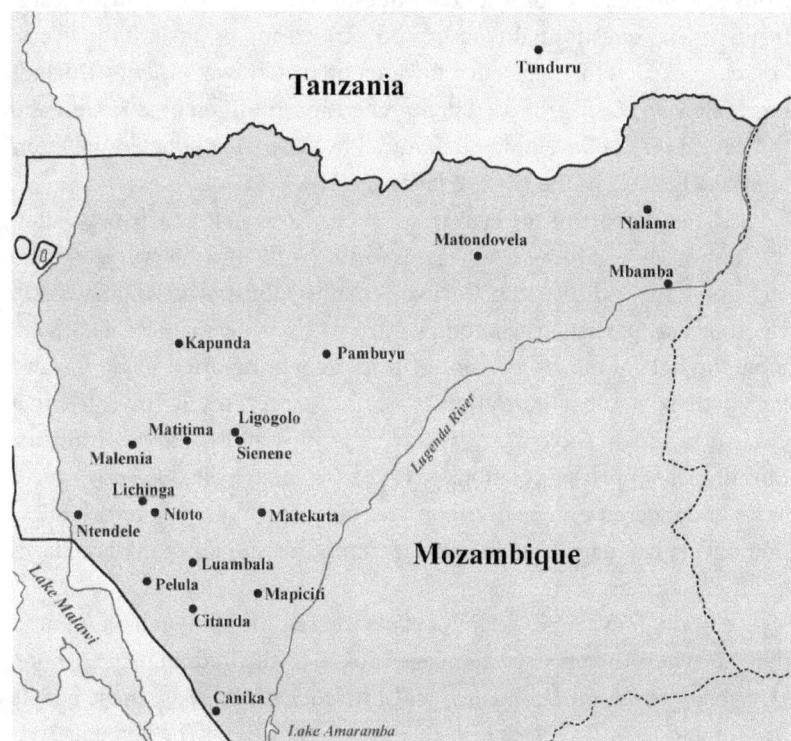

Map of Survey Reference Points

For the survey, all participants were long-term community residents who had not spent significant time away recently. They were required to have Yawo parents and to speak Ciyawo as their first language. Reaching a certain level of education was not a criterion for participation. However, it is notable that about 40 percent of respondents reported never having attended school. Less than 2 percent had reached the twelfth grade, and only 13 percent had completed up to the fifth grade in primary school. I conducted one hundred and twenty-eight interviews across more than fifteen villages that participated in the questionnaires. Each location provided an equal number of male and female interviewees: two men over thirty-five, two women over thirty-five, two men aged eighteen to thirty-four, and two women aged eighteen to thirty-four.

The questionnaire comprised fifty-nine primary questions adapted from Catherine Showalter's work *Getting What You Ask For: A Study of Sociolinguistic Questionnaires.*[37] Additionally, I asked one key person from each village a set of secondary questions tailored for knowledgeable insiders. The questionnaire addressed various topics, including Ciyawo language use, vitality, attitudes towards other Ciyawo varieties (including Malawian), self-professed comprehension of different varieties, and the desirability of developing literature in Ciyawo. I conducted the interviews exclusively in the Ciyawo language.

The early part of the survey considered the state of Ciyawo's vitality. Responses regarding language use with family members and in various situations indicate that Ciyawo remains robust. The language is in vigorous use, particularly among rural Yawo people, many of whom are monolingual. About 95 percent of respondents reported using Ciyawo for all their significant relationships. The survey results revealed that Ciyawo is widely spoken across all age groups and genders within the Mozambican Yawo population surveyed. The language does not appear to be endangered except in urban areas like Lichinga, where urbanization affects language use, which is a common issue for many languages in urban settings.

Although my survey did not explicitly test for bilingualism, I found that Ciyawo is the primary language spoken until children begin school. Due to poor school attendance and low education levels, most people continue to use Ciyawo exclusively in their daily lives. The language's vitality is further affirmed by its use in various domains. Most respondents reported using Ciyawo for storytelling, singing, and even when interacting with government officials (particularly in rural centers). In religious settings, Ciyawo is also predominantly used to ensure comprehension and understanding. This widespread use across different aspects of life underscores the robust health of the Ciyawo language.

Expanding beyond individual language use, subsequent sections of the questionnaire examined perceptions of using Ciyawo in public settings. Many respondents indicated that Ciyawo is utilized in public meetings, often with the assistance of interpreters. Radio broadcasts in Ciyawo are prevalent across most Yawo communities, with some areas boasting community radio stations. Moreover, broadcasts originating from central hubs such as Lichinga have considerable reach. Additionally, even the most isolated survey locations receive visits from vehicles equipped with loudspeakers for making announcements.

---

37. Showalter, "What You Ask For."

Other questions in the survey took into account what respondents think *about* certain aspects of life with Ciyawo. The majority of respondents expressed concern that older Yawo individuals would feel disheartened by the increasing use of Portuguese among younger generations. Many respondents expressed optimism that future generations will continue to speak Ciyawo, viewing this as beneficial. Few could envision a scenario where Portuguese becomes more prevalent than Ciyawo in the years ahead. This underscores the enduring use of Ciyawo and the positive outlook toward its continuation for future generations.

However, it's important to note some caveats. Many respondents were not confident regarding using Ciyawo for employment. More than 85 percent of individuals stated that it's unlikely to secure good jobs solely with Ciyawo proficiency. Additionally, over 60 percent explicitly mentioned Portuguese as the preferred language for work. While these observations may hold true within the Mozambican Yawo context, they don't negate the need for developing Ciyawo literature. Creating literature and literacy materials in Ciyawo can serve as a foundational step towards achieving the level of proficiency enjoyed by Portuguese, which is perceived as essential for employment opportunities by many people.

Considering that Ciyawo serves as the "mother tongue" for most Yawo individuals, receiving education in this language can greatly facilitate the learning of reading and writing in a second language like Portuguese. Most respondents emphasized the importance of formal education for both genders. About three-quarters of participants viewed literacy in Ciyawo positively and expressed interest in reading Ciyawo literature if it were available. However, beyond daily social and familial interactions, Ciyawo is not highly valued as a practical language. While people would welcome literacy in Ciyawo if offered, proficiency in Portuguese (both speaking and reading/writing) is considered more advantageous. It is challenging for individuals to envision a scenario where Ciyawo literature and literacy are both feasible and beneficial.

I examined whether Yawo people in Mozambique hold positive or negative attitudes toward Malawian Ciyawo. Negative perceptions of the Malawian variety would make using Malawian Ciyawo literature unviable in Mozambique. According to survey results, most respondents reported understanding Malawian Ciyawo to some extent. However, this is counterbalanced by a more significant number of individuals claiming better comprehension of all other Ciyawo varieties compared to the Malawian one. Most Yawo people in Mozambique stated that the Malawian variant of Ciyawo is the least understood among all Ciyawo varieties. This claim does not reflect people's *actual* understanding but only their *perceived* capability to understand. Nonetheless, the attitude is important at this point, and most respondents said that if differences exist between Ciyawo varieties, those differences are not a good thing.

In the end, the sum of all the survey results indicated that, from a sociolinguistic perspective, the development of specifically Mozambican Ciyawo materials (including Bible translation) is necessary for a full engagement of Ciyawo literature (whether written or oral). These results were further compounded by actual testing of Malawian Ciyawo Bible materials, which found Mozambican comprehension of these materials to be quite low.[38] For my purposes here in this book, the results of my survey show that to be loyal to the Yawo in Mozambique, an adequate response means taking their individual circumstances seriously and not simply assuming that the materials produced in another dialect of the language will do for them. This might be the same in other contexts; it is best not to assume that what is good enough for one dialect is good enough for another. It is imperative to assess the sociolinguistic circumstances properly because it is an important bead on the beaded necklace of any Bible translation situation.

THE RELIGIOUS "BEADS"

The Yawo predominantly identify as Muslim, although it is important to note exceptions, as there are some Christian Yawo in urban areas such as Mangochi and Zomba in Malawi and Lichinga in Mozambique. In particular, there is a Yawo Anglican community in Mozambique that traces its roots back to late nineteenth-century efforts by English missionaries of the Universities' Mission to Central Africa (UMCA). While the Yawo predominantly adhere to Islam as their "structural" religion, it is also accurate to acknowledge that the Yawo people are heavily influenced by their traditional religious beliefs. This recalls the idea espoused by anthropologist Robert Redfield about the "great tradition of the reflective few" and the "little tradition of the largely unreflective many" and how "the great tradition is cultivated in schools or temples; the little tradition works itself out and keeps itself going in the lives of the unlettered in their

---

38. To see the full results, including appendices of word lists and data, see Houston, "Sociolinguistic and Extensibility Survey."

village communities."³⁹ Warrick Farah is also undoubtedly correct with his idea "that there are great variations among individuals in cultures. ... Any approach focusing on a large grouping of people will have to acknowledge such inherent limitations."⁴⁰ In other words, "we should indeed be good students of Islam, but we should be even better students of Muslims."⁴¹ Within Yawo traditional religion, the veneration of deceased ancestors stands out as one of the primary characteristics. Additionally, there exists a prevalent fear of witchcraft, along with the practice of sorcery, which is perceived as both benevolent and malevolent. Moreover, using charms and amulets is deeply ingrained within their cultural practices. These traditional beliefs and behaviors are often practiced in parallel with Islam, particularly among adherents of the majority *Qadiriyya* pathway (Arabic, الطريقة القادرية, *al-ṭarīqa al-Qādiriyya*) of Islam in Yawo society. In this sense, I affirm how *Margins of Islam* demonstrates the existence of many variations in Islamic expression around the world and that Islam is at least as diverse as the number of communities in which it is embedded (we can say the same of the myriad Christian expressions globally too).⁴²

The Yawo as Muslims

According to Edward Alpers, the Islamization of the Yawo is traceable to several favorable precolonial and colonial "political, social and religious pre-conditions."⁴³ Prior to substantial European colonization in the interior of Africa, where the Yawo resided, the nineteenth century witnessed the emergence and consolidation of powerful Yawo chiefdoms into distinct and influential entities. The first of these key chiefs to convert to Islam was Makanjila Bonali III in present-day Malawi at around 1870.⁴⁴ These powerful chiefs used Islam to maintain their control over such liminal periods as *jando*, an Islamized initiation ceremony for Yawo boys that was known as *lupanda* prior to Islamization and already included

---

39. Redfield, *Peasant Society and Culture*, 70.
40. Farah, "Adaptive Missiological Engagement," 113.
41. Farah, "Adaptive Missiological Engagement," 114.
42. Daniels and Farah, *Margins of Islam*.
43. Alpers, "Expansion of Islam," 181.
44. Alpers, "Trade, State, and Society," 420.

a form of partial circumcision.[45] Thorold suggests that these powerful chiefs linked initiation rituals to Islam, which helped to reinforce further "their own position as custodians of Yawo tribal identity. The Islamization of rituals emphasized the difference between the Yawo and others . . . and confirmed the authority of the Muslim chiefs."[46]

Furthermore, Liazzat Bonate points out that being initiated under "ritual initiation controlled by chiefs meant achieving adulthood and becoming a proper Yawo."[47] Hence, despite the Yawo's long-standing interactions with the Swahili Islamic coast, evidenced by their engagement with places like Kilwa in present-day Tanzania since at least the seventeenth century[48]—a period of at least two hundred years preceding their Islamization—it was not until these powerful chiefdoms developed in the nineteenth century that Islam began to take root. Another concurrent factor contributing to Islamic conversion was the looming European colonial threat, which posed economic challenges to the Yawo chiefdoms.

Of particular significance to the Yawo situation was the abolition of the slave trade in Britain during the first half of the nineteenth century, marked by the enactment of the Slave Trade Act in 1807 and later the Slavery Abolition Act in 1837. As Britain's influence expanded in Yawo regions of Africa during the latter half of the nineteenth century, it facilitated the involvement of British missionaries and renowned explorers like David Livingstone in efforts to combat the slave trade. These endeavors aimed to either eradicate the practice altogether or mitigate its impact. One such initiative was the establishment of new communities, like the one in Masasi in 1876 in present-day Tanzania, for liberated and rescued slaves.[49]

In 1880, Chief Mataka II Nyenje initially welcomed Anglican Reverend William Johnson from the UMCA into Muembe (Muembe, or "Mataka's," is now Mavago in modern-day Mozambique). Mataka permitted Johnson to carry out mission work in the area. However, tensions arose when British colonists intercepted a slave caravan belonging to Chief Mataka. This incident prompted suspicions of espionage, leading Chief Mataka to order Johnson to leave the village[50] and to burn Johnson's

45. Bonate, "Yao," 3; Thorold, "Yao Muslims," 128.
46. Thorold, "Yao Muslims," 130.
47. Bonate, "Yao," 3.
48. Alpers, "Trade, State, and Society," 406.
49. Ranger, "Missionary Adaptation," 224.
50. Alpers, "Expansion of Islam," 184.

hut in the meantime.[51] Mataka's allegiance to Islam at around this point was then confirmed[52] because his political and commercial needs were dependent on slave trading with the Islamic Arab Swahili traders on the East African coast. Hence, the economic gains from the slave trade combined with British interference of that trade fostered distrust towards European colonial powers among the Yawo people. This situation led to the acceptance of Islam, which offered economic security through trade with the coast. Additionally, it resulted in resistance to Christian missionary efforts, including the rejection of schools and education initiated by missionaries. It is notable that during the early stages of Yawo Islamization, spiritual matters played a minor role, with political and economic stability being the primary concerns for Yawo chiefs in anticipation of colonization by European (Christian) powers. In Mozambique, Portuguese colonists were also viewed in an unfavorable light due to their inhumane treatment at times of the indigenous population.[53] Despite this initial phase, however, this doesn't rule out that the spiritual dimension now has a strong influence on the hearts and minds of the average Yawo person. On a theological level, there seems to be an accommodation for Islam within Yawo traditional religious thought, as long as the fundamental principles of the *oneness* (Arabic, تَوْحِيد, *tawḥīd*) and the supremacy of God remain unchallenged. It appears that these two belief systems are allowed to coexist somewhat in parallel, a phenomenon that persists today.

With the great Yawo chiefdoms weakening in the early twentieth century due to increased colonial pressures from the British, Portuguese, and Germans, in particular, more egalitarian forms of Islam were introduced and began to take root in Yawo communities. These more inclusive Sufi orders, the *Shadhuliyah* and the *Qadiriyya*, first arrived in northern Mozambique towards the end of the nineteenth century and the beginning of the twentieth century.[54] The emergence of these Sufi *pathways* (Arabic, طُرُق, *ṭuruq*) suggests "that Islam was no longer the exclusive prerogative of the chiefs or the coastal Swahili because the religious authority associated with Sufism need not be linked to political power."[55] Years later, with further consolidation of European colonial authorities,

---

51. Anderson-Morshead, *History of the Universities' Mission*, 147; Johnson, *African Reminiscences*, 71.

52. Alpers, "Expansion of Islam," 184.

53. Eyre, "Portuguese Action," 173.

54. Bonate, "Yao," 3; Bonate, "Sufi Orders," 485.

55. Bonate, "Yao," 4.

Yawo chiefs seem to have focused their attention on "recuperating Islam as part of their chiefly domain"[56] as opposed to antagonizing the European colonialists. Eventually, this led to conflicts and debates internally amongst the chiefly elites and Islamic leaders of Yawo communities about "such issues as whether the main ṣūfī ritual of *dhikr* should be performed loudly or quietly, with drums or without them, and in mosques or not."[57] Therefore, because of such debates, the Yawo *Qadiriyya* adherents divided themselves "between those who performed the noisy *dhikr* with drums and the quietists (*sukūtīs*),"[58] with the primary controversy concerning *dhikr* (Arabic, ذِكْر; Ciyawo, *sikili*). *Sikili* for the Yawo is the ritual invocation of the names of God through singing and dancing during funerals and other events.[59] The "quietists" (Ciyawo, *sukutis*) are often referred to as *Qadiyani* in Mozambique,[60] even though this nomenclature is vague and not necessarily indicative of a singular organized group. In other countries, such as Pakistan, the term *Qadiyani* even appears to be a slur referring to Ahmadi Muslims. In 1968, the Portuguese even sought a sheikh from Mozambique Island to issue a legal ruling (Arabic, فتوى, *fatwā*) on the drumming issue, resulting in the statement that "the funerals should be neither silent nor noisy, but performed in a normal voice."[61] Despite this ruling, both *Qadiriyya* and *sukuti* groups persist in Yawo communities today, and debates continue. For example, in a Mozambican Yawo village I visited recently, one group antagonized the other by closing and padlocking the mosque of the other group over a minor dispute and would not allow the other group to enter their mosque for Friday prayers.

From the 1960s onwards, the so-called Islamists began to emerge in Mozambique when graduates of the Islamic university at Medina in Saudi Arabia returned home. These "Wahhabi" Muslims in Mozambique seem to have developed out of the *sukutis*.[62] They are far less tolerant of many traditional practices, such as the veneration of deceased ancestors and magical practices like witchcraft (Ciyawo, *wusawi*). Indeed, the celebration of the Prophet Muhammad's birthday is also considered to

56. Bonate, "Yao," 4.
57. Bonate, "Yao," 4.
58. Bonate, "Yao," 4.
59. Bonate, "Islamic Funeral Rites," 43.
60. Dicks, *African Worldview*, 210.
61. Bonate, "Yao," 5.
62. Bonate, "Yao," 5.

be *bid'a*, or "innovation."⁶³ Ian Dicks refers to these more "scripturalist" Muslims as "New Reformists" and suggests that they are a difficult group to distinguish from the contemporary *sukutis* because they both "hold a scripturalist perspective of Islam."⁶⁴

At present, most Yawo people identify themselves as *Qadiriyya*, and in particular, those who do use drums for their ceremonies. Those who remain silent, the *sukutis*, are in the minority. The "Islamists" or "Wahhabi" among the Yawo are even fewer, with the sphere of their influence primarily concentrated in urban centers where there is an increased opportunity to receive external Islamic teaching. For the majority of Yawo *Qadiriyya*, this means that they practice many traditional customs in parallel to Islam. For more thorough analyses of the development of Islam among the Yawo, and discussions on the varieties of Islam with Yawo communities and their practices, see in particular the writings of Liazzat Bonate,⁶⁵ David Bone,⁶⁶ Ian Dicks,⁶⁷ and Alan Thorold.⁶⁸ The nature of traditional Yawo religion appears in the following section.

The Yawo and African Traditional Religion

In contrast to Islam, the traditional religious context of the Yawo people does not revolve around any formal sets of doctrines or teachings. Instead, a general amalgamation of various religious ideas and beliefs permeates the entirety of Yawo life.⁶⁹ These beliefs among the Yawo are not necessarily unique to them, for African Traditional Religion (ATR) serves as an overarching designation of the multiplicity of religious beliefs, practices, and ideas among a wide variety of African peoples. While each African culture possesses its distinctive religious character, many of these cultures, particularly in sub-Saharan Africa, share common features. One of the most prominent features of ATR is the veneration of deceased

---

63. Bonate, 5; Dicks, *African Worldview*, 197.

64. Dicks, *African Worldview*, 210.

65. Bonate, "Matriliny, Islam and Gender"; Bonate, "Roots of Diversity"; Bonate, "Traditions and Transitions"; Bonate, "Islam in Northern Mozambique"; Bonate, "Yao"; Bonate, "Islamic Funeral Rites"; Bonate, "Sufi Orders."

66. Bone, "Islam in Malawi"; Bone, "Establishment of Islam."

67. Dicks, *African Worldview*.

68. Thorold, "Yao Conversion to Islam"; Thorold, "Metamorphoses"; Thorold, "Yao Muslims."

69. Heckel, *Yao Tribe*, 14.

ancestors. The Yawo, like many other African peoples, hold their ancestors in high regard, believing that the spirits of the deceased continue to play an active role in the lives of the living. These ancestors in ATR are often referred to as the "living dead," indicating this ongoing interaction.[70] This veneration manifests in various rituals and practices designed to honor and appease the ancestors, ensuring their favor and guidance. There is a widespread fear of witchcraft among the Yawo, which significantly influences their daily lives and social interactions. Witchcraft and sorcery are perceived as potent forces capable of causing harm or misfortune, and this belief instills a sense of caution and vigilance within the community. Untimely deaths and sicknesses are usually attributed to malevolent causes. Indeed, this suspicion of malevolent forces causing things to go wrong seems common to all African societies.[71] These causes may include sorcery (Ciyawo, *kuloga*) and witchcraft (Ciyawo, *wusawi*), but also the breaking of cultural taboos and upsetting deceased ancestors. The most common ways to protect oneself and one's property from the evil machinations of others through sorcery and witchcraft involve a combination of traditional practices and Islamic religious elements. One of the primary methods is the use of charms, known locally as *ciwindo*, which are believed to possess protective powers. These charms are often carried on the person or placed in strategic locations around one's home or property to ward off malevolent forces. In addition to charms, traditional medicines, referred to as *mitela*, play a crucial role in safeguarding against witchcraft. These medicines are typically prepared from various herbs, roots, and other natural ingredients believed to have protective or healing properties. Individuals can request these medicines through a *jwamtela*, who is a traditional medicine person skilled in the preparation and application of *mitela*. The *jwamtela* utilizes their extensive knowledge of local ingredients to create remedies tailored to specific needs and circumstances. This person also prepares medicines for other benevolent uses, such as to improve sexual performance or to treat common ailments. This form of medicine can involve the use of purely herbal treatments to other substances or herbs and plants enchanted with traditional magic. Local Muslim *shehes* (Arabic singular, شَيْخ, *shaykh*) can also prepare *matalasimu*, or "talismans," which incorporate religious elements from the Qur'ān. These talismans are made by writing specific verses or

---

70. Mbiti, *African Religions*, 82.
71. Mbiti, *Introduction*, 166.

prayers from the Qurʾān on paper,[72] which is then used to create a form of protective medicine. Often, the person must drink a solution in which the paper has been placed. This practice blends traditional beliefs with Islamic teachings, providing a unique form of spiritual protection that resonates with the religious and cultural context of the Yawo people.

Another important aspect of protection involves seeking information about the causes of misfortune or illness from traditional diviners (Ciyawo, *ŵacisango*). These diviners use a variety of techniques, such as interpreting dreams, to diagnose the source of a problem and recommend appropriate protective measures or treatments. If a person dreams about a deceased ancestor, for example, the diviner may deduce that the issue affecting the person is due to the deceased ancestor requiring that their descendant sweep their grave (Ciyawo, *kupyajila malembe*) to appease them. The guidance provided by *ŵacisango* is highly valued in the community and is often sought in times of crisis or uncertainty. A traditional type of sorcery is *citega*, a form of entrapment whereby people can place specific medicines under paths and thoroughfares to cause harm upon a target as they pass over the medicine.[73]

These various protective measures, whether through *ciŵindo*, *mitela*, the guidance of *ŵacisango*, or *matalasimu* prepared by *shehes*, illustrate the deeply ingrained belief in the need for spiritual protection against witchcraft and sorcery. They also highlight the syncretic nature of Yawo religious practices, where traditional and Islamic elements coexist and complement each other in the daily lives of the people.

We need to further understand these specific characteristics of the Yawo within the overarching context of ATR as a whole. Generally speaking, ATR is usually monotheistic and mirrors the cultural system in which it finds itself.[74] It follows an organic and holistic worldview.[75] These elements essentially mean that there is no stark contrast between the spiritual and material worlds, as is often found in contemporary Western dualism (the separation of the spiritual from the physical and material). In ATR, the spiritual and material realms are more closely interconnected, creating a cohesive understanding of existence where every aspect of life is imbued with spiritual significance.

---

72. Dicks, *African Worldview*, 103.
73. Dicks, *African Worldview*, 355.
74. Lugira, *African Traditional Religion*, 38.
75. Walt, *Understanding and Rebuilding Africa*, 62.

ATR is very much centered upon the present desires and foci of the community in the here and now. It is in this sense that "God and the rest of the spirit world exist for the sake of the human community."[76] This perspective underscores the immediate relevance and practical nature of ATR, which prioritizes the well-being and prosperity of the community in the present moment. The focus is on addressing current needs and ensuring harmony in daily life. ATR is rarely oriented to the future. Instead, it looks continuously to the past as it remembers and venerates deceased ancestors. Their remembrance is essential, as a failure to honor them can result in calamity and misfortune in the present.

Another distinct feature of ATR is that it is not a "book" religion. Unlike Islam and Christianity, which are centered around sacred texts and prescribed doctrines, ATR does not have a canon or written scriptures. There are no prescribed doctrines or teachings that are universally followed. Instead, ATR relies heavily on oral traditions that are passed down through generations. These traditions are maintained by certain individuals within the community who are considered keepers of traditional religious knowledge. These custodians play a crucial role in preserving and transmitting the beliefs, practices, and rituals that define ATR. Each expression of ATR is deeply rooted in its local context, reflecting the peculiarities, experiences, and histories of the community. This localized nature means that ATR can vary significantly from one community to another, even within the same ethnic or cultural group. The oral traditions that sustain ATR are adapted to the specific needs and circumstances of each community, making ATR a highly dynamic system of belief.

Another common theme in ATR is the notion of a cosmic life force, or "cosmic totality."[77] This conviction refers to the belief that everything that exists does so in harmony or totality and interdependence with one another. Positive "cosmic totality" for the Yawo is explainable in terms of living in healthy relationships with others in the community and maintaining accepted societal taboos. When life is troublesome, or things are going badly, then it may be that the cosmic life force is deficient in that community, which could be due to broken relationships or broken societal taboos. The traditional diviner is often required to determine the cause. This cosmic totality is available to all, but it is limited in quantity,

---

76. Walt, *Understanding and Rebuilding Africa*, 64.
77. Crafford, "African Traditional Religions," 9.

and so this basically means that there is only a certain amount of good to go around. This belief in a finite cosmic life force also extends to practical aspects of life, such as agriculture. For example, the reluctance to adopt scientifically improved farming techniques among many Africans, including the Yawo, might be traced back to this worldview. The idea is that increasing one's harvest through new methods would essentially mean taking more than one's fair share of the limited cosmic life force available, thereby depriving others in the community. This perspective underscores the deep-seated communal values and the intrinsic sense of balance that permeates many African cultures, including the Yawo.

The veneration (not worship) of deceased ancestors is one of the ways in which the cosmic life force is positively maintained in societies such as the Yawo. Ancestor veneration for the Yawo is most prominently expressed through remembrance feasts held at specific intervals after death, known as *sadaka*. The term *sadaka* is derived from the Arabic word صدقة (*ṣadaqah*), meaning "almsgiving" or "charity." The fortieth-day *sadaka* is particularly significant, as it is believed to be the occasion when the deceased's spirit finally progresses to its final dwelling place.[78] In addition to these *sadaka* feasts, various other practices are associated with ancestor veneration. One such custom is the aforementioned "sweeping the graves" of deceased ancestors. This ritual, along with other occasional *sadaka* events, is often performed in response to perceived ancestral discontent, which is usually revealed through dreams. Ancestors are frequently invoked during liminal periods, such as initiation ceremonies and the enthronements of village headpersons. They are also called upon during rain prayer ceremonies, highlighting their integral role in various aspects of community life.[79]

Ancestral spirits can affect the lives of their living descendants in both positive and negative ways. They may bless their families with good health and fortune (Ciyawo, *wupile*) or, conversely, cause sickness and accidents if they feel neglected. By remembering and honoring their ancestors, the Yawo believe they can ensure a prosperous and healthy life. Conversely, forgetting the ancestors or failing to perform the necessary rituals is often seen as the cause of negative occurrences and calamities (or the malice of others through witchcraft and sorcery). For the Yawo, one term for deceased ancestors, *acinangolo*, is notably the same word used

---

78. Dicks, *African Worldview*, 175.
79. Dicks, *African Worldview*, 102.

for living elders. This linguistic nuance reflects a cultural belief that the distinction between the living and the dead is not as stark as it is from a Western Enlightenment perspective. In the Yawo worldview, and in ATR more broadly, deceased ancestors play a vital mediatory role between the community and the supreme being. It is assumed that because they are now closer to God, ancestors can intercede on behalf of the living. Living humans are unable to mediate directly with God and are, therefore, dependent on the mediation provided to them by their deceased ancestors.

In contrast to some colonial-era assumptions that suggested Africans lacked a theology of God[80] prior to the arrival of Christianity on the continent,[81] most African cultures nevertheless already assumed the existence of and maintained belief in an invisible and omnipotent supreme being.[82] This colonial-era assumption was not universal. For example, David Livingstone acknowledged in his journal from 1866 that the indigenous people living near the Rovuma River held to belief in a supreme being. These people included the Yawo. In the present day, the Rovuma River serves as a border between Mozambique and Tanzania. Specifically, Livingstone wrote, "They have a clear idea of the Supreme Being, but do not pray to Him."[83] The supreme being in ATR is often the singular source and creator of all that is.[84] Indeed, according to Yusufu Turaki, "It is not necessary to prove to Africans that God exists."[85] The Yawo commonly refer to this supreme being using the term *Mlungu*, or more accurately, according to Mozambican pronunciation, *N'nungu*. In ATR, this "God" typically occupies the highest position in a hierarchical structure that includes lesser divinities, ancestors, and spirits.[86] However, despite acknowledging a supreme being in the traditional African worldview, this being is often perceived as distant from the world, delegating

---

80. Brown, "Concepts of God in Africa," 5.

81. Not to mention that Christianity actually first arrived on the African continent within a generation after the death of Jesus. Some of the early church's most prominent theologians were Africans, including Athanasius, Augustine of Hippo, Tertullian, and Origen.

82. Crafford, "African Traditional Religions," 8.

83. Waller, *Last Journals*, 57.

84. Brown, "Concepts of God in Africa," 16.

85. Turaki, *Engaging Religions and Worldviews*, 173. I am not personally claiming that Africa has no atheists but just pointing out that the majority of Africans hold to a worldview more accommodating to supernatural matters than the West generally does at present.

86. Walt, *Understanding and Rebuilding Africa*, 63.

the responsibilities of maintaining creation to lesser deities and ancestral spirits.[87] The delegation of tasks to minor deities is well represented in a Yawo myth regarding *Mlungu*'s agent of creation, *Mtangaluwembe* or simply just *Mtanga*, who is said to have carried out the actual work of creating on *Mlungu*'s behalf.[88] In Western theology, this view might be akin to deism—the idea that God set the world in motion and then left its control to other powers and natural laws after its creation. In ATR, because the supreme being is seen as transcendent and not intimately involved in the everyday lives of people, ancestral spirits play a crucial role. These spirits are believed to be intimately involved in the daily affairs of the community,[89] acting as mediators between the people and the supreme being, especially during difficult times such as drought and famine. Although these spirits and deceased ancestors are not worshipped—worship is reserved for the supreme being alone—the actual worship of the supreme being is rare in ATR.[90] This context is significant because it demonstrates that the traditional religious worldview of the Yawo does not fundamentally challenge the core tenet of Islam, which is the oneness of God (Arabic, تَوْحِيد, *tawḥīd*). If the Yawo people had worshipped their ancestors, it would be unlikely that monotheistic Islam would have been able to take root among them. Instead, the ATR worldview, which acknowledges a supreme being without challenging God's oneness as stipulated in Islam, allows the traditional belief system to coexist with Islamic beliefs. Thus, as long as the concept of *tawḥīd* is upheld, the majority of the Yawo people can maintain their traditional practices alongside their Islamic identity. This reality challenges any simplistic assumptions about the nature of African religious systems and their compatibility with monotheistic religions like Islam. For Bible translation contexts, the possibility of such syncretism may frighten Christians. Aside from any point about how much syncretism is tolerable, we should at least be aware of the worldview of many Africans as we translate the Bible so that we can understand what is going on for them when they encounter the biblical

---

87. Crafford, "African Traditional Religions," 8.
88. Dicks, *African Worldview*, 338.
89. Crafford, "African Traditional Religions," 13; Oborji, "Dialogue," 18.

90. Brown, "Concepts of God in Africa," 11. I am saying here that, although the supreme being is the only one who can be worshipped, worship of the supreme being is rare in ATR because of the belief that this supreme being is too great to approach. The influence of Islam and Christianity in Africa certainly challenges this traditional outlook.

claims about the nature of God. The Bible should speak to people without the imposition of foreignness from outsiders.[91]

In ATR, the supreme being is generally considered omnipresent and, therefore, unconfinable to a specific place such as a temple or altar. This contrasts with the organized religion of the Israelites, who believed that YHWH dwelt in the sanctuary of the tabernacle and later in the temple. However, this does not imply that the supreme being is unimportant in ATR. Rather, it is suggested that, to the African, this being is *too important* to disturb with our measly and insufficient offerings.[92] Indeed, in ATR, the supreme being is viewed very highly but is effectively neglected by people[93] because he seems disinterested in the affairs of humankind and prefers to remain estranged from creation.[94] This preconception of the supreme being poses a challenge in Bible translation given that the Bible centers itself around the intimate activity and involvement of the supreme being (Hebrew, אֱלֹהִים, 'ĕlōhîm; Greek, θεός, theos) in human history. The involvement of God in human affairs is a recurring theme throughout the biblical narrative, which contrasts with the ATR perspective, where the supreme being is seen as detached from daily life. Therefore, translating the Bible into the context of ATR requires careful consideration of these theological differences to ensure that the message of an actively involved God is communicated effectively. The immanence of God is most purely seen in the belief in Jesus as God "with us." Both Muslims and adherents of ATR may struggle to comprehend this notion because Muslims reject Jesus as God and ATR does the same when it assumes God's transcendence without immanence.

The greatness and transcendence of the supreme being is often reflected in the names given to him in various African languages. For instance, the Gikuyu, Maasai, and Wakamba of Kenya use variations on the name *Ngai* or *Enkai*, which means "creator" and "giver of all things."[95] The Yoruba of Nigeria refer to the supreme being as *Ọlọrun*, a name synonymous with a term for "sky,"[96] which reflects the profound loftiness of the supreme being as "the owner or chief of heaven."[97] Similarly, the Zulu

---

91. Dapila, "Need for Indigenization," 37–38.
92. Bolink, "God in Traditional African Religion," 23.
93. Ubah, "Supreme Being," 92.
94. Oborji, "Dialogue," 18.
95. Brown, "Concepts of God in Africa," 9.
96. Brown, "Concepts of God in Africa," 7.
97. Awolalu, "Yoruba Concept of God," 6.

of South Africa use the name *uNkulunkulu*, which alludes to the ancientness of the supreme being.⁹⁸

The etymology of the term for the Yawo's supreme being, *Mlungu*, is subject to some debate, and yet I can make some suggestions. One proposal connects it to the word *kulangama* or *kulunga*, which, at least in neighboring Chichewa, is related to the verbs "to be straight" and "to put together rightly," respectively.⁹⁹ However, the name *Mulungu*, as it is spelt in Chichewa, is generally recognized as an introduced term, with the Chewa preferring *Chiuta* or *Chauta* for their supreme being. These words literally mean "the big bow" or "the Great (One) of the rainbow."¹⁰⁰ Another possibility for the etymology of the Yawo's *Mlungu* from within the Ciyawo language is that it derives somehow from the verb *kulungwa*, which means "to make big" or "be great." In this case, *Mlungu* would emphasize the supreme being's greatness.¹⁰¹

Frankl provides a valuable discussion on the etymology of the word as it relates to Kiswahili, suggesting associations with "clouds" and "sky."¹⁰² Indeed, Henry Salt even applies the link between "sky" and "molungo" to the Yawo, whom he calls the "Monjou."¹⁰³ Regardless of these etymological possibilities, Chakanza convincingly argues that all the various proposals regarding the etymology of *Mlungu* ultimately point to his unfathomable greatness anyway.¹⁰⁴ We must also guard against what Carson calls the "root fallacy" in relation to biblical exegesis, which is the mistaken belief that the meaning of words continues to be made up of their underlying components.¹⁰⁵ Furthermore, the etymology is no longer critical to Bible translation because *Mlungu* is now widely recognized by the Yawo as a proper noun for what in English is rendered as *God*. Another reason to guard against this etymological fallacy is that, historically, *Mlungu* in Ciyawo seemed to have a broader meaning than just a referent to a supreme being. Early missionaries recorded that this term was also used generally to refer to spirits, with the "spirit" of a deceased person also being called

---

98. Brown, "Concepts of God in Africa," 14.

99. Breugel, *Chewa Traditional Religion*, 31; Wendland, "Case for Chauta," 433.

100. Breugel, *Chewa Traditional Religion*, 29–30.

101. For other examples of the names and meanings given to the supreme being in various African cultures, see the discussion in Mbiti, *African Religions*, 30–36.

102. Frankl, "Word for 'God.'"

103. Salt, *Voyage to Abyssinia*, 41.

104. Chakanza, "Some Chewa Concepts," 4.

105. Carson, *Exegetical Fallacies*, 28–33.

"Mulungu."[106] What is critical here, however, is to show that these traditional terms can be used as terms for *God* in Bible translations regardless of their etymology when that etymology has become redundant.

Loyalty in Light of the Religious "Beads"

I already established the predominant Muslim identity of the Yawo in this book, and it requires no further emphasis now. However, for a Bible translation project in this context, it is crucial to acknowledge and respond to the prevalent Islamic influence among the Yawo. Given that the Yawo community is predominantly Muslim, they already possess a rich Islamic religious vocabulary and hold certain convictions about the word of God. Not all of these convictions are incompatible with a Christian view of the Bible.[107] Therefore, a Mozambican Ciyawo Bible translation should incorporate familiar vocabulary to resonate with the existing religious and cultural framework (the only other available vocabulary would be foreign to most Yawo people and therefore not comprehensible). In this Islamic context, there are already commonly used terms available derived from the Qur'ān that correspond to many biblical characters including, but not limited to, Abraham (Arabic, إبراهيم, *Ibrāhīm*), Moses (Arabic, موسى, *Mūsā*), Elijah (Arabic, إلياس, *Ilyās*), and Jesus (Arabic, عيسى, *'Īsā*). The majority of previous Ciyawo Bible translations have opted for terms derived from other languages, such as Chichewa, as opposed to using the commonly used words in Ciyawo that have Islamic origins. Although Chauncy Maples's 1880 Ciyawo translation of the Gospel of Matthew frequently used Islamic terminology, those responsible for past Ciyawo Bible translations have generally aligned with foreign terminology. They often adopted terms used by Christian communities of other language groups, such as the Chewa/Nyanja. This tendency is not inherently erroneous, but if the intended *skopos* involves a Bible translation project aimed at a Muslim community yet to embrace the Christian message, an "indigenizing" approach to translation is recommended. Such an approach would serve the Yawo Muslim community better as it focuses

---

106. MacDonald, *Africana*, 1:59–60.

107. Although Christians do, of course, speak of the "Word of God" as the Bible, the true "Word" of God in Christianity is the person Jesus, God's ultimate revelation. This view differs distinctly from the Islamic view that God's ultimate revelation is in a book (the Qur'ān).

"upon the understandability and acceptability of the ideas within the biblical text for a reader within an Islamic cultural milieu."[108]

Apart from using Islamic terminology, where linguistically appropriate and faithful to the source text, another crucial consideration in response to the religious frame of Islam pertains to the issue of metatexts. This aspect particularly applies to the physical presentation of the translation product. This means that any printed Bible translation among the Mozambican Yawo should conform to the established forms expected of authoritative scriptural texts. In accordance with the work of Jacobus Naudé and Cynthia Miller-Naudé, who demonstrate that "metatexts are a critical component of the translation of religious texts" and that they "foreground the role of the translator as an agent in shaping the interpretation of the text theologically and ideologically,"[109] it will not do to produce low quality products that disrespect the biblical text in the eyes of the end users. While this does not necessarily imply that stapled booklets, for instance, are inherently unacceptable or would be outright rejected by a Yawo Muslim audience, it does mean that a Bible translation product is more likely to succeed if its form is readily identifiable as respectable and fitting for Scripture—particularly among the influential people of Yawo societies. In practical terms, this might entail using certain colors (such as green or red) for the cover rather than others (like black) and incorporating Arabesque borders and embellishments to surround the text. However, outside organizations should not unilaterally dictate the inclusion of such features; instead, they should involve appropriate Yawo stakeholders in the decision-making process. It is crucial to recognize that despite expectations based on an understanding of the context that the majority of Mozambican Yawo people would prefer Arabesque forms, style, and language, the Yawo stakeholders may opt for alternative decisions. We must duly respect these preferences and expectations. Simultaneously, the Yawo themselves should be able to make informed decisions about what is possible. This respectful approach can only truly occur if the various contextual frames are known and understood and the right individuals are engaged in the process.

---

108. Miller-Naudé and Naudé, "Covert Religious Censorship," 822. The term "indigenizing" here echoes Dapila's use of the term above. I am using the term synonymously with "domesticating."

109. Naudé and Miller-Naudé, "Theology and Ideology," 287.

It is evident that Islam is one of the beads of the Yawo situation in Mozambique.[110] The Yawo, primarily a homogeneous people group, predominantly identify with Islam, except for minority Christian Yawo populations, which are mainly located in urban areas. Any Bible translation endeavor seeking to be sensitive to Yawo culture must pay attention to this Islamic reality.[111] While Islam is not the sole narrative frame or necessarily the most important one, a recent sociolinguistic survey sheds light on its prominence. For example, out of 268 Mozambican Yawo male and female respondents across more than fifteen distinct locations, over 98 percent identified themselves as Muslim.[112] The predominance of Islam among the Yawo in Mozambique is undeniable. For many, being Yawo equates to being Muslim. Ignoring this reality would undoubtedly hinder the success of Bible translation efforts in the Mozambican Yawo context, especially if success is measured by how well the translation fulfills an established translation covenant, shaped by a thorough understanding of the context. A Bible translation intended solely for Yawo churches would likely only reach a tiny fraction of the population, and that without considering other narrative frames that influence how Bible translation efforts in Ciyawo should occur. That said, an analysis of the Yawo situation can still involve church communities in the process of translation and distribution, particularly those sympathetic to the majority Muslim population. Best efforts should also be made to incorporate the role of the local church into the translation covenant itself as well, without inhibiting the primary purposes of the translation.

Understanding the characteristics of ATR, especially in the context of the Yawo people, provides valuable insight into how their traditional beliefs and practices shape their worldview. It also highlights the importance of considering this narrative frame in any efforts to engage in Bible translation in such a context (and in missionary work in general, for that matter). By appreciating the deeply ingrained nature of ATR and its influence on the Yawo, one can approach Bible translation with greater

---

110. Although there is also the overarching religious "bead," it is also appropriate to break down the narrative frames into subframes as necessary so that Islam can be considered as a "bead" in its own right.

111. This focus on the Islamic Yawo community does not mean that Yawo Christians are to be ignored. However, the reality is that there are not really "Yawo churches" so much as there being churches that have Yawo in them. Most Yawo remain impacted by Islam and so this is my main focus here when it comes to discussing the socioreligious realities of Yawo society.

112. Houston, "Sociolinguistic and Extensibility Survey," 3.

sensitivity toward their cultural and spiritual heritage and underlying worldview. Although the influence of ATR is, perhaps, less obvious in terms of concrete examples of vocabulary that might enter into a new Bible translation, the reality remains that African cultures, including the Yawo, are deeply and inevitably influenced by their traditional worldview. Therefore, it makes sense that a translation would show loyalty to the Yawo by accepting this reality. The most obvious example of such acceptance is seen in the use of the term *N'nungu* for God. This word is a traditional term used since the beginning of Yawo Bible translation, despite the fact that it predates any introduced monotheistic conceptualization of God—whether Christian or Islamic. Also, although the Ciyawo word *wupile* (English, *fortune, luck*) is an example of Ciyawo Bible translation using a traditional term (one that was mentioned above), it is not exclusively a religious term but simply the most natural equivalent available and used in normal life—in spite of its sometime traditional religious connotations. The word itself is used in instances of *bless* and *blessings* in both verbal and substantive senses. These examples show that it is fine to use traditional vocabulary in a Ciyawo Bible translation, fully expecting that the Bible's narrative will be part of the evolving and expanding conceptual landscape of the Yawo.

THE HISTORICAL "BEAD"

The historical bead in any Bible translation situation would involve looking at existing translations and previous work done in a given community. This bead involves the overall history of the people and how they got to where they are now. This section discusses the historical context of the Yawo in Mozambique as its own bead on the necklace in that situation.

Setting the Scene: Early Christian Mission Among the Yawo

The Yawo people are not a group who have benefited from centuries of interaction with the Christian "good news" nor its primary vehicle, the Bible.[113] Instead, significant Christian contact with the Yawo appears to have first taken place in the nineteenth century, notably when explorer missionaries such as David Livingstone encountered the people he

---

113. Much of the discussion here follows an earlier version I wrote but has since been updated here with new discoveries. See Houston, "Utenga Wambone."

referred to as the "Ajawa."[114] Today, this term is used by speakers of other languages, such as Portuguese, and by the Makhuwa people of Mozambique to refer to the Yawo. The Yawo refer to themselves as Ŵayawo, with the Ŵa prefix indicating the people class of nouns. Sometimes, Yawo people will also call themselves Ŵaciyawo, meaning "people who speak the Ciyawo language." It is theoretically possible that the Yawo were exposed to Christian theology earlier than the nineteenth century by virtue of their contact through slave trading with other peoples on the East African coast. However, it is more likely that their conceptions of Abrahamic monotheism were influenced primarily by their Muslim business partners—the Swahili Arabs along the east coast of Africa. This relationship was significant in shaping the Yawo's religious landscape. This mention of Abrahamic monotheism among the Yawo does not downplay the significance, though, of the many African religious traditions, including those of the Yawo, that independently conceptualized a single supreme being. As mentioned, African traditions across various cultures on the continent often already included the belief in an omnipotent supreme being prior to and independent of Christian or Islamic influence.[115] This was certainly the case for the Yawo.

The two Christian missions that worked most closely among the Yawo during the relatively early days of the late nineteenth century were the Church of Scotland's Blantyre Mission and the Anglican Universities' Mission to Central Africa (UMCA). Others, such as the Free Church of Scotland's Livingstonia Mission, had also established themselves on Lake Malawi around the same time, but the Blantyre Mission and the UMCA are the two groups that had significant early input into Ciyawo Bible translation. Both missions worked among Yawo communities and used the Ciyawo language in their work and interactions.

The UMCA was uniquely situated in prime Yawo territory. It played a pivotal role in the early Christian missionary efforts among the Yawo people. The formation of the UMCA was inspired in part by David Livingstone's call to establish mission work in Central Africa during his influential visits to various universities in the United Kingdom in 1857. These visits galvanized support and enthusiasm for missionary work in Africa, leading to the establishment of the UMCA shortly thereafter. By the middle of 1861, Charles Mackenzie, its leader and the first missionary

---

114. Livingstone and Livingstone, *Narrative of an Expedition*, 355.
115. Lugira, *African Traditional Religion*, 39.

bishop in what is now Malawi, traveled on an expedition up the Zambezi River, choosing Magomero, with the help of David Livingstone, in the Shire Highlands of Malawi as the site for a new mission. However, only months after setting out, in January 1862, Mackenzie died from complications from malaria after his medicines were lost when the boat he was traveling on sank. Under the guidance of Mackenzie's successor, Bishop William Tozer, the UMCA instead established itself at Zanzibar in 1864.[116] In subsequent years, the mission expanded to the interior of Central Africa, with settlements established at Masasi in 1876[117] and Newala in 1878,[118] both in present-day Tanzania. The Masasi community was formed with freed slaves and founded by the UMCA missionaries. The UMCA also established a presence on Likoma Island on Lake Malawi by 1886,[119] a site that became a crucial hub for the mission's work on the lake. The construction of the immense St. Peter's Cathedral on Likoma Island, completed in 1909 and still in use today, underscores the island's significance for the UMCA. This grand cathedral stands as a symbol of the mission's commitment and the substantial investment they made in their work.[120]

In the heart of Yawo territory in Mozambique, after William Percival Johnson was kicked out of Muembe in 1880, the UMCA established more permanent mission stations at Unangu in 1893[121] and Mtonya in 1905.[122] Like Muembe, these locations are far closer to the Yawo heartland than Blantyre. Mtonya and Unangu are located approximately twenty and fifty kilometers from Lichinga respectively. Lichinga is the present-day capital of Niassa Province. The impact of the two stations of Unangu and Mtonya on Yawo society is significant. The efforts of the UMCA in these areas laid the foundation for the minority Anglican Yawo Church that still exists in Mozambique today. Despite the predominant Islamic faith among the Yawo, the legacy of the UMCA's work is evident in the active Anglican fellowship found in present-day Machemba, situated near the now-abandoned Mtonya mission site. Additionally, there

---

116. Anderson-Morshead, *History of the Universities' Mission*, 47–50.

117. Anderson-Morshead, *History of the Universities' Mission*, 128.

118. Anderson-Morshead, *History of the Universities' Mission*, 132.

119. Anderson-Morshead, *History of the Universities' Mission*, 322; Maples, "Lukoma," 60.

120. Bremner, "Architecture of the Universities' Mission," 516.

121. Hine, *Days Gone By*, 131.

122. Winspear, "Short History," 31.

are now Anglican congregations in various locations across Niassa Province, including prominent ones in Lichinga, Marrupa, and Messumba, the latter being near Metangula on the lakeshore. A notable symbol of this Anglican presence is the large church building in Lichinga named after Yohanna Abdallah, a significant Yawo Anglican figure from the early twentieth century. Abdallah's contributions to the Anglican community have left a lasting legacy, and his name continues to be honored within the church. Abdallah is also remembered as one of the first African writers to author a book in an East African language—*The Yaos: Chiikala Cha Wayao* (1919).[123] Despite the continued presence of the Anglican community, the proportion of Yawo Anglicans compared to Yawo Muslims remains very small. The Yawo are predominantly Muslim, a reality that has significantly shaped the religious landscape of the region. The small Anglican minority in Niassa is composed mainly of individuals from other ethnic groups, such as the Nyanja, rather than the Yawo themselves. This demographic situation is likely a result of the UMCA's strategic shift in focus to Likoma Island, where the Nyanja population was more receptive to Christian mission efforts.

As mentioned briefly above, one of the UMCA's missionaries, William Johnson, was welcomed at Chief Mataka II's village, Muembe, in November 1880 with the aim of establishing mission work.[124] But after the British authorities intercepted a caravan transporting Mataka's slaves, this led to a sharp turn in the chief's attitude and trust towards the mission.[125] Chief Mataka suspected that Johnson had colluded with the British authorities and so kicked him out in retaliation.[126] It is undoubtedly partly due to incidents like this that Mataka and other Yawo chiefs eventually chose to embrace the Islamic religion of their coastal business partners rather than the Christian message brought by the European missionaries.[127] By the time of his death in the 1880s, Mataka II appears to have become a Muslim. He was remembered as "Mataka of the Mosque"[128]

---

123. Abdallah, *Yaos*. This book also includes a contemporary English translation by a British medical officer.

124. Barnes, *Johnson of Nyasaland*, 34–36; Johnson, *African Reminiscences*, 57.

125. Anderson-Morshead, *History of the Universities' Mission*, 147; Johnson, *African Reminiscences*, 69; Winspear, "Short History," 19.

126. Anderson-Morshead, *History of the Universities' Mission*, 147; Johnson, *African Reminiscences*, 71.

127. Bone, "Islam in Malawi," 128; Thorold, "Yao Muslims," 123–25.

128. Abdallah, *Yaos*, 56.

and buried beneath the veranda of the mosque at Muembe, symbolizing his commitment to his adopted faith.[129]

It is noteworthy for Yawo history that the European, mainly British, colonial efforts to abolish the slave trade likely thwarted the widespread acceptance of the Christian *utenga wambone* ("good news," and also the title of some early Gospel translations into Ciyawo) of justice and love. The economic ties of Yawo leaders, particularly Chief Mataka II, to the slave trade were too lucrative for them to embrace the contrarian antislavery message that missionaries such as William Johnson brought to them. The missionaries represented a broader Christian movement, epitomized by figures like William Wilberforce in England, who had vigorously campaigned for the abolition of the slave trade in the first place. The abolitionist stance of these Christians put them in direct conflict with the economic interests of Yawo chiefs, for whom the slave trade was a significant source of wealth and power. Mataka's economic interests and political alliances were deeply intertwined with the slave trade, making it exceedingly difficult for him to consider the acceptance of Christianity, which Mataka likely perceived as a threat to those interests. While the religious truths offered by Islam may have genuinely appealed to Mataka and other Yawo chiefs, it is essential to recognize that the initial conversion of the Yawo to Islam was likely influenced more by economic and political conditions than by purely theological factors. The Swahili Arab traders, who were the primary Muslim influences in the region, provided not only religious teachings but also lucrative economic opportunities through the slave trade. Accepting Islam allowed Yawo chiefs to maintain and even enhance their economic and political power as opposed to the disruptive consequences that would have accompanied a conversion to Christianity. Moreover, the perception of Christian missionaries as agents of European colonial powers further complicated the religious landscape, particularly towards the end of the nineteenth century. This association added another layer of resistance, as embracing Christianity could be seen as a capitulation to foreign influence and control.

Another significant figure of Protestant Christian mission to the Yawo in this early period was Duff MacDonald, a Scottish missionary based in Blantyre, Nyasaland (now Malawi), from 1878 until 1881. Despite his relatively brief tenure in Blantyre, MacDonald managed to acquire considerable knowledge of the Yawo people and their language.

---

129. Abdallah, *Yaos*, 56; Alpers, "Trade, State, and Society," 420.

Although he served in Blantyre only for a few years until his controversial dismissal for his handling of the so-called Blantyre Scandal of 1879,[130] he was nevertheless able to produce the two-volume *Africana: Or the Heart of Heathen Africa*.[131] This work is a significant contribution that describes the Yawo people at considerable length in the fashion of an ethnographical and anthropological study. MacDonald devoted the second volume primarily to mission life issues, and it contains an appendix of "native tales" translated into English.[132] An expansion on this theme was published as "Yao and Nyanja Tales" in 1938 after a manuscript by Duff MacDonald was discovered among the papers of Alice Werner. This manuscript was "evidently [intended] as a supplement to [MacDonald's] well-known publication in Africana."[133] After this early work, another Scotsman, Alexander Hetherwick, emerged as the most famous figure of the Blantyre Mission. Hetherwick arrived in 1883, following the turmoil of the Blantyre scandal, and later went on to have a significant and well-recognized impact on Malawi's Christian history. He became a leading figure in linguistic and Bible translation efforts in both the Chichewa and Ciyawo languages.[134] He became the head of the Blantyre Mission in 1898[135] and continued in this role until his retirement in the late 1920s.

Many of these nineteenth-century missionaries seemed to believe that Ciyawo was more challenging to learn as a language than the other languages used within the geographical areas where the respective missions worked. The other languages used among the UMCA and Blantyre Mission included predominantly Kiswahili and Chichewa/Nyanja, as well as Emakhuwa. Individuals such as Bishop John Edward Hine[136] and Bishop Edward Steere[137] of the UMCA asserted that Ciyawo was indeed particularly difficult to learn. For example, Hine, reflecting on his

---

130. Chirnside, *Blantyre Missionaries*; Hinchliff, "Blantyre Scandal." In short, the scandal involved the punishment of Africans at the hands of some mission staff who considered Blantyre as an ecclesiastical colony over which the church possessed civil jurisdiction. The scandal arose after several people were flogged and imprisoned and a suspected criminal was executed. Although Duff Macdonald was likely more a scapegoat than actual perpetrator, his reputation nonetheless suffered.

131. MacDonald, *Africana*, vol. 1; MacDonald, *Africana*, vol. 2.

132. MacDonald, *Africana*, 2:319.

133. MacDonald and Doke, "Yao and Nyanja Tales," 251.

134. Ross, *Mission in Malawi*, 101.

135. Livingstone, *Prince of Missionaries*, 95; Ross, *Blantyre Mission*, 224.

136. Hine, *Days Gone By*, 128.

137. Steere, *Collections for a Handbook*, iii.

experience, wrote that after he began learning Ciyawo, he found it to be "quite different from the ChiNyanja of the Lake, and of all the many languages used in the mission, I think the hardest for an Englishman to acquire. The grammar is more complicated and the accent is peculiar, and not many can speak it correctly."[138] Although the assertion about Ciyawo's difficulty for foreigners is not unfounded, the UMCA's Chauncy Maples found his portions of the Emakhuwa Gospel of Matthew more challenging to work on than the Ciyawo translation.[139] Regardless of these perceived difficulties in learning Ciyawo, many early missionaries made historic contributions to the linguistic study and development of Ciyawo as a written language. The missionaries' linguistic endeavors were crucial in creating the first dictionaries, grammar guides, and translated texts in Ciyawo.

The Historical Background to Ciyawo Bible Translations

In terms of language development and published literature, Ciyawo remains quite limited, especially in terms of its actual use in written form by Yawo people. While there are established orthographies[140] and some materials have been published in Ciyawo, including even the United Nations' Universal Declaration of Human Rights,[141] the majority of Yawo individuals are unable to engage with these resources due to high levels of illiteracy and limited accessibility. Moreover, the inconsistency between the orthographies used in Mozambique, Tanzania, and Malawi poses an additional challenge. Like many other African contexts, the vast majority of Yawo people are functionally nonliterate and rely primarily on oral communication. This situation is influenced by various factors, including the absence of suitable educational materials, insufficient funding for education, and a range of historical and cultural issues.

The most significant works of literature in the Ciyawo language that exist to date are undoubtedly translations of the Bible. The first published portion of the Bible in Ciyawo, and indeed one of the earliest examples of written literature in the language, was the Gospel of Matthew translated

---

138. Hine, *Days Gone By*, 128.

139. Maples, *Chauncy Maples*, 134; Maples, *Anjili ya Mattayo*.

140. Center for Language Studies, *Orthography of Ciyawo*; Ngunga and Faquir, *Padronização da Ortografia*.

141. UN Office of the High Commissioner for Human Rights, "Mkamulano."

by Chauncy Maples of the UMCA and printed in 1880.[142] Early in his time in Africa, Maples had envisioned himself and his colleague, William Johnson, as the most likely candidates within the mission to undertake translation work in Ciyawo,[143] a vision later realized with the publication of Matthew. Although Johnson later shifted his focus to other languages, such as Chinyanja and Mpoto,[144] he also contributed to Ciyawo Bible translation to some extent.[145] Even though Johnson had made early attempts at translating portions of Ciyawo Scriptures,[146] it is also possible that he worked again on translating Scripture portions into Ciyawo due to an immediate evangelistic need during his stint at Muembe living among Yawo people. However, it seems that any efforts to that effect were never published. Given Johnson's close relationship with Maples, it is likely that he benefited from Maples's translation of Matthew, published in the same year that Johnson arrived at Chief Mataka's Muembe for his residence there.

Following Maples's pioneering translation of Matthew in 1880, Alexander Hetherwick embarked on his own translation efforts, independently from Maples. In 1889, Hetherwick published translations of the four Gospels[147] and Acts.[148] Subsequently, he translated Paul's Letter to the Romans[149] and the Letters to the Corinthians[150] in 1891, with further translations released in the following years. By 1898, Hetherwick had completed a translation of the entire New Testament in Ciyawo, and by 1902, he had already revised his translations of the Gospels and Acts. Prior to Hetherwick's formal publications and around the time Maples published his translation of Matthew, Duff MacDonald in Blantyre also engaged in translating portions of the Bible into Ciyawo. In his work *Africana*, MacDonald mentioned that he had prepared some parts for printing by 1879.[151] Indeed, in that same year, he published a collection

---

142. Maples, *Anjili ja Ambuje Wetu*.

143. Maples, "'My Dear Bishop'" (March 6th, 1877); Maples, *Chauncy Maples*, 84.

144. Mojola, *God Speaks My Language*, 211.

145. Barnes, *Johnson of Nyasaland*, 210; Maples, "'My Dear Mr. Heanley.'"

146. Maples, "'My Dear Randolph.'"

147. Hetherwick, *Matayo*; Hetherwick, *Marko*; Hetherwick, *Luka*; Hetherwick, *Yohana*.

148. Hetherwick, *Masengo ga Wandumitume*.

149. Hetherwick, *Kalata jua Paolo*.

150. Hetherwick, *Achikalata jua Paolo*.

151. MacDonald, *Africana*, 2:127.

of Bible lessons[152] and then in 1881 a selection of Gospel extracts.[153] He expressed his eagerness to accelerate the translation process, stating in 1881 that "we knew the time required to translate the whole Bible was about fifteen years, and Buchanan and I were anxious to try whether we might not, by working as for a wager, complete the task in a much shorter time."[154] According to Chauncy Maples, John Buchanan also contributed positively to Ciyawo Bible translation by completing a translation of the Gospel of Luke. Maples noted that Buchanan's translation, while not on par with Hetherwick's work, still represented a commendable effort, claiming that "Mr. Buchanan of Zomba, whose translation of St Luke, though certainly inferior to the St Mark [of Hetherwick], is still an excellent specimen of what good work in this line may be done by one who has had no special training in linguistics."[155] Buchanan himself lists the availability of his Luke translation in *The Shire Highlands*, alongside a collection of hymns copublished with Alexander Hetherwick.[156]

For Duff MacDonald, however, any plans he may have had to continue with Ciyawo Bible translation were unfortunately curtailed by his enforced absence following the fallout of the Blantyre scandal. Despite the brevity of his time, MacDonald made some headway in translating the historical parts of the Old Testament and the Gospels,[157] although it remains uncertain whether these translations were ever formally published. MacDonald himself mentioned in 1881, "besides having [the Gospels of] Matthew and Mark ready for the printer, I had translated the historical parts of the Old Testament, and hoped to get these printed and illustrated."[158] Even though it is unclear as to whether any more of MacDonald's Ciyawo translation efforts actually ever saw the light of day beyond his Gospel extracts, Hetherwick notes that "before his [MacDonald's] retirement in 1881, he was enabled to publish a selection of Scripture passages in Yao, together with a small collection of native stories for use in the mission schools."[159] Duff MacDonald undeniably accomplished a significant amount of Ciyawo Bible translation work during

152. MacDonald, *Bible Lessons*. Cf. Buchanan, *Shire Highlands*, 221.
153. MacDonald, *Masagulo*.
154. MacDonald, *Africana*, 2:234.
155. Maples, *Yao-English Vocabulary*, 7.
156. Buchanan, *Shire Highlands*, 221.
157. MacDonald, *Africana*, 2:95.
158. MacDonald, *Africana*, 2:260.
159. Hetherwick, *Introductory Handbook*, vi.

his brief tenure among the Yawo. Indeed, it is conceivable that some of Hetherwick's translations were informed by MacDonald's earlier efforts.

As previously mentioned, after the initial efforts in translating the Bible into Ciyawo by Chauncy Maples of the UMCA, followed by Duff MacDonald and John Buchanan of the Blantyre Mission, Alexander Hetherwick began translating parts of the Bible into Ciyawo. After a meeting between Maples and Hetherwick in 1886,[160] Maples appears to have ceased further translation efforts, leaving Hetherwick as the primary and most prolific translator of Ciyawo Scriptures at that time. Regarding Hetherwick's translation of Mark's Gospel, Maples himself lauded it as "a genuine triumph of translation, and I cannot refrain here from expressing my admiration for this splendid achievement."[161] Similarly, Johnson also acknowledged Hetherwick's "well-known work in Yao translations,"[162] indicating recognition and appreciation from within the wider missionary community for Hetherwick's contributions to Bible translation in the Ciyawo language.

After Hetherwick's completion of the entire New Testament by 1898, and over the next two decades, the translation of the Old Testament books began, undertaken by various missionaries, many of whom were associated with the UMCA. The Yawo Anglican priest Yohanna Abdallah also contributed to the translation effort, with the Old Testament eventually completed by 1920 following the publication of Job, Ecclesiastes, and Song of Solomon. At least two different versions of Genesis were translated during this period, appearing in 1904[163] and 1906.[164] The 1904 version was published with only the first twenty-five chapters, for unknown reasons. A Swahili teacher apparently translated the 1906 version with revisions by W. B. Suter of the UMCA. The UMCA published an edition of the first five books of the Bible, the Pentateuch, at Likoma Island in 1913 or 1914.[165] Throughout this period and up to the 1930s, individuals such as Edith How of the UMCA, along with others, engaged in revisions and new translation work. These efforts were likely sometimes done in committee until the final approval of a completed New Testament in 1936, but actual publication as a whole book was delayed until 1952 for

160. Maples, *Yao-English Vocabulary*, 2.
161. Maples, *Yao-English Vocabulary*, 7.
162. Johnson, "Mohammedanism and the Yaos," 105.
163. *Chipeperu Chakutanda Cha Musa Chichitelwe Genesis*.
164. Suter, *Genesis in Chiyao*.
165. Suter and Ker, *Genesis–Deuteronomy*.

uncertain reasons. This delay may have been due to existing stocks, but perhaps the situation was also impacted by the global geopolitical situation at the time and the breakout of the Second World War in 1939. It is also worth noting that Christian communities throughout Yawo lands, such as the Anglican church, have produced some of their own texts in Ciyawo, such as hymnals and prayer books, ever since the first missionaries began the practice of translating "mattins, litany, and evensong."[166] Still, these documents are not widely published or circulated.

Sadly, despite the significant effort and remarkable accomplishments of these early Ciyawo translators, their works are not readily accessible today. Most of these texts are only found in archives, hidden away from the public eye. The National Archives of Malawi in Zomba house an incomplete collection of biblical books translated into Ciyawo, as do a few other libraries scattered around the world. The most comprehensive collection of early Ciyawo Bible translations can be found in the archives of the British and Foreign Bible Society at Cambridge University in England. It is lamentable that there are no extant copies of any Ciyawo literature at Likoma Island's Anglican cathedral, where a UMCA printing press was once active. Many of their texts, including translations of biblical books into Ciyawo, were transferred to the Malawian national archives at Zomba. This general loss of tangible historical artifacts represents a missed opportunity for future generations to engage with and appreciate the linguistic and cultural heritage of the Yawo people.

Since the delayed 1950s publication of the New Testament text, which was approved in 1936, there was a notable gap in fresh Bible translation work in Ciyawo until the 1981 publication of the Gospel of Luke by the Malawian Bible Society[167] and the subsequent 1992 publication of selections from the New Testament, such as the Gospel of Mark (now archived at Cambridge in the UK). This hiatus in translation efforts is understandable, considering the sociopolitical context of the time. Many African nations, including Mozambique, were grappling with the struggle for independence amid the political turbulence of the Cold War era. Mozambique, in particular, endured a prolonged civil war that severely hindered the country's capacity to undertake Bible translation work. Indeed, it is only now, after around thirty years since the end of the civil

---

166. Maples, "'My Dear Bishop'" (October 10th, 1880), 2.
167. *Ngani Syambone Syakwamba Yesu Kristo siŵalembile Luka.*

war in 1992, that the Mozambican Bible Society has been able to begin thinking about its own Ciyawo Bible translation endeavors.

After the 1990s, the Malawian Bible Society's full Bible (*Buku Jeswela*) in Ciyawo appeared, which was translated in the urban center of Mangochi and published in 2014. This publication came about due to the rejection that the 1992 version experienced among Yawo communities. This rejection was due, in part, to using difficult and archaic words, inadequate interpretations, Chichewa "mixing," incorrect orthography, stylistic problems, and "expressions that do not convey the meaning properly."[168] *Injil Jeswela*, or the "Holy Gospel," which contains the books of Luke and Acts, came out of a project based in the village of Chiutula in rural Malawi and was aimed at the majority Muslim Yawo audience; it was published a few years before the Bible Society's full Bible.

Most recently, the Seed Company initiated a Bible translation project for Yawo churches in Tanzania, while a revision of *Buku Jeswela* (but realistically, it is more of a fresh translation) is nearing completion in Namwera, Malawi. This version is supposed to align the Bible more closely with the predominantly Muslim majority Yawo demographic. In addition, the Bible Society of Mozambique commenced a translation project in Lichinga in 2019 for use by Yawo churches in Mozambique (of which, if there are any, there aren't many exclusively Yawo churches). The entire New Testament has been completed by the team in Tanzania, with work underway on the Old Testament. One of the initial publications by the Tanzanian project was the Gospel of Luke[169] with the rest of the New Testament now published and available online.

The most recent endeavors in Ciyawo Bible translation are oral translations of Genesis, Exod 1–20, Matthew, and a selection of Psalms under the auspices of Baptist Mission Australia in collaboration with the Baptist Convention of Mozambique and with assistance from Faith Comes By Hearing. This project, which commenced in Lichinga in 2021, has already released audio portions of Genesis, Exodus, Psalms, and Matthew to the public. While initially oral, the project has already produced a transcription of Genesis alongside the audio and published it as a book with Arabesque design. Targeted at the Muslim-majority Yawo population, this translation is expected to be valuable for Christian Yawo in Mozambique as well because the language used is distinctly Mozambican.

---

168. Bister et al., "Sociolinguistic Survey."
169. See *Ngani Jambone*.

The oral format and approach is chosen due to the widespread illiteracy among the Yawo, preventing them from engaging with written translations. Finally, although it may seem strange that Malawi, Tanzania, and Mozambique each have Ciyawo Bible translations underway in one regard or another, in my survey I demonstrated conclusively that there are sufficient differences between Ciyawo variants to warrant their own versions (notwithstanding differences between orthographies anyway).[170]

As the latest translations into Ciyawo are unveiled and distributed to the public in the forthcoming months and years, it is imperative to assess their impact. There has been a varied history of Ciyawo Bible translation since the nineteenth century, yet most Yawo remain Muslim. Despite the various attempts over the years to translate the Bible into Ciyawo, it is debatable whether these were successful when measured by the lack of ongoing use and availability. Analyzing whether the oral Bible translation currently underway in Mozambique and the latest translations from Malawi effectively address the Islamic context of the Yawo, as outlined in their respective covenants and briefs, will be a crucial area of investigation in the future.

Loyalty in Light of the Historical "Bead"

Responding to the historical context of Ciyawo Bible translation is less crucial than addressing the Islamic context, as there is no specific historical community or previously spoken vocabulary in active use today. By this I mean that the Yawo audience that existed at the time of the first Ciyawo Bible translations are no longer with us, and the language has evolved since then. A response to the historical frame is more honorary in character, serving to acknowledge past efforts and learn from them rather than replicate them. It is essential to recognize that certain approaches to Ciyawo Bible translation have been attempted before and that it is not necessary to repeat these efforts, particularly if they were unsuccessful. One of the main lessons from the historical frame is that Ciyawo Bible translation has broadly been ineffective, as evidenced by the fact that most Yawo have mainly remained unengaged with the Bible throughout each iteration of a Ciyawo Bible translation or its portions—especially for those Yawo outside the Anglican communion. This indicates that something crucial has been missing in the strategies employed,

---

170. Houston, "Sociolinguistic and Extensibility Survey," 92.

and a change is required for the future of Ciyawo Bible translation. Additionally, no formal Ciyawo Bible translation efforts had been conducted in Mozambique after the early twentieth century until the newly initiated translation for existing Yawo churches by the Bible Society of Mozambique, which began in 2019. This marked a significant milestone but even this project highlights a clear gap in Mozambican Yawo Bible translation for Muslim audiences, underscoring the need for a contemporary and culturally relevant Ciyawo Bible translation in Mozambique. Thus, the historical frame teaches us that it is time for Mozambique to have its own Ciyawo Bible translation, one that addresses the needs of the modern Yawo community and engages effectively with their predominantly Islamic context. By learning from past efforts and avoiding previous mistakes, future translations can be more successful in reaching and resonating with the Yawo people.

THE ORALITY "BEAD"

When the Mozambican Yawo situation is analyzed, it is clear that orality is one of the "beads" on the necklace. For this discussion, orality is defined as dependence on verbal language for communication instead of written language.[171] It is less about a preference for one communication style over another but more about which is predominantly relied upon in life. Ernst Wendland's definition is also applicable here: "The term 'orality' refers generally to the characteristic modes of thought and verbal expression in societies that depend for communication essentially upon the spoken word, accompanied by various associated non-verbal techniques, such as gestures, facial features, and body movements."[172]

Like most African cultures, the Yawo people rely upon oral means of communication in most aspects of their lives. Even the minority of literate Yawo individuals generally prefer oral communication over written communication when interacting with their peers. This preference for orality extends beyond practical communication; it is deeply embedded in the fabric of Yawo culture. Oral traditions such as stories, myths, proverbs, and riddles play a crucial role in preserving and transmitting cultural values, knowledge, and history from one generation to the next.

---

171. Lovejoy, "Extent of Orality," 121–22.
172. Wendland, *Orality and the Scriptures*, 12–13.

Oral communication among the Yawo is not merely a practical choice but a necessity for life. Let us consider the nature of Yawo orality further.

Orality in Yawo culture manifests practically in the fact that the majority of Yawo people are unable to read or write (in any language) and rely on oral means of communication to carry out their everyday activities. There are exceptions to this inability to read or write, particularly in urban settings where there is greater opportunity for formal education. For the majority of Yawo who do not read and write, though, this does not mean that their language is unsophisticated. On the contrary, Ciyawo and the people who speak it are deeply versed in their own "oral literature"[173] and tradition.

The Yawo people have a rich tradition of riddles, proverbs, songs, and other forms of oral literature (*yakuŵeceta*, literally, "spoken things"). The most predominant forms of Yawo include what are termed *yitagu* (proverbs), *adisi* (parabolic story), *misyungu* (initiation advice), *ngani/ndano* (story), *nyimbo* (song), and *mapopelo* (informal prayers).[174] For example, Yawo proverbs encapsulate wisdom in concise, memorable phrases that are easily recalled and applied to various situations in daily life. A Yawo proverb might be used to advise someone on appropriate behavior, to offer comfort in difficult times, or to convey a complex idea succinctly. Using proverbs enriches everyday conversation, making it more layered and meaningful. The same can be said about riddles, as they are often used as a form of intellectual play, challenging listeners to think creatively and critically. Dance also plays an important role in Yawo culture and so the use of movement and gesture would be interesting to further study alongside the various modes of oral communication.

These oral art forms are also used during village headperson enthronement ceremonies (*kutaŵa dina*, literally, "tying of the name"), rain-prayer ceremonies, and other significant occasions. In other words, the contexts in which the different *yakuŵeceta* appear are as varied as the distinct forms of oral literature themselves. Ian Dicks suggests that *yakuŵeceta* can occur in both formal and informal settings, such as "initiation events, religious occasions, traditional court cases, as well as official discussions by kin or marriage sureties about marriage, other family

---

173. Finnegan, *Oral Literature in Africa*. The term "oral literature" may seem contradictory at first, but a broader definition of literature does not limit expression to the written word. An alternative term, "orature," is used by some scholars to refer to what I call oral literature in this book.

174. Dicks, *African Worldview*, 254–55; MacDonald, *Africana*, 1:47–50.

matters or sexual taboos" (formal), and in "everyday conversations, discussions at mealtimes, informal advice given by peers, storytelling and minor disciplinary measures by relatives" (informal).[175]

A further explanation of each of the predominant forms of Yawo oral literature follows:

1. *Yitagu* (singular, *citagu*): a type of proverb. Ian Dicks characterizes these as "spoken, non-narrative, factual wisdom, [which can be] formal and informal and profane."[176]

2. *Misyungu*: initiation advice, often in the form of a song.

3. *Ngani, ndano*: the Yawo story or narrative. Any retelling of an event can be *ngani*, and if it is a myth or sacred story, the term *ngani yakala-kala* (English, "story of long ago") may be used.

4. *Adiri*: parabolic story. The word itself seems to derive from the Arabic حديث (*ḥadīth*), which generally refers to traditions of the words and actions of the Prophet Muhammad. I've heard Mozambican friends distinguish between the pronunciation of the terms *adiri* and *adisi*, with the latter being *ḥadīth* of the Prophet Muhammad and the former being any parabolic story. The pronunciation distinction would only really make sense in Mozambique, where there is a difference between the *r* and *s*—Mozambicans more readily pronounce the *r* in words than in Malawi, where the *r* becomes *l* as in the name *Robert*, which is pronounced as *Lobet*. Clearly, this informant views the word pronounced as *adisi* as a somewhat foreign word with foreign pronunciation. Sometimes, a parabolic story may also be connected to a *citagu*.

5. *Mapopelo* (singular, *lipopelo*): traditional prayer that, although not memorized, tends to be formulaic. *Mapopelo* are spoken at rain-prayer ceremonies and other occasions. *Mlungu* (English, "God") may be the recipient of such prayers, often via the ancestral spirits who act as intermediaries.

6. *Nyimbo*: a song, whether traditional or originating from outside the culture; can even include popular Western music.

The importance of orality in Yawo society is vividly demonstrated during serious life cycle rituals such as *malilo* (funerals), *ditiwo* (birth

---

175. Dicks, *African Worldview*, 255.
176. Dicks, *African Worldview*, 256.

rites), and *unyago* (initiation) ceremonies. For instance, during *msondo* (girls' initiation) and *jando* (boys' initiation), dance and song are integral components of the teaching process and include more than just *misyungu*. These initiation ceremonies mark the transition from childhood to adulthood and are fundamental to the cultural identity of the Yawo people. Throughout these rites, specific songs and dances, which are characteristically Yawo in rhythm and timbre, are used to impart crucial life lessons, social responsibilities, and cultural heritage. The songs used during these ceremonies are not only a medium of instruction but also a means of reinforcing community bonds and ensuring the continuity of cultural traditions.

These examples of Yawo oral literatures highlight that, despite the absence of a written tradition, the Yawo have developed sophisticated oral forms for teaching and disseminating valuable information. This reliance on orality is not a sign of cultural deficiency but rather a testament to the adaptability and richness of Yawo traditions.[177] Oral communication allows for a dynamic and interactive exchange of knowledge, fostering a deep sense of communal and cultural continuity. Notably, though, urbanization does seem to interfere with preserving these traditions, with variations to the traditional ways of doing things under threat—including changes to initiations and the practices associated with them.

Considering the historical context of previous work in Ciyawo, which suggests that those efforts have not been particularly effective, clearly change is necessary to achieve better engagement with Bible translations. Despite numerous attempts at translating the Bible into Ciyawo, engagement with these texts has remained limited, indicating that traditional written translations have not resonated deeply with the wider Yawo community. The hints provided by the orality frame of the Yawo situation may offer a viable solution. The Yawo people are predominantly reliant on oral communication, which is deeply embedded in their cultural practices. Oral literature, such as proverbs, parabolic stories, initiation advice, and songs, plays a crucial role in their daily lives and important rituals. This cultural reliance on orality suggests that a Bible translation in the Mozambican Yawo context must take this aspect seriously into account.

---

177. As I do not intend for this book to provide a detailed exploration of Yawo oral literature, I am directing you as the reader to actual examples of the different kinds of Yawo literature and discussions concerning them as found in the following works (among others): Amaral, *O Povo Yao*; Dicks, *Wisdom of the Yawo People*; Dicks, *African Worldview*; MacDonald, *East African Tales*; MacDonald, *Africana*, vol. 1; MacDonald and Doke, "Yao and Nyanja Tales"; Stannus, "Wayao."

Therefore, to enhance Scripture engagement among the Mozambican Yawo, a Ciyawo Bible translation project in Mozambique should explicitly and openly embrace orality in both the translation process and its eventual distribution. Such an approach could also be beneficial for other cultures around the world that rely heavily on oral communication. Embracing orality in Bible translation projects can lead to greater acceptance and engagement, ensuring that the translated Scriptures resonate deeply with the target communities. This strategy acknowledges the sophistication and richness of oral traditions and leverages them to translate the Bible effectively. As Makutoane and Naudé remind us: "a translation designed for oral communication should have suitable rhythm and sound forms. It must also be understandable with ease and incorporate features of orality like an additive style rather than a subordinate style. It must be aggregative rather than analytic and to reinforce information there must be some redundancy."[178]

Practically speaking, features such as ideophones and existing oral genres should be encouraged in contexts such as the Yawo situation because "presentations without ideophones are unnatural."[179] Irresponsible use of oral features must be resisted, of course, but it is worth remembering that the Bible itself was composed in cultures dominated by orality.

In her thesis on orality in the context of Bible translation, Robin Green makes several helpful claims and suggestions that can also apply specifically to the Mozambican Ciyawo Bible translation situation. Firstly, she guards against the temptation to produce a print translation simply because it is easier to do[180] and suggests that "the most natural sounding translation will be obtained through oral composition."[181] This further means that one can see oral Bible translation as a legitimate form of translation itself and not merely a "stopgap measure"[182] before graduation to the supposedly superior print translation—as though print is the only medium by which to engage with the Bible properly. Herbert Klem writes that "if we are serious about reaching the unreached peoples of the world, we cannot afford to rely on a strategy that half the world does not use or understand."[183] In line with my sociolinguistic survey results

---

178. Naudé and Makutoane, "Reanimating Orality," 737.
179. Green, "Orality Strategy," 27; Klem, *Oral Communication*, 122.
180. Green, "Orality Strategy," 71.
181. Green, "Orality Strategy," 87.
182. Green, "Orality Strategy," 106.
183. Klem, "Dependence on Literacy Strategy," 59.

that suggest that the Yawo value tradition,[184] Klem also indicates that "it is possible ... that we are actually not dealing with an inability to read, *so much as a resistance to literacy and education out of loyalty to the group*, to a set of traditions, which are seen to be in conflict with books and book learning."[185] Fundamentally, and despite the literary bias of much Bible translation work across the world and even in the oral Yawo context, it must be acknowledged, as John Wilson writes, that "since total literacy in an oral society is a remote, if not impossible, prospect, and since the reality is often quite a high degree of illiteracy or inadequate literacy, one must conclude that in terms of the Protestant tradition, the Bible as Scripture is not the heritage of every man in an oral culture."[186]

Loyalty in Light of the Orality "Bead"

As much as literate Western missionaries may exhibit a text-based bias, the reality is very different in many of the world's Bible translation situations. It is time to show loyalty to these oral contexts by actually engaging with them on their own terms, not ours. This section of the book highlights what both a literary and orality-based approach to Bible translation in the Yawo context would look like before discussing loyalty in response.

A Literary-Based Approach: Pros and Cons

One of the most apparent risks in pursuing a literary-based approach to Bible translation in the Mozambican Yawo context is that it inherently limits access to the text to those who are literate. In this book, I define a literary-based approach as one that approaches the translation task from written texts in order to produce written texts, excluding orality in both the translation process and the features of the final product. Given the low literacy rates among the Yawo, especially in rural areas, this approach would likely mean that only some Yawo males and very few females would be able to read and engage with the translated Bible. Literacy levels are notably lower among females due to lower levels of formal education, compounding the problem of accessibility. Several other issues arise with a literary-based approach. Orthographical concerns are significant, and

---

184. Houston, "Sociolinguistic and Extensibility Survey," 60.
185. Klem, "Dependence on Literacy Strategy," 62 (emphasis original).
186. Wilson, "Scripture in an Oral Culture," 36.

cultural factors also play a crucial role; there is a possible stereotype that printed material equates to foreignness. Consequently, the message within printed texts may be perceived as foreign and irrelevant, making it less acceptable to the Yawo community. Furthermore, producing a written translation may constrain the translation to a genre that feels non-Yawo, given that the Yawo traditionally do not compose in written form.

On a very practical level, then, it is essential to emphasize that the vast majority of Yawo people are unable to read in any language. Thus, despite any well-intentioned (yet idealistic) desire to produce a quality written translation, most Yawo would not benefit from a literary-based approach. The reality is that those who can read are usually men, meaning that women, and the majority of other men who cannot read Ciyawo, are generally excluded from accessing the Bible in this form. Another significant risk is the potential for hundreds of printed Bibles in Ciyawo to remain on the shelves of missionaries and translation offices. Even if a Yawo person does purchase one, it is likely to be left unused at home due to the difficulty of engaging with it. As well as this very conceivable issue of having endless copies of the Bible sitting on shelves, "putting those same print-influenced sermons [or Bible translations] into audio form ... does make them audible, which is a step in the right direction, but their print-based way of organizing and expressing truth is still an obstacle in communication."[187] Therefore, even if people are buying printed Bible translations, there is still a genuine concern that they will not be able to engage with what they have acquired because, in general, we are devoting our energies to "providing materials for only a small portion of the population"[188] and "even when the message is recorded, the audio presentation of a literate-styled message is difficult for an oral communicator to understand."[189] These are very likely realities in the Yawo context, where the majority of people will struggle to engage with a printed book.

Unfortunately, "the assumption that all people should be literate is well intentioned but egocentric, when more than half the world's population prefers to communicate orally rather than via print."[190] In light of these considerations, it is essential to recognize the limitations of a literary-based approach and to explore alternatives that align more closely with the Yawo's cultural and communicative practices. Embracing

187. Lovejoy, "Extent of Orality," 11.
188. Stine, "Experiment in Audio Scriptures," 419.
189. Green, "Orality Strategy," 29–30.
190. Green, "Orality Strategy," 12.

orality in both the translation process and its eventual distribution could significantly enhance Scripture engagement among the Yawo, making the Bible more accessible and meaningful to them.

While the drawbacks of a literary-based approach to Bible translation in the Mozambican Yawo context are evident, it is essential to acknowledge that there are potential benefits to this approach as well. For example, one significant advantage is the perceived authority of a printed, literary-based translation as "Scripture," especially within the Islamic contextual frame of the Yawo people. The tangible presence of a written text may lend it greater legitimacy and reverence among Yawo communities. Moreover, a literary-based translation offers practical advantages in terms of permanency, form, and presentation. Unlike oral transmissions, written texts are less susceptible to technology and equipment changes over time. They provide a stable and consistent medium for preserving and disseminating the translated Scriptures. Additionally, the availability of a vernacular text can create opportunities for literacy and education because individuals gain access to reading materials in their own language. From a pragmatic standpoint, a literary-based translation may also facilitate engagement with government authorities or other stakeholders. Tangible written documents are often perceived as more credible and substantial, making them useful for reporting and advocacy purposes by mission or translation organizations. Culturally, the production of a newly written text in Ciyawo has the potential to expand the possibilities of Yawo literary genres. Rather than viewing written material as foreign and something to be avoided, creating indigenous written works could foster a sense of cultural pride and identity among the Yawo people. While there are overlaps between the features of orality in Yawo culture and those of the biblical milieus of the ancient Near East, Israel, and "Hellenized Roman Palestine,"[191] there are also significant differences.[192] It is essential to carefully analyze these variances, utilizing methodologies such as biblical performance criticism, when embarking on a new translation that effectively captures the distinctiveness of the biblical text in the Yawo context. By acknowledging and addressing these differences, translators can ensure that the translated Scriptures resonate meaningfully with Yawo audiences while honoring the alterity of the biblical text.[193]

---

191. Naudé and Miller-Naudé, "Alterity, Orality and Performance," 300.
192. Makutoane et al., "Similarity and Alterity," 156.
193. Naudé and Miller-Naudé, "Alterity, Orality and Performance," 310.

It is undeniable that throughout the history of Bible translation and the transmission of Scriptures, authoritative versions of the text have predominantly existed in written form, even though the original autographs may be lost to us. Regardless of whether most people engaged with it as written text or heard it read aloud, the textual nature of the Scriptures remains unchanged. Whether the extant text was initially produced and transmitted orally is a moot point at this juncture,[194] as what we have preserved is in written forms. In this sense, then, a written form of a Bible translation in Ciyawo is more likely to be viewed as authoritative and recognized as "Scripture" than an oral-only product. This is because the tradition of preserving sacred texts in written form is deeply ingrained, not only in the Christian tradition but also in other religious contexts. For example, the Qurʾān, the holy text of Islam, exists primarily in written Arabic as the verbatim record of Allāh's words as revealed to Muhammad by the angel Gabriel.[195] While the level of reverence accorded to the Bible compared to the Qurʾān may differ among Muslims, it is essential to consider the reverential attitude Muslims have towards their sacred text when contemplating the nature of Scripture among the Yawo, who are predominantly Muslim. Understanding the Yawo's cultural and religious context is crucial for shaping approaches to Bible translation and ensuring that the translated Scriptures are received with respect and recognition among Yawo communities.

An Orality-Based Approach: Pros and Cons

In addition to the risk of an orally based Bible translation potentially lacking the authority of Scripture, there is a significant concern regarding the reliance on available technologies for distribution, especially if the desired end product is in audio format. Technological advancements occur rapidly, particularly in the realm of media technologies. For instance, a charging cable that currently connects to a mobile phone may become incompatible in the future, even in the short-to-medium term. This technological concern not only poses challenges associated with the technology itself but also presents difficulties in the case of incorporating metatextual features such as footnotes and explanatory information in

---

194. Wegner, *Journey from Texts*, 75.
195. Naudé and Miller-Naudé, "Theology and Ideology," 283.

the translation product.¹⁹⁶ Furthermore, the technological issue extends into the long term, as audio files must be archived and preserved for future generations. If an audio version of the Bible is merely a recording of a written text read aloud, then theoretically, it can be replicated by reading afresh from the text. However, if the Bible translation exists solely in an audio format, archiving and preserving it becomes more complex. Stakeholders involved in an entirely oral Bible translation project must address the challenge of finding sustainable methods to store or archive audio files permanently. This technological dependence highlights the importance of considering both short-term compatibility issues and long-term preservation strategies when developing an orally based Bible translation. Stakeholders must navigate these challenges to ensure the accessibility and longevity of the translated Scriptures in oral formats.

Some scholars have also critiqued the exclusive adoption of an orality-based approach, suggesting that it borders on "soft racism"¹⁹⁷ by potentially denying opportunities for literacy and further education. However, one could also argue that the belief that people should be "like us" in conforming to literacy norms is soft racism because it disregards the preferences of orally dominant communities.¹⁹⁸ Despite the good intentions and efforts to promote literacy in communities worldwide, Gilbert Ansre reminds us that "illiteracy is preponderant and the many efforts to increase literacy through the years have not been spectacularly successful."¹⁹⁹ Another potential negative of an orality-based strategy, especially in the early stages of developing oral Bible translation (OBT) as a formalized approach to translation, is that it may be more difficult to achieve. This challenge is likely to persist, for example, until someone produces standardized guidelines or handbooks like those produced by the United Bible Societies for typical literary translations. In this sense, OBT is still somewhat experimental, albeit with massive potential in contexts such as the Mozambican Yawo situation. The development of tools like Render Software is a major leap forward in what is technologically

---

196. Kelly, "Preliminary Questions to Consider," 5.

197. Gravelle, "Literacy, Orality, and the Web," 16.

198. I do not believe that most scholars and practitioners who are against orality-based approaches are intentionally racist but rather that there could be a hint of unconscious bias, as is the case for all of us. There is also a lot to be said for the preservation of the Bible throughout history as a written text.

199. Ansre, "Crucial Role of Oral-Scripture," 65.

possible now that wasn't before. Even OBT using free audio recording programs like Audacity is making this translation approach achievable.

An oral approach can still "produce a high-quality draft ... that is both accurate and natural"[200] and invites the opportunity to exegete texts orally as a group in a way not generally possible with an exclusively literary-based approach. There are many benefits to an oral approach. Firstly, it ensures more comprehensive access, as individuals across all demographics of Yawo society can engage with an oral translation through audio formats, aside from those with hearing impairments. Secondly, an oral translation resonates more naturally with typical Yawo speech patterns and communication styles, seamlessly integrating into the existing oral-centric context. Thirdly, involving nonliterate individuals in the translation process as translators and reviewers enhances community participation and ownership.

Additionally, a notable advantage of an oral approach is its ability to incorporate ideophones and other oral features of speech that can actually be heard, enriching the translation with authentic linguistic elements. A written translation can include representation of these features, too, especially for the common purpose of public reading, but an out-loud reading of Scripture (or audio Bible), as common as it is in churches and group settings, is not the same thing as an oral translation. By planning for the translation as audio from the outset, stakeholders can "approach the translation process as an act of [natural] communication."[201] It also means that the end product is not reliant on superior education levels, making it accessible to both men and women, regardless of their formal education. This inclusivity is particularly significant in contexts where males typically receive higher levels of education than females. Of course, seeing such contextualization as a reasonable outcome in the first place does depend on the assumption that contextualization itself is a worthy goal to pursue and that the male gatekeepers or formal religion in Yawo society will tolerate spiritual truth being so widely accessible to all.

While there are significant challenges to face with adopting an orality-based approach to Bible translation projects, particularly in the Yawo context where oral communication predominates, there are also numerous advantages to consider. As highlighted earlier, the majority of Yawo individuals lack proficiency in reading written texts in any language,

---

200. Kelly, "Preliminary Questions to Consider," 3.
201. Kelly, "Preliminary Questions to Consider," 3.

underlining the importance of oral-based initiatives. It is also important to recognize that "it is not adequate just to read a literary translation onto tape. The translation must be designed and tested from the start to be suitable for audio presentation."[202] Instead, translations must be meticulously designed and tested with audio presentation in mind from the outset. This approach ensures that the translation is optimized for oral delivery and adheres to the unique conventions of audio communication. In essence, "the world of audio has its own rules and we need to play audio by its rules and not by the print-based rules."[203] As far as evangelistic efforts are concerned, it is a troubling bias if missionaries and others refuse to embrace Scripture engagement with orally reliant communities using only literary means. The reality for the Yawo and other people like them is that "it is simply not possible to effectively reach most . . . with a written message."[204] Indeed, communicating effectively with people necessitates embracing diverse methods of communication, particularly those rooted in oral traditions. By acknowledging the limitations of literary approaches and embracing the rich oral heritage of communities like the Yawo, Bible translation efforts can become more inclusive and impactful.

Loyalty in Light of Both Islam and Orality

Even though the need is clear for a Bible translation in the Mozambican Yawo context that takes orality seriously, it is essential to recognize and balance various competing frames, with Islam being one of the most prominent. The notion of written scripture holding authority is deeply ingrained within the Islamic frame. Therefore, it is crucial to transcribe and print the orally produced version of the Ciyawo Scriptures as a tangible book. This response is closely tied to the Yawo's Muslim identity and their reverence for written scripture. As a people of a book, it is important to the Yawo that they see the oral product as having come from a written source. This ensures that the oral Scriptures are accorded the respect and authority befitting Scripture itself rather than being dismissed as something lesser. One potential approach worth exploring is creating an oral translation in Ciyawo designed for recitation, aligning with the tradition

---

202. Brown, "Designing Programs for Oral Cultures," 29.
203. Sundersingh, *Audio-Based Translation*, 54.
204. Klem, *Oral Communication*, xvii.

of qur'ānic recitation. However, regardless of stylistic considerations, it is pragmatically advisable to produce a printed transcription alongside the orally produced Mozambican Ciyawo Bible translation. Furthermore, the transcription process should involve personnel distinct from those primarily responsible for the oral product. This separation is crucial because "oral communicators quickly develop a written style after seeing their language on paper."[205] Therefore, involving different individuals can help maintain the authenticity and integrity of the oral translation.

Further reasons for continuing to produce a written text alongside an oral translation are rooted in the heritage of the global church for the written word of God, in that "the written Mosaic laws were preserved for succeeding generations and were expected to be, and were, referred to."[206] Additionally, technological challenges associated with audio preservation highlight the longevity and durability of printed books.[207] In other words, "books live longer than spoken words, and they certainly outlive their writers, rekindling the best ideas of the authors generations after their death."[208] This push for a printed product must not neglect the fact that the majority of Yawo do not prefer written communication, and indeed, many are incapable of engaging in printed texts. In light of this reality, advocating for literacy alongside the distribution of a printed Mozambican Ciyawo Bible translation becomes imperative. By promoting literacy initiatives, communities can empower individuals to access a wealth of knowledge and to participate more fully in societal and educational spheres—and not just for engaging with the Bible—even if the pessimism of Ansre's statistics rings true. That is, based on an approximate extrapolation of the data provided by Ansre[209] and applied to the Yawo context, we would see something like only 0.5145 percent of the population being able to engage in a written text. Pragmatically, the benefit of producing both an oral product and a printed adaptation of that product is so that "every segment of society"[210] can engage with it. This means that a variety of different media is required[211] because, as Wilson identifies,

---

205. Green, "Orality Strategy," 35.
206. Wilson, "Scripture in an Oral Culture," 35.
207. Wilson, "Scripture in an Oral Culture," 48.
208. Ansre, "Crucial Role of Oral-Scripture," 65.
209. Ansre, "Crucial Role of Oral-Scripture," 66.
210. Wilson, "Scripture in an Oral Culture," 63.
211. Green, "Orality Strategy," 36; Kilham, "Written Style," 46.

the literate can benefit from the use of oral skills applied in education to help in the understanding and application of Bible content. He or she can also use oral skills to communicate what can be read. Through their common orality, members of an oral culture—both literate and non-literate—can participate equally and fully in the life and ministry of the Church.[212]

We should not view the transcription of an orally produced product merely as a mechanical process of converting spoken words into written text; instead, we should recognize it as its own unique medium with distinct characteristics. While the transcription remains an entirely written product, it should embody the fluidity and simplicity of the oral translation process. It also must be truly recognizable as a transcription so that when audiences follow along, they can see that it is one and the same as the audio version. The structure of a transcription will be very oral by reflection of its original nature, but certain features will have to be introduced to then make the transcription easy to read. Ernst Wendland suggests using "dashes or double hyphens for marking 'rhetorical pauses,' those added to create effect, and the marking of 'rhythmic speech units.'"[213] Wendland also encourages features like "a clear type style, dark ink, larger type size, a sufficient amount of interlinear spacing, more white space on the page . . . a format that reproduces key aspects of the discourse organization of a given pericope."[214] For the Yawo context, we should also consider Islamic influences when it comes to the design of the printed product. Ultimately, transcribing an orally produced product represents a nuanced interplay between oral and written modes of communication. By embracing the unique features of both mediums and employing strategies to bridge the gap between them, the transcription can serve as a faithful representation of the original oral translation while catering to the needs of a written audience—even if such an audience in Yawo societies is small.

While the allure of an oral Bible translation may evoke romantic notions of cultural authenticity and visions of utopia, its practical longevity in the face of technological advancements remains uncertain. Indeed, the rapid pace of technological evolution raises concerns about

---

212. Wilson, "Scripture in an Oral Culture," 63.

213. Wendland, "Duplicating the Dynamics," 36; see also Green, "Orality Strategy," 37.

214. Wendland, "Duplicating the Dynamics," 38; see also Green, "Orality Strategy," 38.

the preservation of oral translations over time, highlighting the need for a more durable solution. Therefore, despite the initial production of a Bible translation using oral methods, the subsequent creation of a written transcription seems imperative to safeguard the translation in Ciyawo for future generations. Acknowledging this imperative underscores the importance of promoting literacy initiatives, albeit with a realistic understanding of the limited reach of written Bible translations within the wider Yawo community. Nonetheless, transcribing the text ensures that a literate individual could read and record the translation for posterity, mitigating the risk of loss associated with technological obsolescence—even if rerecording a written text is far from ideal. Looking ahead, the prospect of rerecording audio translations underscores the value of integrating oral features into the written text to start with, thereby enhancing accessibility for future generations of Yawo speakers who, upon potentially losing the audio, might encounter a written version. In combination with the Islamic frame, creating mechanisms to facilitate memorization and recitation could also be helpful.

Furthermore, while honoring the oral tradition of the Yawo, it is essential to recognize the broader literacy agendas pursued by national governments. Embracing these efforts entails not only producing oral translations but also developing written versions that are natural and easy to comprehend. Such written translations, crafted in an oral manner, can serve as a gateway to further learning and literacy development in societies such as the Yawo, but including others as well.

THE ORGANIZATIONAL "BEAD"

The success or failure of a Bible translation project hinges on various factors. Often, the measure of success is viewed through the lens of accuracy, naturalness, clarity, or appropriateness/acceptability.[215] However, an aspect frequently overlooked is the organizational frame, wherein the decisions and directions within a project are influenced by the ideologies and biases of the involved organizations. Often these decisions are made at an organizationally subconscious level, or by translators making automatic choices without much active reflection. Those choices then impact on the criteria mentioned above—accuracy, naturalness, clarity, and appropriateness/acceptability.

215. Barnwell, *Bible Translation*, ch. 5.

At the core of understanding Bible translation projects lie the questions: Why do we translate the Bible? What drives the organizations and individuals spearheading these endeavors? Exploring the motivations behind renowned Bible translation organizations can shed light on the objectives they seek to achieve and the values they prioritize. With these motivations and aims established, we can see which kind of translation approach might achieve their goals. For example, take the following statements concerning a sampling of some major Bible translation organizations' comments on their mission and vision:

1. *Wycliffe Bible Translators*: "For people from every language to understand the Bible and be transformed" (vision). "Serve with the global body of Christ to advance Bible translation and work together so people can encounter God through his Word" (mission).[216] Aside from the vision and mission statements, Wycliffe Bible Translators also explain their motivation explicitly:

   > The Bible is one of the oldest and most popular books of all time. But is it just a book, or is it much more? We believe that the Bible is God's Word to us—something that everyone should be able to understand in a language and format that clearly speaks to their hearts. More than 1,600 languages around the world are still waiting for a translation project to start. When people finally get Scripture in their own language, lives often change in amazing ways. People are transformed as they discover Jesus Christ and enter into a right relationship with God.
   >
   > That's why Wycliffe Bible Translators exists—to help speakers of these remaining languages get the Bible for themselves. And we won't stop until all people have God's Word in a language they understand.[217]

2. *Pioneer Bible Translators*: "Pioneer Bible Translators exists to disciple the Bibleless, mobilizing God's people to provide enduring access to God's Word" (mission); "Transformed lives through God's Word in every language" (vision).[218]

---

216. Wycliffe Bible Translators, "Beliefs."
217. Wycliffe Bible Translators, "Why Bible Translation?"
218. Pioneer Bible Translators, "Bible Translation to Life Transformation."

3. *American Bible Society*: "Making the Bible available to every person in a language and format each can understand and afford, so all people may experience its life-changing message."[219]

4. *Seed Company*: "To accelerate Scripture translation and impact for people without God's Word through Great Commission partnerships" (mission). "God's Word transforming lives in every language in this generation" (vision).[220]

5. *FOBAI*: "The Forum of Bible Agencies International is a network of 40 leading international Bible Agencies and other mission organizations with a shared vision: 'working together to maximize the worldwide access and impact of God's Word.'"[221]

Each of these organizations and collaborations listed above are clearly motivated by the belief that the Bible and translations of it are transformative for the communities that use them. For this reason, loyalty to the Bible's author and loyalty to the target audience are vitally important. Theologically speaking about the motivation for Bible translation, we can reflect on the following, for instance:

> Yet Jesus told us to make disciples to Him in every ethnic group (Matthew 28:19). God's love for ethnic diversity is so great that Jesus will not return until this has happened (Matthew 24:14). The result is seen in an end-time vision of heaven that includes people "from every nation, tribe, people, and language" (Rev 7:9). This surely includes people from every Muslim dialect and culture.[222]

This perspective underscores the importance of translating the Bible into diverse linguistic and cultural contexts to fulfil the divine mandate of reaching every corner of the world. Similarly, Timothy Tennent draws attention to the significance of Pentecost, where people from various backgrounds heard the wonders of God in their own language.[223] This event serves as a powerful demonstration of God's commitment to speaking in the vernacular, emphasizing the importance of translating the gospel into the heart language of every culture. Furthermore, "Kwame Bediako

---

219. American Bible Society, "Share the Life-Changing Message."
220. Seed Company, "Unleashing the Potential."
221. Forum of Bible Agencies International, "Mission and Vision."
222. Brown et al., "Muslim-Idiom Bible Translations," 88–89.
223. Tennent, *Invitation to World Missions*, 335.

insightfully reminds us that Pentecost is not just a *sociological* event but a *theological* statement demonstrating God's ongoing commitment to translate the good news of Jesus Christ into the heart language of every culture in the world."[224]

In light of these perspectives, the overarching goal of Bible translation organizations is to facilitate access to the Scriptures in languages and cultural contexts where they are needed most. By embracing linguistic diversity and cultural specificity, these organizations aim to fulfil the biblical mandate of making the gospel accessible to all, echoing Jesus's commission to "go and make disciples of all the nations, baptizing them in the name of the Father and the Son and the Holy Spirit" (Matt 28:19 NLT). Thus, understanding the motivations behind Bible translation endeavors can inform the selection of translation approaches that effectively resonate with the objectives and values of the organizations involved.

In choosing a particular approach to translation from within the framework of Skopos theory, organizations and practitioners should be aware that there is not necessarily always a right or wrong translation philosophy. Adopting a domesticating, foreignizing, or hybrid approach often depends on the identity of the organization and its overarching vision and mission. However, we should not disregard the desires and needs of the community. Instead, let us take the options into account in conjunction with the community's involvement as stakeholders in the translation project's development. This is all part of the process of deciding upon the details of a translation covenant that adequately deals with all of the narrative frames relevant to the situation. The needs of the community should trump the needs of an initiating organization (and foreign influence)—while maintaining loyalty to the source, of course. For instance, if the aim is to promote a high level of Scripture engagement, or if the objective is to provide a liturgical text for church use, or if the translation product is intended for private or corporate reading, these considerations should inform the translation approach.

Ideally, organizations engaged in Bible translation endeavors should collaborate with local community partners to address these questions and make informed decisions. Nonetheless, the stance of the initiating organization also plays a role, as various approaches can be undertaken based on the desired outcomes. The notion of ideology comes into play here too, particularly when considering such aspects as Islamic and orality frames.

---

224. Tennent, *Invitation to World Missions*, 335 (emphasis original).

The ideologies of the stakeholders, especially those of the initiating organization, profoundly influence how these frames are addressed and acted upon. Different ideological perspectives can lead to significantly varied translation strategies and outcomes. For instance, an "insider movement" ideology, which seeks to integrate and work within the existing sociocultural context, would likely advocate for Muslim-idiom translations. This approach utilizes language and cultural references familiar to the Muslim community, aiming to make the translated Scriptures resonate deeply with their lived experiences and religious background. Such translations might incorporate common Islamic terms and concepts. This strategy aligns with the principle of contextualization, ensuring that the translation is not only accurate but also culturally relevant and easily accessible to its intended audience. On the other hand, an ideology that is more traditional and possibly more apologetic in nature might adopt a different approach. This perspective might view the Islamic context as a challenge to be addressed head-on, aiming to produce a translation that encourages people to move away from their Islamic milieu and towards a foreign version of Christianity. Such translations might consciously avoid Islamic terminology and opt instead for language and forms that clearly demarcate the Bible from Islamic texts. The goal here would be to create a clear demarcation between the two religious traditions, potentially creating a more disruptive experience. These differing ideologies highlight that while the sociocultural and narrative frames may remain consistent, the organizational ideology profoundly influences the response to these frames. An organization with an insider-type ideology will focus on harmonizing the translation with the current cultural and religious landscape, shaping a translation as a natural extension of their existing culture. Conversely, a traditional ideology might prioritize supposed theological clarity and doctrinal purity, even if that means disrupting the existing context for no other reason than the belief that our garb is meant to be the norm for everyone.

The implications of these ideological differences are significant. They affect not only the translation approach but also the reception and effectiveness of the translation itself. A translation that respects and incorporates local cultural and religious elements is more likely to be accepted and utilized by the community. In contrast, a translation that is overtly evangelistic and seeks to fundamentally alter the community's beliefs may face resistance and rejection before anyone even picks up the translation. The interplay of ideology with sociocultural and narrative frames in Bible translation, therefore, underscores the need for a thoughtful and reflective approach. Organizations must be clear about their own goals and values and how these shape their translation efforts. By doing so, they can better serve their communities and contribute to successful translations.

Moreover, it is worth briefly mentioning that, given the diverse genres within the source material alone, it is possible to employ different approaches within the same Bible translation. It is, therefore, helpful if the organizational frame is appreciated because, in one sense, the means (choice of translation strategy) is a way to the ends (the *skopos*, or function), and so the ends in mind will determine which means are used. That is, certain approaches and translation philosophies will result in specific outcomes. This proactive approach ensures alignment between the chosen strategy and the ultimate goals of the translation project from the beginning.

Furthering the discussion of narrative frame theory and the presentation of various Yawo narrative frames, it is crucial to recognize the significant role of organizational frames in Bible translation among the Yawo of Mozambique. Indeed, according to the complexity thinking of Kobus Marais, "in open systems, with the slightest difference in initial conditions, one cannot predict the outcome; that is, one could not have identical translations."[225] This suggests that even with identical narrative frames, the differing "conditions" or ideologies between two organizations will lead to different translation outcomes. Understanding these organizational frames alongside the other frames is, therefore, essential for proposing a suitable trajectory for future Mozambican Ciyawo Bible translation work. For instance, Baptist Mission Australia, as a stakeholder, brings its own set of values, mission, and vision that will shape its approach to translation in the Yawo context. Therefore, in this section, we consider Mozambican Ciyawo Bible translation within the context of Baptist Mission Australia as the initiating organization. Baptist Mission Australia serves as the intercultural ministry arm of the Australian Baptist Churches and maintains a presence of "intercultural team members" in both Malawi and Mozambique, specifically to work among the Yawo people.

Baptist Mission Australia's core vision is summed up in their public tagline: "Empowering communities to develop their own distinctive ways

---

225. Marais, *Translation Theory*, 10.

of following Jesus." And so an associated value would be that "everyone should have access to his translation in culturally appropriate ways, and in the language and mode (print or oral) that he understands best."[226] In addition to the tagline above, Baptist Mission Australia historically has in their work the focus to serve among "least reached" communities, which, according to this vision, includes the Muslim Yawo of Malawi and Mozambique (and Tanzania). Although Bible translation work does not appear to be the clear focus of Baptist Mission Australia's work in the same vein as, for example, Seed Company, Pioneer Bible Translators, or Wycliffe Bible Translators, Baptist Mission Australia has a long history of involvement in Bible translation work if there is a clear need. In other words, if the realization of Baptist Mission Australia's intention to "empower communities to develop their own distinctive ways of following Jesus" is compromised by a lack of a suitable Bible translation in the vernacular language of the people group in question, then Baptist Mission Australia will not hesitate to address that need.

Baptist Mission Australia prioritizes using the local languages of the communities they serve rather than relying on a language of wider communication, such as Portuguese, or depending on interpreters. This commitment ensures that team members conduct their ministry in the local language and that vernacular Bible translations are profoundly important. This is not to say that languages of wider communication are abandoned. This all depends on the contextual reality on the ground. In urban areas, in particular, it is possible that communities use these local languages exclusively.

As we consider the skopos of a Bible translation project undertaken by Baptist Mission Australia within the Mozambican Yawo context, it becomes essential to identify the primary function of the final product. This project aims to create a vernacular Bible translation that serves as a foundational tool for fostering a new faith community movement among the Yawo people, who have not yet embraced Jesus. By translating the Bible into their native language, the project seeks to make the Scriptures accessible and comprehensible, ensuring that the Yawo people can engage with the biblical text in a way that resonates deeply with their cultural and linguistic background. An indigenizing translation can provide this because translators act as agents of change that facilitate "understanding through a non-offensive biblical text which may, in turn, assist a community in

226. Green, "Orality Strategy," 11.

developing their religious identity."[227] This purpose means that the Bible translation product must be acceptable to the majority of the Mozambican Yawo people and must reflect the vernacular that is predominantly used and understood by most of the Yawo community. In other words, in line with Baptist Mission Australia's vision to empower "communities to develop their own distinctive ways of following Jesus," the *skopos* of a Bible translation project can develop around and embrace the various contextual frames that I discussed earlier in this book. With this all in mind, let us delve into the selected approach(es) for Bible translation within the context of the Mozambican Yawo community in the next chapter.

---

227. Miller-Naudé and Naudé, "Ideology and Translation Strategy," 186.

4

Loyal Bible Translation in Action and the Translation Covenant

It doesn't matter who you are or what you look like so long as somebody loves you. —Roald Dahl, *The Witches*, 1983

Love is something more stern and splendid than mere kindness. —C. S. Lewis, *The Problem of Pain*, 1940

As previously mentioned, a key aspect of Skopos theory and functional approaches to translation is the production of a "translation brief" document. In this book, I adapted this concept into what I refer to as a "translation covenant." This covenant not only outlines the specific aims, functions, and target audience of the translation project, as would a standard translation brief, but it also serves as a relational guide and a formal commitment to maintain loyalty. This loyalty extends to both the source-text author and the people for whom the Bible translation is intended. The translation covenant goes beyond the technical aspects of translation, embedding the process within a committed relationship of mutual respect, collaboration, and accountability. It signifies a solemn agreement between the translators, the commissioning organization, and the community stakeholders. By establishing clear expectations and commitments, as with a regular brief, the covenant also ensures that all parties are aligned in their objectives and approach to the translation project.

The translation covenant serves as a relational compass. It emphasizes the importance of maintaining strong, respectful, and collaborative relationships among all participants in the project. This relational aspect is crucial because Bible translation is not merely a technical task but a deeply human endeavor that impacts the spiritual and cultural life of the community. Firstly, understanding and respecting the Yawo's cultural and religious context is paramount. This means engaging with local traditions, beliefs, and linguistic nuances to produce a translation that resonates with the community. Involving community leaders, religious figures, and other stakeholders in the decision-making process is also vital. This collaborative and participatory approach ensures that the translation is not only accurate but also culturally appropriate and widely accepted.

The covenant also represents a formal pledge of loyalty—both to the source text and to the community that will use the Bible translation. This loyalty is multifaceted, ensuring that the translation remains faithful to the source-text author. This loyalty also means ensuring that the translation is accessible and resonates with the Yawo people in all their complexities. This includes using language and expressions that are familiar to them and natural in their historical, cultural, social, and religious contexts.

Practically, the translation covenant means that any issues or challenges that arise during the translation process are to be resolved within the context of this relational and committed framework. For example, when linguistic challenges arise, such as finding equivalent terms in Ciyawo for biblical concepts, these issues are addressed through collaborative discussions and community consultations. Addressing cultural sensitivities, such as the use of Islamic terminology, requires careful consideration and dialogue with community leaders to ensure that the translation is both respectful and conveys the intended message of the source. The covenant also fosters a relationship whereby robust feedback mechanisms are in place so that the community can provide input and feedback on the translation drafts, ensuring continuous improvement to accuracy, naturalness, clarity, and acceptability/appropriateness.

The translation covenant is a cornerstone of my Loyal Bible Translation model. It encapsulates the goals, relational dynamics, and commitments essential for a successful translation effort. By adhering to this covenant, all stakeholders can work together towards a common goal: producing a Bible translation that is loyal to the author and profoundly meaningful to the people for whom it is intended. This approach not only enhances the quality and acceptance of translations but also strengthens the relationships and collaborations between the translators and the communities served.

Bible translation in any context is a complex affair. For the Yawo in Mozambique, I discussed a whole host of different aspects that impact the situation. For example, if a Bible translation project in the Yawo context embraces an oral translation strategy, what does this mean for concerns such as equivalence or loyalty to the source text? A short answer is simply to state that, although the format may differ, the chosen translation strategy can still be effectively maintained alongside loyalty (and equivalence if that is relevant for the context). Skopos theory emphasizes that the intended aim and function of the translation are central to determining its adequacy. In the Yawo context, orality is a crucial factor because a written translation alone would be inadequate for the predominantly nonliterate population. While orality is essential, other aspects of translation remain important. For instance, we must still pay attention to the genre of the source text to ensure loyalty to it.[1] Due to such loyalty requirements, oral Bible translation can actually achieve high levels of fidelity to the source text, especially on occasions when the source text includes oral elements. Features such as alliteration, direct speech, or song may be effectively represented in an oral translation by replicating these forms in the new language (where possible). For example, songs can be translated as songs, and direct speech can be creatively rendered using different voices to represent various speakers. No single translation can capture every aspect of the source text perfectly, and oral translations are no exception. However, oral Bible translation offers unique opportunities that traditional written translations do not. We should pursue these characteristics in oral Bible translation, balancing them with loyalty to the source text and the translation's desired aim as outlined in the translation covenant.

In exploring orality in this book, I noted some of its many facets: as a manifestation of biblical culture, as elements within the written Scriptures that are oral in nature, and as a predominant mode of communication in contemporary cultures like the Yawo. The Yawo have a rich tradition of sophisticated oral forms but are largely unable to engage with written texts. This oral dominance significantly influences the approach needed for Bible translation among the Yawo. The indigenous translators themselves rely heavily on oral communication, and the target audience is an orally dominant people, too. Thus, an orality friendly Bible translation product is essential in this context. As stated by Kroneman,

---

1. Nord, "Loyalty Revisited"; Nord, "Function and Loyalty."

"By presenting the scriptures and scripture-based products in oral form, we reach a much broader audience by sidestepping the literacy barrier."[2] Gone are the days of *having to* develop an orthography and teach literacy before an audience can engage with the Bible—a process that surely takes years, if it is ever successful in orally reliant communities.[3] Indeed, Cleaver suggests that oral Bible translation will likely grow in importance as the remaining languages of the world have Bible translations undertaken among them.[4] Therefore, by taking the contextual frame of Yawo orality seriously, a translation that will engage the Mozambican Yawo adequately can be produced. This approach not only caters to their communication preferences but also allows the inherent orality of the biblical source text to be appreciated and utilized in the translation into Ciyawo. Such an approach ensures that the translation is loyal to both the source-text author and the target audience, happily fostering better engagement and understanding among the Yawo community as it maintains this loyalty.

In the context of this book, this all means that the new project begins with orality by working on an oral Bible translation project in Mozambican Ciyawo. Oral Bible translation involves utilizing oral methods throughout the entire process. Although the steps of the workflow resemble those of traditional, literary-based translation, every stage—from the initial translation to community checking and consulting—is conducted orally. The core hallmark of oral Bible translation is a determined focus on "internalization." When done well, internalization leads to no loss of accuracy and a distinct improvement in naturalness and clarity.[5] These three characteristics—accuracy, naturalness, and clarity—are the classic criteria for evaluating a "good" Bible translation in contexts like that of the Yawo in Mozambique.[6] It is important to recognize, however,

---

2. Kroneman, "Translation, Literacy, and Orality," 51.

3. It seems to be a lacuna in Strauss's recent book that, when discussing the challenges associated with Bible translation in "illiterate populations," he neglects to mention the great progress being made in oral Bible translation. Not to mention that the term "illiterate" is out of favor as it can suggest an inherent deficiency of a people where there is none. I do not believe Strauss is deliberately demeaning, but he seems to stick to a paradigm whereby Scripture *must* be written. The best he can suggest is that beyond establishing schools and "resources for literacy," it "may also entail producing audio versions of the Bible translation, which do not require reading skills" (Strauss, *40 Questions About Bible Translation*, 330.) Audio recordings of written translations and oral Bible translation are not the same thing.

4. Cleaver, "Oral Bible Translation," 18.

5. Toler, "Internalization," 99.

6. Barnwell, *Bible Translation*, 29–30.

that a good translation must not only be measured by these equivalence criteria but also by the adequacy of the translation in accordance with the desired function outlined in the translation covenant,[7] after careful consideration of the narrative frames associated with the context. Appropriateness/acceptability has, more recently, also been attached to the three characteristics named above—aligning here with the idea of the adequacy of the translation according to its purpose. That is, the desired function of the translation, as detailed in the translation covenant, is crucial in determining the adequacy of the translation. This function is developed through careful consideration of the narrative frames associated with the Yawo context, resulting in loyalty to the contextual realities at play.

Oral Bible translation goes beyond simply making the Scriptures accessible; it also empowers the community. By utilizing oral methods, the translation process involves the community directly in ways not possible with a written translation, encouraging participation and ownership. This involvement can lead to greater acceptance and use of the translated Scriptures, as the community feels a sense of connection and responsibility for the translation. Moreover, the focus on orality addresses the literacy barrier that exists in many parts of the Yawo community. While efforts to promote literacy are important and should continue, the reality is that unless something unprecedented happens, many Yawo people will remain nonliterate for at least the next generation. An oral Bible translation ensures that these individuals are not excluded from engaging with the Scriptures.

But what of the fact that the Yawo are Muslims too? Their adherence to Islam significantly shapes their cultural and religious outlook. This Islamic context presents unique challenges and opportunities for Bible translation efforts among the Yawo. In fact, the translators themselves are all Muslims. To effectively engage this audience, a Bible translation project must be strategically designed to resonate with their existing religious framework while maintaining the integrity and message of the translated Bible, in *ḥesed* loyalty. The Qurʾān, revered as the ultimate authority in Islam, is highly esteemed in its written form. In apparent contrast to the prevalence of orality, we must consider this reverence for written scripture when approaching Bible translation for the Yawo. And so, given the Yawo's oral culture and Islamic identity, an oral Bible translation plus transcription strategy offers a compelling approach. This strategy

---

7. Nord, *Purposeful Activity* (2018), 33–35.

involves translating the Bible using oral methods throughout the entire process, ensuring that the final product is delivered in a form that is appropriate. But, this strategy also involves transcribing the oral translation into a written form to conform to the Yawo's expectations for authority in the written Scriptures. However, this strategy must go beyond merely transcribing the text. It should also incorporate elements familiar to the Yawo's Islamic context in the translation itself. This includes using Islamic terminology where appropriate, provided it does not compromise loyalty to the source-text author. For instance, using terms that align with the Yawo's understanding of religious concepts can bridge the gap between the Bible and the Yawo. Given the Yawo's predominantly Islamic faith, the translation must navigate Islamic terminology and concepts carefully but be willing to use them when linguistically and pragmatically appropriate. This means potentially adopting an ideology that utilizes familiar Islamic idioms and expressions to convey the source text message in a way that resonates with the Yawo people's existing religious framework. This strategy could foster a deeper understanding and acceptance of the translated Bible. Community involvement is, therefore, essential in this process. Collaborating with local Yawo leaders—both village leadership and religious leadership, along with regular Yawo people—ensures that the translation is relevant and acceptable to the community. In the active context of the Mozambican Ciyawo oral Bible translation project ("PROMOTYPAD," *Projecto Moçambicano de Tradução Yaawo da Palavra de Deus*, or, in English, Mozambican Project of the Yawo Translation of the Word of God), this involvement takes many forms, from translators and advisors to active participation in community testing sessions. For example, in each community testing group, there are both men and women, as well as local Muslim *shehes* (clerics). This participatory approach fosters a sense of ownership and responsibility, increasing the likelihood of the translation being embraced and utilized effectively. When it comes to distribution, we liaise with the local village leadership for advice to ensure that they, as the gatekeepers in their communities, are part of the process. Distribution itself involves disseminating audio on microSD cards that people can use in their existing mobile phones as well as radio broadcasting of the translations. Hence, a Mozambican Ciyawo Bible translation that embraces an oral strategy while respecting the Islamic and traditional contexts of the Yawo people is both necessary and strategic.

The rationale presented here is intentionally succinct, providing a concise overview of the considerations and strategic direction for a

Mozambican Ciyawo Bible translation project. This brevity stems from the understanding that the actual initiation of the project and the decisions associated with it must be made in collaboration with the Yawo stakeholders themselves. Effective Bible translation, especially in a complex sociocultural and religious context like that of the Yawo people, requires deep, participatory engagement with the local community to ensure that the translation is culturally relevant, acceptable, and functional. Specifically, the following discussion primarily outlines how we responded to the various contextual frames, including the religious, cultural, and oral traditions of the Yawo people. And so while these suggestions provide a strategic starting point, they are not definitive prescriptions for all contexts. Additionally, I don't claim that this response is absolutely correct. However, what is certain is that being loyal to both God as the source-text author and the target audience are crucial imperatives for the Bible translation task.

Despite the large amount of data gathered in my own sociolinguistic and extensibility survey,[8] which was designed to lend an ear to the desires and attitudes of the Yawo people themselves, the path forward for Mozambican Ciyawo Bible translation remains ambiguous on its own. This ambiguity arises from the various ways one might respond to a single phenomenon or narrative frame. For instance, should we use Islamic terminology in a Ciyawo Bible translation because the Yawo are predominantly Muslims? Or should we avoid Islamic terminology for the same reason? These questions underscore the complexity and multifaceted nature of Bible translation in this context.

I already referred to some translation issues and gave some examples from the Mozambican Yawo context in the previous chapter, but what does an adequate translation of the Bible look like in actual practice? What does it mean to consider the Yawo's beaded necklace and the string of loyalty that permeates it? In response to this, my first point is about how the translation gets referred to in light of the Yawo's contextual situation or narrative frames—that is, the beads on the necklace.

In responding to Islam amongst the Yawo, the Bible translation project now underway amongst the Mozambican Yawo is not usually talked about in general discourse as a "Bible" translation using the Christianized terminology of "Bible." Although the reality of it being a Bible translation is not hidden, it is rather referred to as a translation of the

---

8. Houston, "Sociolinguistic and Extensibility Survey."

malowe ga N'nungu" ("word of God"). The term equivalent to "Bible" is deliberately avoided in favor of "the word of God" because the term *Bayibolo* (a term borrowed from English) carries unhelpful and even negative connotations among the Yawo. In their minds, this term refers exclusively to a Christian book, leading Yawo Muslims to reject it outright as irrelevant to them, for it is not their book—to say nothing of the fact that Jews also justifiably consider part of the Christian Bible as their own Scripture. I conducted research that indicated that using the term "Bible" results in a conscious disconnect and lack of engagement from the Yawo community. For them, a "Bible" holds no relevance and is seen as a book for Christians alone. In other Muslim contexts, keeping the word "translation" in a description can be problematic because translation is sometimes unfavorable in Muslim circles. Typically, for example, translations of the Qur'ān into languages other than the original Arabic are known as "interpretations" and not "translations" because the Arabic Qur'ān is believed to be the verbatim words of God revealed to Muhammad via the angel Gabriel. However, in Mozambique, the Ciyawo term used for "translation" is happily used for "interpretation" as well, so this concern is not really an issue, even if it is worth mentioning for the sake of other situations.

For rather pragmatic reasons, the Mozambican Ciyawo translation project began with Genesis. We made this strategic choice because Genesis is not entirely new to Yawo Muslims; it contains themes and characters already familiar to them from their own religious traditions. Hence, Genesis was the natural and most acceptable choice as the first biblical book translated into Mozambican Ciyawo. Starting with another book would not have made sense when considering the Islamic Yawo context and the absence of other suitable Bible translation materials for Mozambican Ciyawo speakers. To further mitigate this irrelevance issue and foster better engagement, we've carefully titled the new Mozambican Ciyawo Genesis oral translation as *Cibuku Candanda ca N'nabi Musa Ca Cidi mu Tawureta ca Kuŵilanjigwa 'Ndandidilo,'* which translates in English to *The First Book of the Prophet Moses Which Is in the* Taurāt [Torah]*, Called 'Beginnings.'*[9] We crafted the title to resonate with Yawo Muslims by referring to Moses as a prophet (*n'nabi* in Ciyawo; Arabic, نبي, *nabī*) and the book itself as being part of the *Tawureta* (Arabic, توراة,

---

9. The transcribed book version is published by PROMOTYPAD as *Ndandidilo: Cibuku Candanda ca N'nabi Musa ca Cidi mu Tawureta*, or *Beginnings: The First Book of the Prophet Moses Which Is in the Torah*.

taurāt)—terms they are familiar with. The book is usually just referred to by its short non-Arabic influenced title of *Ndandidilo* (English, "Beginnings"). This reflects the concepts of origins and beginnings inherent in both the commonly used Greek Septuagint title *Genesis* (ΓΕΝΕΣΙΣ) and the Hebrew title *bᵉrē'šît* (בראשית). This approach is not to say that Islamic terminology is always used in all cases. Rather, the title above also shows the pragmatic choice to use *cibuku* for "book," as derived from English. An alternative could have been *citabu* (Arabic, كتاب, *kitab*) to reflect Arabic influence. But it so happens that *cibuku* is more commonly used for books and is perfectly acceptable in this context, even in Mozambique. The overall project designation, "the Mozambican Project of the Yawo Translation of the Word of God," will be the name used for translating other books of the Hebrew Bible and New Testament moving forward. These terminology choices are not an attempt to hide the Bible's Jewish and Christian roots but rather to acknowledge that Islam already recognizes the value of many of these Scriptures, which they refer to as *taurāt* (Arabic, توراة), *zabūr* (Arabic, زَبُور), and *injīl* (Arabic, إنجيل)—or *Tawureta*, *Zaburi*, and *Injili* in Ciyawo. By avoiding terms that are presupposed to be strictly "Christian" and thus "other," the project opens the door to meaningful dialogue about the nature of the Scriptures. This thoughtful approach has already yielded positive results. By avoiding terminology that might cause misunderstanding before the conversation even begins, the project has facilitated the inclusion of Yawo *shehes* (Muslim clerics, or *sheikhs*) as members of community checking and as advisory groups. Although it is no secret to the community that we are translating the Bible, these efforts in terminology and approach have led to fruitful dialogue. A Yawo Muslim community leader encapsulated this sentiment by saying to me, "This translation is not religion; this is God's word."

So far, in its early stages, the translation project has already garnered far greater comprehension and enthusiasm from the Yawo community than any previous attempts using Malawian literary-based material in Mozambique, as indicated by my language survey.[10] The *Mozambicanness* of the new Genesis product largely helps. This is partly due to attitudinal factors but also because of the use of familiar vocabulary, which is less influenced by other languages such as Chichewa. Furthermore, the project has responded to the Islamic context by producing a printed version of the oral translation. This approach addresses the Yawo Muslim

---

10. Houston, "Sociolinguistic and Extensibility Survey."

expectation for written scripture as the proper authority, even though most Yawo people currently lack the ability to read it. The physical presence of a written text lends credibility and authenticity to the translation in the eyes of the Yawo Muslim community—which means most people. This decision to print the oral translation underscores the importance of understanding and respecting the cultural and religious frames within which the translation is being introduced, ensuring that the translated Scripture meets the expectations and needs of the Yawo people effectively. The cover of our printed version of our translation of Genesis appears below in figure 4.

FIGURE 4

Book Cover of Mozambican Ciyawo Genesis

By carefully considering the Yawo's sociocultural and religious context(s), this translation project aims to create translations that are both respectful and engaging for Yawo Muslims. This nuanced approach underscores the importance of contextual sensitivity and open dialogue in achieving a successful translation—one that achieves its intended purpose and remains loyal to the source and audience.[11]

EXAMPLES FROM LOYALLY TRANSLATING GENESIS[12]

Regarding individual vocabulary choices in the new translation of Genesis, *Ndandidilo*, the translation teams have begun to use Arabic/Islamic terminology in specific instances when Yawo Muslims understand these terms better than the alternatives. Even when dealing with words and names that are relatively unfamiliar in Yawo society, the translation follows the Arabic/Islamic context whenever appropriate. For instance, the Hebrew proper nouns חִדֶּקֶל (hereafter "*ḥiddeqel*") in Gen 2:14 and קַיִן and הֶבֶל (hereafter *qayin* and *hebel*, respectively) in Gen 4 are rendered in the new translation in ways that are more accommodating to the Yawo Islamic context. This methodology involves using Arabic equivalents or transliterations that are more likely to be recognized and accepted by the Yawo audience. An illustrative example is the rendering of names like Adam and Abraham. The new translation presents these names as "Adamu" and "Ibrahima," respectively. These forms are familiar to the Yawo because of their frequent use in Islamic discourse. This familiarity helps to bridge the cultural and linguistic gap, making the text more approachable for Yawo Muslims. However, the approach extends beyond well-known names. We also translate less familiar terms such as *ḥiddeqel* in this domesticating manner, which might be less immediately obvious

---

11. Some might distinguish between using Arabic and the use of Islamic terms. Given that Arabic is an entire language used by Christians as well as Muslims, using Arabic does not necessarily mean Islamic. In the Yawo context, there are some words from Arabic that are clearly known as having come through interaction with Islamic ritual and theology. However, there are plenty of words in Ciyawo that have come from Arabic but have no lingering sense of being exclusively Islamic. Languages shift and change constantly and so it is unreasonable to dismiss the use of Arabic terms simply because of fears that Arabic and Islamic mean the same thing. Even if they do, this does not negate using such terms for translating the Bible. The Bible has always adopted the existing terminology of its communities to express its message.

12. I presented some of the discussion here on Genesis in an earlier form in Houston, "Deciding to Translate."

to the audience but equally important for ensuring comprehension and acceptance. This deliberate approach to terminology reflects an appreciation for the Yawo's linguistic and cultural narrative frames. By using terms already part of the Yawo's Islamic vocabulary, the translation avoids unnecessarily alienating the audience.

To delve deeper into the examples mentioned above, let us examine the translation of *ḥiddeqel* in Gen 2:14.[13] This term is well-known in English as Tigris, the name of the third of the four rivers of Eden, with the other rivers named in English as Pishon, Gihon, and Euphrates. In older English Bible versions, translators usually transliterated the Hebrew *ḥiddeqel*. This practice is evidenced in, for example, the King James Bible / Authorized Version (1611), the New King James Version (1982), the American Standard Version (1901), the Geneva Bible (1560), the Tyndale Bible (with revisions to Genesis in 1534), and the Bishops' Bible (1568). Most recent English translations tend to translate *ḥiddeqel* with its commonly used English equivalent Tigris. The name Tigris itself derives from the name of this river in Greek via Persian, as it appears in the Septuagint translation of Gen 2:14.[14] Etymologically, the biblical Hebrew term seems to borrow from or exist as a cognate of Sumerian and Akkadian languages.[15] In most Portuguese Bibles, a language relevant to Mozambique due to its colonial history, the chosen term is *Tigre*, which is a form that also means "tiger" (as in the animal). For instance, in the *A BÍBLIA para Todos* (BPT) translation,[16] the Hebrew *ḥiddeqel* is preserved via transliteration as *Hidéquel* and *Tigre* is avoided but with a footnote offered to explain that it refers to the Tigre River.

In previous translations of Genesis into Ciyawo, versions appearing in 1904,[17] 1906,[18] 1913,[19] and 1933[20] all employed transliterations of the Hebrew *ḥiddeqel*. The 1904, 1906, and 1913 versions all used *Hiddekel* and the 1933 translation used *Heddekel*. It was not until the far more

---

13. This term also appears once in Dan 10:4.

14. The Greek term in the LXX here is Tigris (Τίγρις), which also appears in Sir 24:25, Tob 6:2, and Jdt 1:6.

15. Köhler and Baumgartner, "חִדֶּקֶל," 1:293.

16. *A BÍBLIA para Todos* (BPT).

17. *Chipeperu Chakutanda cha Musa Chichitelwe Genesis*.

18. Suter, *Genesis in Chiyao*.

19. Suter and Ker, *Genesis–Deuteronomy*.

20. How et al., *Genesis Ne Exodus*.

recent Malawian translations of Genesis published in 2004[21] and 2014[22] that a transliteration from English was introduced (*Tigilisi* and *Taigilisi*, respectively). Even the recent 2020 revision[23] of the 2014 translation, intended for Muslim Yawo audiences in Malawi, maintains the use of English transliteration with *Tayigilisi*. It seems clear that these recent Ciyawo translations used modern English Bibles as their source text. The decision to use transliterations from other languages highlights the complexities and considerations involved in Bible translation. For the Yawo people living in a Muslim context, using transliterations from Hebrew or English might not be as effective or meaningful as employing terms that resonate more closely with their linguistic and cultural background. This insight underlines the importance of choosing terminology that facilitates better understanding and engagement with the text.

On a practical level, *ḥiddeqel*, *Tigris*, and *Tigre* are unfamiliar to the Yawo as names of a real river in modern-day Iraq. Although the actual river in Iraq is indeed called *Tigre* in Portuguese and *Tigris* in English, this holds little significance for most Yawo people, who are unacquainted with either term. Consequently, to align with the Yawo's Islamic identity and the reality of influence from the Arabic language, the new Mozambican Ciyawo translation of Genesis has opted for a different approach by using the term *Dijlah* (دجلة), the contemporary Arabic name for this very same river. The name *Dijlah* appears to derive from earlier etymologies. It bears some resemblance to the Aramaic *Diglath* (דִּגְלַת)—a form carried over into Greek texts such as Josephus's *Antiquities*, also transliterated as *Diglath* (Διγλάθ).[24] Given the Yawo people's predisposition to Arabic influences in their language, and considering that Yawo men, in particular, occasionally travel to the Middle East to study Arabic and Islam, the choice of *Dijlah* is both logical and practical. Indeed, this translation strategy demonstrates a keen awareness of the Yawo's existing cultural and religious narrative frames and that their frames are not our frames.

The second example involves the pairing of the Hebrew *qayin* and *hebel*. In the modern Malawian Ciyawo versions of 2004, 2014, and 2020, the translators opted for transliterations of the English Cain and Abel as represented by the forms *Kayini* and *Abele*. Similarly, the Portuguese

---

21. *Ndandililo Ni Kutyoka: The Books of Genesis and Exodus in Chiyao.*
22. *Buku Jeswela: The Bible in Chiyawo.*
23. *Jenesesi Ni Ekisodo: Genesis and Exodus in Ciyawo.*
24. Josephus, *Jewish Antiquities* 1.39.

translation for these names is *Caim* and *Abel*, respectively. Even though the 2020 Ciyawo translation from Malawi renders other names such as Adam (Arabic, آدم, *'Ādam*), Eve (Arabic, حَوَّاء, *Ḥawwā'*), and Abraham (Arabic, إبراهيم, *Ibrāhīm*) using the commonly accepted Islamic forms (adjusted for pronunciation into Ciyawo as *Adamu*, *Hawa*, and *Ibulahima*), the apparent lack of engagement with the Muslim Yawo community for other terms and names is startling. In contrast, in the new Mozambican Ciyawo translation, *qayin* and *heḇel* are rendered using the terms already familiar through Islam. Specifically, the translation opts for the Arabic terms *Qābīl* (قَابِيل) and *Hābīl* (هَابِيل), albeit adjusted for ease of pronunciation in Ciyawo, resulting in *Kabili* and *Habili*. Using *Kabili* and *Habili* instead of the transliterations from English (or Portuguese), *Kayini* and *Abele*, ensures that the translation feels more natural and less foreign.

In the same part of Genesis that recounts the narrative about Cain and Abel (Gen 4), we also encountered a "key term" that was also best translated using a word with an Arabic origin. The Ciyawo term we chose for the "offering" (Hebrew, מִנְחָה, *minḥâh*) that Cain and Abel each offer to God is *sadaka*. This term was previously discussed in this book in the context of how the Yawo also use the term as a name for a specific religious ceremony that is practiced in intervals after the death of a person. However, the term *sadaka* in Ciyawo has broader application beyond this ritual. It can also be used in the context of a "sacrifice" or offering to God—which is more in keeping with its original Arabic (صدقة, *ṣadaqah*) sense. In Arabic, *ṣadaqah* normally refers to a charitable act or gift given in sincerity and devotion, often as an expression of faith and gratitude to God. This connection enhances the resonance of *sadaka* in Gen 4, where Cain and Abel's offerings are acts of worship (whether or not they were deemed adequate). Also, aside from the use of *sadaka* in Gen 4, the Ciyawo translation of the narrative concerning the sacrifice of Abraham's son in Gen 22 also uses the term *sadaka*, but this time it is paired with an adjective to indicate that Isaac was to be offered as a "burnt" *sadaka*. This addition of "burnt" (Ciyawo, *ja kutinisya*) is in keeping with the common way this type of offering is translated from Hebrew into other languages, including English. For example, English translations often render the Hebrew term עֹלָה (*'ōlâ*) as "burnt offering," to clarify the nature of the act being described, given that the original audience would already know that. In these examples, the use of *sadaka* bridges the ancient Hebrew worldview and the Yawo context, capturing not only the act of offering itself but also its spiritual weight and significance. This is one of the ways in which this new translation shows loyalty to the source text and to the target audience.

In each of these examples, *ḥiddeqel* and *qayin/heḇel*, and key terms such as *minḥâ* and *ʿōlâ*, the new Mozambican Ciyawo Bible translation of Genesis employs forms that are both appropriate and adequate by drawing on their current use in Islam or as they are known in contemporary Arabic. This approach recognizes the narrative frame of the Yawo as a Muslim people deeply influenced by Islamic teachings and the Arabic-speaking world. Consequently, the translation choices made in these instances reflect a robust engagement with the Yawo contextual frames and further enhance the cultural and religious relevance of the text in this setting. It also acknowledges that the Yawo are not just speakers of Ciyawo in a void but are also part of a larger Islamic sphere. This dual influence means that their comprehension and acceptance of Bible translations are significantly enhanced when the translation aligns with terms they already recognize and use—all without compromising loyalty to the source-text author.

EXAMPLES FROM LOYALLY TRANSLATING EXODUS

After completing our translation of Genesis, we began work on Exodus. In keeping with the precedent set by the Genesis translation's title, Exodus follows the pattern with the title *Cibuku Cawîdi ca N'nabi Musa Ca Cidi mu Tawureta ca Kuŵilanjigwa 'Kutyoka,'* which translates in English to *The Second Book of the Prophet Moses Which Is in the Taurāt [Torah], Called 'Exits.'* At the time of writing, the project is focusing first on Exodus 1–20, with any future work beyond the twentieth chapter deferred to the future. As of writing, the entirety of chapters 1–20 are complete as oral Bible translations and are undergoing transcription for later printing.

Some specific ways in which we can highlight the loyalty to the target audience in this instance is seen in the use of the names for Moses and his siblings. Firstly, Moses (Hebrew, מֹשֶׁה, *mōšeh*) himself is rendered as *Musa* as per the Arabic form of the name (موسى, *Mūsā*) and in keeping with the Yawo's existing knowledge of him. Secondly, Aaron's name (Hebrew, אַהֲרֹן, *ʾAhărōn*) is rendered as *Aruni* (Arabic, هارون, *Hārūn*), also in keeping with Islamic influence and existing Yawo knowledge and expectations. Thirdly, Moses and Aaron's sister Miriam (Hebrew, מִרְיָם, *miryām*) is rendered as *Maryamu* (Arabic, مَرْيَم, *Maryam*), in keeping again with the Islamic tradition. It is worth pointing out that Jesus's mother, Mary, is actually also the same name—a fact that may be missed by readers of English Bible translations that distinguish between *Miriam* and *Mary*.

Another vocabulary choice that utilizes a form influenced by Arabic and existing Yawo knowledge is that of the Egyptian pharaoh. This title is known to Yawo audiences as *Firiyawuni* from the Arabic فرعون (*fir'awn*), and so this is what is used to render the term in the new translation. This same word is also used in Genesis of other pharaohs.

For other vocabulary, it is not necessary to seek out Islamic terminology—not that this is the *modus operandi* anyway but rather a loyal response to who the Yawo are and the words they use. For example, when talking about the plagues and God doing wonders among the Egyptians, it is perfectly adequate and loyal to the Yawo to utilize terminology that is more in keeping with their African traditional religious perspective and worldview. After all, I am writing here about a Ciyawo Bible translation, not an Arabic one. A question we ask ourselves when translating is, How would we (the Yawo) say this? If the best term happens to have an Arabic background, then so be it. If it does not, then this is also fine. An aim is to produce the most natural Mozambican Ciyawo possible.

EXAMPLES FROM LOYALLY TRANSLATING MATTHEW

Concurrently with starting our translation work on Exodus, we also began translating Matthew. The New Testament, being written in Koine Greek, introduced some new concepts and challenges to the Yawo translators who were operating in Genesis before this. The first challenge was deciding on the name of the book. In this case, the Arabic versions of "Matthew," متى (*Mattā*) and متتيا (*Matatiyā*), are not well-known. The most familiar rendering of Matthew in Ciyawo is *Mateyu*, so this is what we used—in keeping with other Ciyawo translations from other countries that do basically the same. Specifically, though, the full title of this gospel is *Cibuku ca Ntenga Wambone wa Mateyu Ca Cidi mu Injili*, which translates in English to *The Book of the Good News by Matthew That Is in the Injil (Gospel)*. In this way, we identify the book within the Yawo's existing understanding of where different parts of the Bible fit into the picture.

Interestingly, the very first Bible portions ever published in Ciyawo, from 1880, used an approach that we would these days call Muslim-idiom translation. This pioneering portion was also a translation of Matthew and was entitled *Anjili ja Ambuje Wetu na Mkulamya Isa Masiya kwa Mattayo*, which translates in English to *The Gospel of Our Lord and Savior Jesus the Messiah by Matthew*. From the title alone, one can see that it uses words derived from Arabic—*Anjili*, *Isa*, and *Mesiya*. This translation includes other Muslim-idiom translation-like features, such as having Jesus greet his disciples with *Salaamu* (e.g., Matt 28:9) and Jesus saying "amin" for each *verily/truly* statement as in Matt 5:18, 5:26, 6:2, 6:5, and other occasions.[25] This use of *amin* is more in keeping with the original Greek word (ἀμήν, *amēn*), which is itself a transliteration of an original Hebrew term (אָמֵן, *'āmēn*). Other examples of Muslim-idiom-like features include *Msham* for *Syria* (Matt 4:24), *nabii* for *prophet* (Matt 27:9), and *sheria* for *law* (Matt 22:35, 23:23).[26] Similarly, many names were rendered using their Islamic equivalents, including the name of Jesus himself, who is *Isa* in this translation. All subsequent New Testament translations avoided calling Jesus *Isa* until far more recently, even though this is the normal name for Yawo people to use. In the new Mozambican oral Bible translation project, the name of Jesus is also rendered *Isa* in the translation of Matthew, which was underway at the time of writing this book. The rebuttals that point out that even Arabic-speaking Christians use an alternative to Arabic-speaking Muslims for the name of Jesus is a nonstarter for the Yawo.[27] The Muslim Yawo simply know Jesus as *Isa*, and so this is what we use. Otherwise, we would be using a term that the Muslim Yawo do not. For most occurrences of Jesus as *Christ*, we use *Mesiya* from the Arabic المسيح (*al-Masīḥ*). This is because the title is known to the Yawo, and an alternative descriptive term for the meaning of Christ as "anointed one" is awkward in Ciyawo, given that the relevant concept of anointing is itself rather strange to the Yawo.

Contrary to the 1880 translation, however, the Mozambican oral Bible translation does not say *amin* each time Jesus begins with *verily/truly*. Instead, we use more natural expressions in Ciyawo that bring attention to the importance of what Jesus is about to say, such as *wune ngusadila yisyene kuti* (English, *I speak truly thus*), as in Matt 6:5. Furthermore, in

25. By this I mean the occasions common in Matthew's Gospel where Jesus introduces a teaching with "verily I say unto you" (KJV), "truly I tell you" (NIV), "I tell you the truth" (NLT), and so on in other English versions.

26. *Msham* derives from the Arabic ٱلشَّام, *Ash-Shām*, *nabii* from نَبِي, *nabī*, and *sheria* from شريعة, *sharīʿah*.

27. Arabic-speaking Christians in modern times tend to use عُوسٰيَ (*Yasūʿ*) for the name Jesus.

keeping with the 1880 version that uses Arabic-influenced place names such as *Sham* for *Syria*, the Mozambican oral Bible translation also uses known Arabic-influenced equivalents such as *Suri* (Arabic, صُور, *Ṣūr*) for the city known as Tyre in English (Matt 11:21, 22). Concerning the "divine familial terms" issue, the Mozambican oral Bible translation avoids the matter because, unlike actual Arabic-speaking contexts, the Yawo's ordinary language allows for metaphorical meanings for divine familial terms. That is, when speaking of God as Father (Ciyawo, *baba*) and Jesus as Son (Ciyawo, *mwanace/mwana*), the Yawo do not have to assume a biological relationship. A conundrum that Ciyawo faces here, though, is that there are no gendered words for *son* or for *daughter* per se. Therefore, the translation uses the non-gendered *Child of God*, where we might expect the masculine *Son of God*. This shows the reality that "literal" translations that convey the "exact" same meaning are simply the stuff of dreams. The most straightforward way to get around this in Ciyawo is to say *male child*, but this becomes awkward and loses its naturalness. In this translation we, therefore, rely on the assumption of all Yawo people that Jesus was male.

Another example of vocabulary choices in the Mozambican Ciyawo oral Bible translation project is that we decided not to translate "John the Baptist" with a transliterated form of "the Baptist" despite this being a very traditional, Christianized, way to translate it. We used a term that indicates a ceremonial washing or pouring of water on a person in the Yawo's expression of Islam—*kusingula*—a term which can be used for an act done in repentance of sin. Although the term itself is a Ciyawo term and not an Arabic one, it is a term used in the context of Yawo Islam.[28] So, in this translation, it is "John the Baptizer" in the sense of "John the one who ceremoniously washes/pours water." This choice is far better than the meaningless "Yohana M'Batiso" transliterated from Greek (or English, or Portuguese, or Chichewa). Indeed, by translating the meaning of "Baptist" and "baptize" in chapters such as Matt 3, the text carries far more meaning and weight than sticking to tradition (remember that, once upon a time, the Greek text was meaningful in its context too). Also, the name *John* is here rendered in Ciyawo as *Yahaya* using the Arabic name for this person: يحيى, *Yaḥyā*.

---

28. Dicks, *African Worldview*, 150.

EXAMPLES FROM LOYALLY TRANSLATING PSALMS

In the case of Psalms, the Mozambican oral Bible translation refers to them as *Zaburi*, using the name given to them in Islam (Arabic, زَبُور, *zabūr*) rather than using another name of less significance. The Psalms are different from Genesis, Exodus, and Matthew, which we have worked on so far. They are, for the most part, musical compositions intended to be sung. Given that the project is firstly oral Bible translation, the Psalms are recorded in two ways: as songs in the style of traditional Yawo music and as more straightforward renditions without accompaniments. The Psalms are meant to engage their audience, and so the project seeks to do just that, adjusting the music style according to the genre of a given psalm. Psalms of lament are sung a certain way and psalms of celebration are sung in another way, and so on. Beyond only a cappella song renditions, however, the recordings also use traditional instruments, including drums and other percussion instruments. This exciting mixture of psalms as *zaburi* and psalms as song shows loyalty to the Yawo people, taking both their Islam and their orality seriously.

In terms of individual vocabulary choices, we follow a similar pattern to that discussed above in relation to other books of the Bible. For example, when translating Ps 2:6, we translated צִיּוֹן, *ṣîyōn* (Zion), as *Siyuna* as influenced from the Arabic صهيون, *Ṣahyūn*, given that there is no other natural Ciyawo equivalent for the name of this hill.

The above examples from Genesis, Exodus, Matthew, and the Psalms show that loyalty to the Yawo is not blind capitulation to Islam or to unfettered orality. Rather, it is about paying attention to the relevant contextual frames and translating accordingly. A difference, perhaps, is that the Mozambican oral Bible translation is not afraid to use Islamic/Arabic terms simply because of their origin. The Bible has always transformed language and the meanings given to the words it uses. There is no reason to believe that the same is not true for the Yawo.[29] It is also the case that the Mozambican oral Bible translation is more than content with working from an oral basis in its approach to translation. These examples show what it means to respond to the beads on the necklace of a specific situation, highlighting what it means to be loyal to both the source-text author, God, and the target audience.

---

29. For example, the English word God has pagan roots and yet no one complains about its use.

Postscript

"Why did you do all this for me?" he asked. "I don't deserve it. I've never done anything for you." "You have been my friend," replied Charlotte. "That in itself is a tremendous thing." —E. B. White, *Charlotte's Web*, 1952

BIBLE TRANSLATION IN THE Majority World is far more than a linguistic exercise of simply rendering words between languages. It is an intricate act of relational engagement that balances loyalty to the source text and the target audience. Throughout this book, we examined how Skopos theory and its functionalist approach lay a theoretical foundation. Translation is a purposeful activity—a reality no less true for translating the Bible than for secular translations. Whether or not translators choose to use specific strategies in their approach to Bible translation, such as formal or functional equivalence, all translation is done according to a purpose. Translators will do a better job if their purposes are openly acknowledged.

The concept of loyalty was enhanced by biblical Hebrew *ḥesed*, bringing depth to the translation process by ensuring that all those involved in a Bible translation honor both the source and the audience in which the translation will be read, heard, and understood. This means that Bible translating is also a loyal activity. In other words, Bible translation involves a committed relationship that exhibits loyalty to both the source-text author and the target audience. Formalizing the relationship between parties can be done practically by creating a translation covenant.

The Beaded Necklace Model was a key metaphor used in this book that demonstrates how we must handle cultural, historical, religious, linguistic, and other factors for adequate Bible translation. This is especially true in Majority World contexts, where it is necessary to navigate complex environments in which Christianity may not be the dominant faith and where the risk of alienating the audience is high if we don't fully consider their context. The Beaded Necklace Model emphasizes that it is essential to understand each "bead" so that a Bible translation resonates with its audience. In the case of the Mozambican Yawo people, understanding the interplay of the various "beads" in their context of Islam and African Traditional Religion and their reliance on oral communication is crucial to producing a translation that they can not only engage with and understand but also embrace as their own. The Beaded Necklace Model is not just a theoretical construct. It is a practical tool that Bible translators, organizations, and initiators can use to ensure that their work remains grounded in the reality of the community. By paying attention to each bead, they can avoid the pitfalls of neglecting critical contextual factors. By integrating all the relevant beads into the design and implementation of a Bible translation project, translators and other stakeholders can work towards crafting a Loyal Bible Translation that speaks meaningfully into the lives of the audience. Without forsaking loyalty to the source, of course, the result will be an authentic and transformative Bible translation that resonates deeply with the lived realities of the people.

Looking to the future, Loyal Bible Translation offers a path forward for Bible translators, organizations, and others involved in the Bible translation movement in the Majority World, where complex cultural and religious landscapes demand both loyalty and creative thinking. By maintaining loyalty to the source and present-day audiences, this model invites a renewed commitment to thoughtful and context-aware Bible translation that respects the sacredness of the biblical text while allowing it to flourish in diverse cultural settings.

I hope that Loyal Bible Translation will make useful, purposeful, and appropriate Bible translations a reality in new places around the world. I showed that it is possible to maintain dual loyalty to the target audience and, ultimately, to God as the author of the source text. I also hope this book provides both the theoretical foundations and the practical tools needed to approach Bible translation with the care and respect it deserves. Given the highly contextual nature of Loyal Bible Translation, you will have to do the hard work of figuring out how to apply the models in your own situation. No translation is perfect, but if you do it well, in and with your communities, you can fully expect to see a meaningful, appropriate, and valuable Bible translation take shape. My prayer, then, is that those involved in translating the Bible in the Majority World will take these lessons to heart, not just for the sake of producing better translations but also for the sake of the communities they serve. These communities should rightly expect to have translations that are relevant, contextual, and deeply connected to their lives and experiences.

As I reflect on my journey of writing this book and the experiences that have shaped my understanding of Bible translation, I am reminded of a core aim that has guided me throughout my work: I want to know, when all is said and done, that I have shown loyalty to the people I worked with, and that my contribution genuinely benefits them. This Bible translation endeavor is not just about completing projects or meeting organizational goals. It is about making sure that we do our work in Bible translation with integrity, with an ethos of respect, and with a deep commitment to the people we serve. Translating the Bible is not just about preserving the sacredness of the text—it is also about ensuring that the message of the Bible is conveyed in a way that honors the sacredness of the image-of-God-bearing people who will receive it.

Bibliography

Abdallah, Yohanna. *The Yaos: Chiikala Cha Wayao*. Edited by Meredith Sanderson. Zomba: Government Printing Office, 1919.
A BÍBLIA para Todos: Edição Comum. Lisboa: Sociedade Bíblica de Portugal, 2009.
Accad, Martin. "Introduction: Engaging Kerygmatically in a Multifaith World." In *The Religious Other: A Biblical Understanding of Islam, the Qur'an and Muhammad*, edited by Martin Accad and Jonathan Andrews, 1–6. Carlisle: Langham, 2020.
Accad, Martin, and Jonathan Andrews. Preface to *The Religious Other: A Biblical Understanding of Islam, the Qur'an and Muhammad*, edited by Martin Accad and Jonathan Andrews, xv–xvii. Carlisle: Langham, 2020.
Acker, Nick. *Exegeting Orality: Interpreting the Inspired Words of Scripture in Light of Their Oral Traditional Origins*. Eugene, OR: Wipf & Stock, 2024.
Alpers, Edward A. "Towards a History of the Expansion of Islam in East Africa: The Matrilineal Peoples of the Southern Interior." In *The Historical Study of African Religion with Special Reference to East and Central Africa*, edited by Terence O. Ranger and Isaria N. Kimambo, 172–201. London: Heinemann, 1972.
———. "Trade, State, and Society Amongst Yao 19th Century." *Journal of African History* 10.3 (1969) 405–20.
Amaral, Manuel Gomes da Gama. *O Povo Yao (Mtundu Wayao): Subsídios para o Estudo de um Povo do Noroeste de Moçambique*. Lisboa: Universidade Tecnica de Lisboa, 1990.
American Bible Society. "We Share the Life-Changing Message of the Bible." Accessed May 29, 2024. https://www.americanbible.org/.
Anderson-Morshead, Anne Elizabeth Mary. *The History of the Universities' Mission to Central Africa, 1859–1896*. Westminster: Universities' Mission to Central Africa, 1897.
Ansre, Gilbert. "The Crucial Role of Oral-Scripture: Focus Africa." *International Journal of Frontier Missions* 12.2 (1995) 65–68.
Awolalu, J. Omosade. "Review of Scholars' Views on the Yoruba Concept of God." *Journal of Religious Thought* 31.2 (Sept. 1974) 5–15.
Baer, D. A., and R. P. Gordon. "חֶסֶד." In *New International Dictionary of Old Testament Theology and Exegesis*, edited by Willem Van Gemeren, 2:211–218. Grand Rapids: Zondervan, 1997.
Baker, Mona. *In Other Words: A Coursebook on Translation*. Abingdon: Routledge, 2011.
———. "Narratives of Terrorism and Security: 'Accurate' Translations, Suspicious Frames." *Critical Studies on Terrorism* 3.3 (2010) 347–64.

———. *Translation and Conflict: A Narrative Account*. Abingdon: Routledge, 2006.
Barker, Kenneth L. "Bible Translation Philosophies with Special Reference to The New International Version." In *The Challenge of Bible Translation: Communicating God's Word to the World*, edited by Glen S. Scorgie, Mark L. Strauss, and Steven M. Voth, 51–63. Grand Rapids: Zondervan, 2003.
Barnes, Bertram Herbert. *Johnson of Nyasaland: A Study of the Life and Work of William Percival Johnson, Archdeacon of Nyasa, Missionary Pioneer 1876–1928*. Westminster: Universities' Mission to Central Africa, 1933.
Barnwell, Katharine. *Bible Translation: An Introductory Course in Translation Principles*. Dallas: SIL International, 2020.
Barton, John. *The Word: How We Translate the Bible—and Why It Matters*. New York: Basic, 2023.
Berger, Klaus, and Christiane Nord. *Das Neue Testament und frühchristliche Schriften*. Frankfurt: Insel, 2000.
Bible Project. "Loyal Love." Jan. 12, 2021. https://bibleproject.com/explore/video/loyal-love/.
Bister, Mikael, et al. "A Sociolinguistic Survey of Yao Variants." Dallas: SIL International, 1996.
Boéri, Julie. "Emerging Narratives of Conference Interpreters' Training: A Case Study of Ad Hoc Training in Babels and the Social Forum." *Puentes* 9 (2010) 61–70.
Bolink, Peter. "God in Traditional African Religion: 'A Deus Otiosus?'" *Journal of Theology for Southern Africa* 5 (December 1973) 19–28.
Bonate, Liazzat J. K. "The Advent and Schisms of Sufi Orders in Mozambique, 1896–1964." *Islam and Christian–Muslim Relations* 26.4 (2015) 483–501.
———. "Dispute over Islamic Funeral Rites in Mozambique." *Le Fait Missionnaire* 17.1 (2012) 41–59.
———. "Islam in Northern Mozambique: A Historical Overview." *History Compass* 8.7 (2010) 573–93.
———. "Matriliny, Islam and Gender in Northern Mozambique." *Journal of Religion in Africa* 36.2 (2006) 139–66.
———. "Roots of Diversity in Mozambican Islam." *Lusotopie* 14.1 (2007) 129–49.
———. "Traditions and Transitions: Islam and Chiefship in Northern Mozambique, ca. 1850–1974." PhD diss., University of Cape Town, 2007.
———. "Yao, Islam and the." Oxford Islamic Studies Online, 2012. https://www.oxfordreference.com/display/10.1093/acref/9780197669419.001.0001/acref-9780197669419-e-477?rskey=OUS62j&result=474.
Bone, David S. "The Establishment of Islam in Malawi." *Society of Malawi Journal* 73.2 (2020) 34–42.
———. "Islam in Malawi." *Journal of Religion in Africa* 13.2 (1982) 126–38.
Botros, Emad. "Jonah: An Encounter with God in the School of Creation." In *The Religious Other: A Biblical Understanding of Islam, the Qur'an and Muhammad*, edited by Martin Accad and Jonathan Andrews, 11–13. Carlisle: Langham, 2020.
Bremner, G. Alex. "The Architecture of the Universities' Mission to Central Africa: Developing a Vernacular Tradition in the Anglican Mission Field, 1861–1909." *Journal of the Society of Architectural Historians* 68.4 (2009) 514–39.
Breugel, J. W. M. van. *Chewa Traditional Religion*. Blantyre: CLAIM, 2001.
Brotherson, Derek. *Contextualization or Syncretism? The Use of Other-Faith Worship Forms in the Bible and in Insider Movements*. Eugene, OR: Pickwick, 2021.

Brown, Francis, et al. "חֶסֶד." In *The Brown-Driver-Briggs Hebrew and English Lexicon*, 338–39. Peabody, MA: Hendrickson, 2017.
Brown, Richard D. "Designing Programs for Oral Cultures." *Notes on Literature in Use and Language Programs* 46 (1995) 14–38.
Brown, Rick, et al. "A Brief Analysis of Filial and Paternal Terms in the Bible." *International Journal of Frontier Missiology* 28.3 (2011) 121–25.
———. "Muslim-Idiom Bible Translations: Claims and Facts." *St Francis Magazine* 5.6 (Dec. 2009) 87–105.
———. "A New Look at Translating Familial Biblical Terms." *International Journal of Frontier Missiology* 28.3 (2011) 105–20.
Brown, William A. "Concepts of God in Africa." *Journal of Religious Thought* 39.2 (Sept. 1982) 5–16.
Bruce, Frederick F. *The Canon of Scripture*. Downers Grove, IL: IVP Academic, 1988.
Buchanan, John. *The Shire Highlands*. Edinburgh: William Blackwood & Sons, 1885.
Buku Jeswela: The Bible in Chiyawo. Blantyre: Bible Society of Malawi, 2014.
Card, Michael. *Inexpressible: Hesed and the Mystery of God's Lovingkindness*. Downers Grove, IL: IVP, 2018.
Carson, D. A. *Exegetical Fallacies*. Grand Rapids: Baker Academic, 1996.
Center for Language Studies. *The Orthography of Ciyawo*. Chileka, MW: E+V, 2005.
Chakanza, J. C. "Some Chewa Concepts of God." *Religion in Malawi* 1 (1987) 4–8.
Chipeperu Chakutanda cha Musa, Chichitelwe Genesis [The First Book of Moses, Called Genesis in Yao]. British Central Africa: n.p., 1904.
Chirnside, Andrew. *The Blantyre Missionaries—Discreditable Disclosures*. London: William Ridgway, 1880.
Clark, Gordon R. *The Word Hesed in the Hebrew Bible*. Sheffield: JSOT, 1993.
Cleaver, Bronwen. "Oral Bible Translation and Its Role in the Future of Bible Translation." *The Bible Translator* 74.1 (2023) 5–20.
Clines, David J. A. "חֶסֶד." In *The Dictionary of Classical Hebrew: Zayin—Teth*, 3:277–81. Sheffield: Sheffield Academic, 1996.
Connelly, Steve, et al. "Translating Research for Policy: The Importance of Equivalence, Function, and Loyalty." *Humanities and Social Sciences Communications* 8.191 (2021) 1–11.
Crafford, Dionne. "African Traditional Religions." In *A World of Religions (A South African Perspective)*, edited by Piet Meiring, 1–26. Pretoria: Kagiso, 1996.
Cross, F. "אֵל." In *Theological Dictionary of the Old Testament*, edited by G. Johannes Botterweck and Helmer Ringgren, 1:242–61. Grand Rapids: Eerdmans, 1974.
Daniels, Gene, and Warrick Farah, eds. *Margins of Islam: Ministry in Diverse Muslim Contexts*. Littleton: William Carey, 2018.
Dapila, Fabian N. "The Need for Indigenization of Bible Translations for African Christians." *African Ecclesial Review* 40.1 (1998) 21–43.
Detienne, Marcel. *The Masters of Truth in Archaic Greece*. New York: Zone, 1996.
Dicks, Ian D. *An African Worldview: The Muslim Amacinga Yawo of Southern Malawi*. Zomba: Kachere, 2012.
———. *Wisdom of the Yawo People [Lunda Iwa Wandu Wa Ciyawo]: Yawo Proverbs and Stories [Yitagu Ni Adisi Sya Ciyawo]*. Zomba, MA: Kachere, 2006.
Dicks, Ian D., and Shawn Dollar. *A Practical Guide to Understanding Ciyawo*. Zomba, MA: Kachere, 2010.

Downie, Jonathan. "The End of an Era? Does Skopos Theory Spell the End of the 'Free vs. Literal' Paradigm?" *Pneuma Review*, Mar. 12, 2014. http://pneumareview.com/the-end-of-an-era-does-skopos-theory-spell-the-end-of-the-free-vs-literal-paradigm-by-jonathan-downie/.

Dye, T. Wayne. "The Eight Conditions of Scripture Engagement: Social and Cultural Factors Necessary for Vernacular Bible Translation to Achieve Maximum Effect." *International Journal of Frontier Missiology* 26.2 (2009) 89–98.

Eberhard, David M., et al. *Ethnologue: Languages of the World*. 27th ed. Dallas, TX: SIL International. http://www.ethnologue.com/language/yao.

EMDC. "Multilingualism Assessment Tool." https://emdc.guide/resources/mat/.

Enns, Peter. *Exodus*. NIV Application Commentary. Grand Rapids: Zondervan, 2000.

Esala, Nathan. "Implementing Skopostheorie in Bible Translation." *Bible Translator* 64.3 (2013) 300–323.

———. "Measuring the Adequacy of the Host Text Using Skopostheorie in Bible Translation: The Ethics of Operational Transparency." *Bible Translator* 65.3 (2014) 308–36.

Eyre, Christopher B. "The Portuguese Action in Central Africa." *Central Africa: A Record of the Work of the Universities' Mission to Central Africa* 20.238 (Oct. 1902) 173.

Farah, Warrick. "Adaptive Missiological Engagement with Islamic Contexts." In *The Religious Other: A Biblical Understanding of Islam, the Qur'an and Muhammad*, edited by Martin Accad and Jonathan Andrews, 108–17. Carlisle: Langham, 2020.

Fee, Gordon D., and Mark L. Strauss. *How to Choose a Translation for All Its Worth: A Guide to Understanding and Using Bible Versions*. Grand Rapids: Zondervan, 2007.

Finnegan, Ruth. *Oral Literature in Africa*. Cambridge: Open Book, 2012.

Follett, Ken. *A Column of Fire*. London: Pan, 2018.

Forum of Bible Agencies International. "Mission and Vision." https://forum-intl.org/about/mission-and-vision/.

Frankl, P. J. L. "The Word for 'God' in Swahili: Further Considerations." *Journal of Religion in Africa* 25.2 (1995) 202–11.

Frederick, John. "Mercy and Compassion." In *Lexham Theological Wordbook*, edited by Douglas Mangum. Bellingham: Lexham, 2014.

Freedman, Harry. *The Murderous History of Bible Translations: Power, Conflict and the Quest for Meaning*. New York: Bloomsbury, 2016.

Gadamer, Hans-Georg. *Truth and Method*. 2nd ed. London: Continuum International, 2004.

Gibson, Gloria D., and Margaret Somers. "Reclaiming the Epistemological 'Other': Narrative and the Social Construction of Identity." In *Social Theory and the Politics of Identity*, edited by Craig Calhoun, 37–99. Oxford: Blackwell, 1994.

Glueck, Nelson. *Das Wort Hesed im Alttestamentlichen Sprachgebrauche als Menschliche und Göttliche Gemeinschaftgemässe Verhaltungsweise*. Berlin: Töpelmann, 1927.

Graham, William A. *Beyond the Written Word: Oral Aspects of Scripture in the History of Religion*. Cambridge: Cambridge University Press, 1987.

Gravelle, Gilles. "Literacy, Orality, and the Web." *Orality Journal* 2.1 (2013) 11–25.

Gray, Andrea, and Leith Gray. "The Imperishable Seed: Toward Effective Sharing of Scripture." In *From Seed to Fruit: Global Trends, Fruitful Practices, and Emerging Issues Among Muslims*, edited by J. Dudley Woodberry, 33–50. Pasadena: William Carey, 2008.

Green, Robin. "An Orality Strategy: Translating the Bible for Oral Communicators." MA diss., Graduate Institute of Applied Linguistics, Dallas, 2007.

Griffith, Sidney H. *The Bible in Arabic: The Scriptures of the "People of the Book" in the Language of Islam*. Princeton: Princeton University Press, 2013.

Grudem, Wayne A., et al. *Translating Truth: The Case for Essentially Literal Bible Translation*. Wheaton: Crossway, 2005.

Guthrie, Malcolm. *The Classification of the Bantu Languages*. London: Oxford University Press, 1948.

———. *Comparative Bantu: An Introduction to the Comparative Linguistics and Prehistory of the Bantu Languages*. Farnborough, UK: Gregg, 1967.

Harding, Sue-Ann. "Narratives and Contextual Frames." In *Handbook of Translation Studies*, edited by Yves Gambier and Luc van Doorslaer, 4:105–10. Amsterdam: John Benjamins, 2013.

———. "Resonances Between Social Narrative Theory and Complexity Theory: A Potentially Rich Methodology for Translation Studies." In *Complexity Thinking in Translation Studies: Methodological Considerations*, edited by Kobus Marais and Reine Meylaerts, 33–52. New York: Routledge, 2019.

Heckel, Benno. *The Yao Tribe*. London: Department of Colonial Education in the Institute: Humphrey Milford, 1935.

Hetherwick, Alexander. *Achikalata jua Paolo jua Ndumitume kwa wa Korinti*. London: British and Foreign Bible Society, 1891.

———. *A Handbook of the Yao Language*. London: Society for Promoting Christian Knowledge, 1902.

———. *Introductory Handbook of the Yao Language*. London: Society for Promoting Christian Knowledge, 1889.

———. *Kalata jua Paolo jua Ndumitume kwa wa Rumi*. London: British and Foreign Bible Society, 1891.

———. *Masengo ga Wandumitume*. London: British and Foreign Bible Society, 1889.

———. *Utenga Wambone wa Luka*. London: British and Foreign Bible Society, 1889.

———. *Utenga Wambone wa Marko*. London: British and Foreign Bible Society, 1889.

———. *Utenga Wambone wa Matayo*. London: British and Foreign Bible Society, 1889.

———. *Utenga Wambone wa Yohana*. London: British and Foreign Bible Society, 1889.

Hill, Margaret V., and Harriet S. Hill. *Translating the Bible into Action: How the Bible Can Be Relevant in All Languages and Cultures*. Carlisle, UK: Langham, 2022.

Hinchliff, Peter. "The Blantyre Scandal, Scottish Missionaries and Colonialism." *Journal of Theology for Southern Africa* 46 (1984) 29–38.

Hine, John Edward. *Days Gone By: Being Some Account of the Past Years Chiefly in Central Africa*. London: John Murray, 1924.

Hjälm, Miriam L. "The Changing Face of the Arabic Bible: Translation Techniques in Early Renditions of Ezekiel." *Open Theology* 2.1 (2016) 832–48.

———. "Qurʾānic Intertextuality in Early Christian Arabic Bible Translations." *Bible Translator* 74.3 (2023) 313–30.

———. "Scriptures Beyond Words: 'Islamic' Vocabulary in Early Christian Arabic Bible Translations." *Collectanea Christiana Orientalia* 15 (2018) 49–69.

Hofstede, Geert. *Cultures and Organizations: Software of the Mind*. Hammersmith: HarperCollins, 1994.

Holt, Mack P. *The French Wars of Religion, 1562–1629*. Cambridge: Cambridge University Press, 2005.

Houston, Tobias J. "Deciding to Translate Genesis Among the Mozambican Yaawo: A Case Study in Narrative Framing." In *Islam and the Bible: Questioning Muslim Idiom Translations*, edited by Ayman S. Ibrahim and Ant B. Greenham, 257–70. Nashville: B&H Academic, 2023.

———. "'Not Getting What You Ask for' from Rapid Appraisal Surveys: A New Model to Assess Bible Translation Needs." *HTS Teologiese Studies / Theological Studies* 78.1 (2022) 1–7.

———. *A Sociolinguistic and Extensibility Survey of Ciyawo Language Communities in Mozambique's Niassa Province.* Journal of Language Survey Reports 4. Dallas: SIL International, 2023.

———. "Towards Redeeming 'Loyalty' in Functionalist Bible Translation Using the Hebrew Ḥesed Concept." *HTS Teologiese Studies / Theological Studies* 79.2 (2023) 1–6.

———. "Utenga Wambone—the 'Good News': An Exploration of Historical Ciyawo Bible Translations and Linguistic Texts." *Studia Historiae Ecclesiasticae* 48.3 (2022) 1–18.

How, Edith A., et al. *Genesis Ne Exodus (Chiyao).* London: British and Foreign Bible Society, 1933.

Injil Jeswela: Utenga Wambone Wa Walembile Luka Ni Yitendo Ya Ndumetume [Holy Gospel: Good Message Written by Luke and the Doings of the Prophets]. Blantyre, MA: Chembecheyo Chasambano, 2011.

Jabir, Jawad Kadhim. "Skopos Theory: Basic Principles and Deficiencies." *Journal of the College of Arts. University of Basrah* 41 (2006) 37–46.

Jenesesi Ni Ekisodo: Genesis and Exodus in Ciyawo. Blantyre, MA: Bible Society of Malawi, 2020.

Jerome. "Letter LVII: To Pammachius on the Best Method of Translating." In vol. 6 of *Nicene and Post-Nicene Fathers of the Christian Church*, Second Series. Edited by Philip Schaff and Henry Wace. Oxford: James Parker, 1893.

Johnson, Dave. "The Familial Language Debate in Muslim Bible Translation." *Asian Journal of Pentecostal Studies* 15.2 (2012) 131–32.

Johnson, William Percival. "Mohammedanism and the Yaos." *Central Africa: A Monthly Record of the Work of the Universities' Mission to Central Africa* 24.340 (Apr. 1911) 101–5.

———. *My African Reminiscences, 1875-1893.* London: Universities' Mission to Central Africa, 1924.

Josephus, Flavius. *Jewish Antiquities.* Edited by Allen Paul Wikgren. Translated by H. St. J. Thackeray, Ralph Marcus, and Louis H. Feldman. Cambridge, Massachusetts: Harvard University Press.

Kadzamira, Zimani David, et al. "Malawi." *Encyclopedia Britannica*, last updated Feb. 3, 2025. https://www.britannica.com/place/Malawi.

Kayambazinthu, E. "The Language Planning Situation in Malawi." *Journal of Multilingual and Multicultural Development* 19.5 (1998) 369–439.

Kelly, Brian. "Preliminary Questions to Consider When Looking at an Oral Translation Approach." *GIALens* 12.1 (2018) 1–8.

Kenmogne, Michel. "At Home in All Languages and Cultures: Bible Translation and World Christianity in the Twenty-First Century." *Journal of Translation* 18.1 (2022) 111–39.

Kilham, Christine. "A Written Style for Oral Communicators?" *Notes on Translation* 123.12 (1987) 36–52.

Klem, Herbert. "Dependence on Literacy Strategy: Taking a Hard Second Look." *International Journal of Frontier Missions* 12.2 (1995) 59–64.

———. *Oral Communication of the Scripture: Insights from African Oral Art*. Pasadena: William Carey, 1982.

Köehler, Ludwig, and Walter Baumgartner, eds. "חִדְקֵל." In *The Hebrew and Aramaic Lexicon of the Old Testament*, 1:293. Leiden: Brill, 2000.

———. "II חֶסֶד." In *The Hebrew and Aramaic Lexicon of the Old Testament*, 1:336–37. Leiden: Brill, 2000.

Kraft, Charles H., and Marguerite G. Kraft. *Christianity in Culture: A Study in Biblical Theologizing in Cross-Cultural Perspective*. Rev. ed. Maryknoll, NY: Orbis, 2005.

Kroneman, Dick. "Translation, Literacy, and Orality: Reflections from the Domain of Bible Translation." *Orality Journal* 6.2 (2017) 41–60.

Lacerda, Francisco José de. *Lacerda's Journey to Cazembe in 1798*. Translated and annotated by R. F. Burton. London: John Murray, 1873.

Livingstone, David, and Charles Livingstone. *Narrative of an Expedition to the Zambesi and Its Tributaries and of the Discovery of the Lakes Shirwa and Nyassa, 1858-1864*. London: John Murray, 1865.

Livingstone, W. P. *A Prince of Missionaries*. London: Clarke, 1931.

Loba-Mkole, Jean-Claude. "Intercultural Translations of Christian Canonical Scriptures." *Acta Theologica* 39.1 (2019) 156–80.

Lovejoy, Grant. "The Extent of Orality." *Journal for Baptist Theology & Ministry* 5.1 (2008) 121–33.

———. "The Extent of Orality: 2012 Update." *Orality Journal* 1.1 (2012) 11–39.

Lugira, Aloysius M. *African Traditional Religion*. 3rd ed. New York: Chelsea House, 2009.

Luther, Martin. *Ein Sendbrief vom Dolmetchen [An Open Letter on Translating]*. Translated by Howard Jones. Treasures of the Taylorian 1. Oxford: Taylor Institution Library, 2017.

MacDonald, Duff. *Africana: Or, the Heart of Heathen Africa*. 2 vols. London: Simpkin, Marshall, 1882.

———. *Bible Lessons in the Yao Language*. Alice, SA: Lovedale, 1879.

———. *East African Tales in Chiyao, Chinyasa, and Machinga with English Translations for Use in Church of Scotland Mission Schools at Blantyre and Zomba*. Edinburgh: William Blackwood & Sons, 1881.

———. *Masagulo ga Malowe Gambone [Gospel Extracts]*. Edinburgh: Edinburgh University Press, 1881.

MacDonald, Duff, and C. M. Doke. "Yao and Nyanja Tales." *Bantu Studies* 12.1 (1938) 251–85.

Maho, Jouni Filip, comp. *NUGL Online: The Online Version of the New Updated Guthrie List; a Referential Classification of the Bantu Languages*. June 4, 2009. https://brill.com/fileasset/downloads_products/35125_Bantu-New-updated-Guthrie-List.pdf

Makutoane, Tshokolo J., et al. "Similarity and Alterity in Translating the Orality of the Old Testament in Oral Cultures." *Translation Studies* 8.2 (2015) 156–74.

Maples, Chauncy. *Anjili ja Ambuje Wetu na Mkulamya Isa Masiya kwa Mattayo [The Gospel of Our Lord and Savior Jesus the Messiah by Matthew]*. London: British and Foreign Bible Society, 1880.

———. *Anjili ya Mattayo (Makua) I-VII [Gospel of Matthew (Makua) I-VII]*. Zanzibar: Universities' Mission to Central Africa, 1881.

———. "Letter to 'My Dear Bishop' 6th March." Kiungani, 1877. In *Correspondence and Papers of Rev. Chauncy Maples 1877-96*. https://britishonlinearchives.com/collections/29/volumes/199/missionaries-correspondence?filters[query]=&filters[className]=document.

———. "Letter to 'My Dear Bishop' October 10th." Masasi, 1880. In *Correspondence and Papers of Rev. Chauncy Maples 1877-96*. https://britishonlinearchives.com/collections/29/volumes/199/missionaries-correspondence?filters[query]=&filters[className]=document.

———. "Letter to 'My Dear Mr. Heanley' 3rd August," 1877. In *Correspondence and Papers of Rev. Chauncy Maples 1877-96*. https://britishonlinearchives.com/collections/29/volumes/199/missionaries-correspondence?filters[query]=&filters[className]=document.

———. "Letter to 'My Dear Randolph' August 2nd," 1877. In *Correspondence and Papers of Rev. Chauncy Maples 1877-96*.https://britishonlinearchives.com/collections/29/volumes/199/missionaries-correspondence?filters[query]=&filters[className]=document.

———. "Lukoma: An Island in Lake Nyassa." *Journal of the Manchester Geographical Society* 5 (1889) 59-68.

———. *Yao-English Vocabulary*. Zanzibar: Universities' Mission, 1888.

Maples, Ellen, ed. *Chauncy Maples: Pioneer Missionary in East Central Africa for Nineteen Years and Bishop of Likoma, Lake Nyasa A.D. 1895; A Sketch of His Life with Selections from His Letters*. London: Longmans, Green, 1897.

Marais, Kobus. "Translation Complex Rather Than Translation Turns? Considering the Complexity of Translation." *Syn-Thèses* 9-10 (2019) 43-55.

———. *Translation Theory and Development Studies: A Complexity Theory Approach*. New York: Routledge, 2014.

Marais, Kobus, and Reine Meylaerts. *Complexity Thinking in Translation Studies: Methodological Considerations*. New York: Routledge, 2019.

Mascarenhas, Adolfo C., et al. "Tanzania." *Encyclopedia Britannica*, last updated Feb. 4, 2025. https://www.britannica.com/place/Tanzania.

Matenga, Jay. "Centring the Local: The Indigenous Future of Missions." Paper presented at Wycliffe Global Alliance / SIL "Together in Christ 2021" Conference, Jan. 2021. https://jaymatenga.com/pdfs/MatengaJ_CentringLocal.pdf.

Maxey, James A. *From Orality to Orality: A New Paradigm for Contextual Translation of the Bible*. Eugene, OR: Cascade, 2009.

Mays, James Luther. *Micah: A Commentary*. Philadelphia: Westminster, 1976.

Mbiti, John S. *African Religions and Philosophy*. Oxford: Heinemann, 1989.

———. *Introduction to African Religion*. Oxford: Heinemann, 1991.

Mburu, Elizabeth. *African Hermeneutics*. Carlisle, UK: Hippo, 2019.

Metzger, Bruce M. *The Bible in Translation: Ancient and English Versions*. Grand Rapids: Baker Academic, 2001.

———. *The Canon of the New Testament: Its Origin, Development, and Significance*. Oxford: Clarendon, 1989.

Miller-Naudé, Cynthia, and Jacobus A. Naudé. "Covert Religious Censorship: Renderings of Divine Familial Imagery in Translations of the New Testament Within Islamic Contexts." *Open Theology* 2 (2016) 818-31.

———. "Ideology and Translation Strategy in Muslim-Sensitive Bible Translations." *Neotestamentica* 47.1 (2013) 171–90.
Mitchell, J. Clyde. *The Yao Village: A Study in the Social Structure of a Nyasaland Tribe.* Manchester: Manchester University Press, 1956.
Mobley, Gregory. "Loving-Kindness." In *Eerdmans Dictionary of the Bible*, edited by David Noel Freedman, et al., 826–27. Grand Rapids: Eerdmans, 2000.
Mohatlane, Edwin Joseph. "Optimality in Sesotho Translation." *Journal of Social Sciences* 39.2 (2014) 149–58.
Mojola, Aloo Osotsi. *God Speaks My Language: A History of Bible Translation in East Africa.* Carlisle, UK: Hippo, 2020.
Moore, Natasha, et al. *For the Love of God: How the Church Is Better and Worse than You Ever Imagined.* Sydney: Centre for Public Christianity, 2019.
Morin, Edgar. "Complex Thinking for a Complex World—About Reductionism, Disjunction and Systemism." *Systema* 2.1 (2014) 14–22.
———. *On Complexity.* Cresskill, NJ: Hampton, 2008.
Mounce, William D. "Do Formal Equivalent Translations Reflect a Higher View of Plenary, Verbal Inspiration?" *Themelios* 44.3 (2019) 477–86.
Munday, Jeremy. *Introducing Translation Studies: Theories and Applications.* 4th ed. London: Routledge, 2016.
Munday, Jeremy, et al. *Introducing Translation Studies: Theories and Applications.* 5th ed. Abingdon: Routledge, 2022.
Naudé, Jacobus A. "Equivalence." In *A Guide to Bible Translation: People, Languages, and Topics*, edited by Philip A. Noss and Charles S. Houser, 415–22. Swindon, UK: United Bible Societies, 2019.
———. "A Narrative Frame Analysis of the 1933 Afrikaans Bible." *Studia Historiae Ecclesiasticae* 37.1 (2011) 255–74.
———. "On the Threshold of the Next Generation of Bible Translations: Issues and Trends." *Meta: Journal Des Traducteurs* 50.4 (2005).
———. "Religious Translation." In *Handbook of Translation Studies*, edited by Yves Gambier and Luc van Doorslaer, 1:285–93. Amsterdam: John Benjamins, 2010.
Naudé, Jacobus A., and Cynthia L. Miller-Naudé. "Alterity, Orality and Performance in Bible Translation." In *Key Cultural Texts in Translation*, edited by Kirsten Malmkjær, et al., 299–313. Amsterdam: John Benjamins, 2018.
———. "Sacred Writings and Their Translations as Complex Phenomena: The Book of Ben Sira in the Septuagint as a Case in Point." In *Complexity Thinking in Translation Studies: Methodological Considerations*, edited by Kobus Marais and Reine Meylaerts, 180–215. New York: Routledge, 2019.
———. "Theology and Ideology in the Metatexts of Bible Translations in Muslim Contexts: A Case Study." In *Ancient Texts and Modern Readers: Studies in Ancient Hebrew Linguistics and Bible Translation*, edited by Gideon R Kotzé, et al., 280–98. Leiden: Brill, 2019.
Naudé, Jacobus A., and Tshokolo J. Makutoane. "Reanimating Orality: The Case for a New Bible Translation in Southern Sotho." *Old Testament Essays* 19.2 (2006) 723–38.
Naylor, Mark. "Consequences of the Divine Familial Terms Controversy in Bible Translation: A Neglected Voice Speaks Out." In *Controversies in Mission: Theology, People, and Practice of Mission in the 21st Century*, 249–68. Pasadena: William Carey, 2016.

Ndandililo Ni Kutyoka: The Books of Genesis and Exodus in Chiyao. Blantyre, MA: Bible Society of Malawi, 2004.
Nelson, Karen. *Ḥesed and the New Testament: An Intertextual Categorization Study.* University Park, PA: Eisenbrauns, 2023.
Newmark, Peter. *About Translation.* Clevedon, UK: Multilingual Matters, 1991.
———. "The Curse of Dogma in Translation Studies." *Lebende Sprachen* 36.3 (1991) 105–8.
———. "The Deficiencies of Skopos Theory: A Response to Anna Trosborg." *Current Issues In Language and Society* 7.3 (2000) 259–60.
Ngani Jambone Mpela Ijitite Pakulemba Ni Che Luka: Gospel of Luke in Kiyao. Morogoro, TZ: Word for the World and Pioneer Bible Translators, 2012.
Ngani Syambone Syakwamba Yesu Kristo siŵalembile Luka [The Good News according to Luke in Chiyao]. Blantyre, MW: Bible Society in Malaŵi, 1981.
Ngunga, Armindo. "Lexical Phonology and Morphology and the Ciyao Verb System." PhD diss., University of California, Berkeley, 1997. https://escholarship.org/uc/item/3xw7j0c2.
Ngunga, Armindo, and Osvaldo Faquir. *Padronização da Ortografia de Línguas Moçambicanas: relatorio do III Seminario.* Maputo, MZ: Centro de Estudos Africanos, 2012.
Nida, Eugene A. *Message and Mission: The Communication of the Christian Faith.* Pasadena: William Carey, 1990.
———. *Toward a Science of Translating: With Special Reference to Principles and Procedures Involved in Bible Translating.* Leiden: Brill, 1964.
Nida, Eugene A., and Charles R. Taber. *The Theory and Practice of Translation.* Leiden: Brill, 1969.
Niebuhr, H. Richard. *Radical Monotheism and Western Culture.* New York: Harper & Brothers, 1960.
Nord, Christiane. "Defining Translation Functions: The Translation Brief as a Guideline for the Trainee Translator." *Ilha Do Desterro* 33 (1997) 41–55.
———. "Function and Loyalty in Bible Translation." In *Apropos of Ideology: Translation Studies on Ideology—Ideologies in Translation Studies,* edited by Maria Calzada-Pérez, 89–112. London: Routledge, 2014.
———. "Functionalism and Bible Translation." In *A Guide to Bible Translation: People, Languages, and Topics,* edited by Philip A. Noss and Charles S. Houser, 459–62. Swindon: United Bible Societies, 2019.
———. "Functionalist Approaches." In *Handbook of Translation Studies,* edited by Yves Gambier and Luc van Doorslaer, 1:120–28. Amsterdam: John Benjamins, 2010.
———. "Function and Loyalty: Theology Meets Skopos." *Open Theology* 2.1 (2016) 566–80.
———. "Loyalty Revisited: Bible Translation as a Case in Point." *Translator* 7.2 (2001) 185–202.
———. "Making Otherness Accessible: Functionality and Skopos in the Translation of New Testament Texts." *Meta* 50.3 (2005) 868–80.
———. "Manipulation and Loyalty in Functional Translation." *Current Writing: Text and Reception in Southern Africa* 14.2 (2002) 32–44.
———. "Quo Vadis, Functional Translatology?" *Target* 24.1 (May 2012) 26–42.
———. "Scopos, Loyalty, and Translational Conventions." *Target* 3.1 (1991) 91–109.

———. "Skopos and (Un)Certainty: How Functional Translators Deal with Doubt." *Meta* 61.1 (2016) 29–41.

———. *Text Analysis in Translation: Theory, Methodology, and Didactic Application of a Model for Translation-Oriented Text Analysis*. Amsterdam: Rodopi, 2005.

———. *Translating as a Purposeful Activity: Functionalist Approaches Explained*. Manchester: St Jerome, 1997.

———. *Translating as a Purposeful Activity: Functionalist Approaches Explained*. 2nd ed. Abingdon, UK: Routledge, 2018.

Norris, Johnathan. "The Familial Language Debate: Understanding a Complex Issue through the Lenses of Theology and Anthropology." *Missiology* 45.2 (2017) 191–203.

Noss, Philip A. "Faithfulness." In *A Guide to Bible Translation: People, Languages, and Topics*, edited by Philip A. Noss and Charles S. Houser, 434. Swindon: United Bible Societies, 2019.

Oborji, Francis Anekwe. "In Dialogue With African Traditional Religion." *Mission Studies* 19.1 (2002) 13–35.

Oyali, Uchenna. "A Critique of Functionalist Approaches to Translation Studies." *Journal of the Linguistic Association of Nigeria* 18.1 (2015) 51–64.

Pioneer Bible Translators. "From Bible Translation to Life Transformation." https://pioneerbible.org/about/.

PROMOTYPAD. *Ndandidilo: Cibuku Candanda ca N'nabi Musa ca Cidi Mu Tawureta*. Maputo, MZ: Ethale, 2023.

Ramm, Bernard. *Special Revelation and the Word of God*. Grand Rapids: Eerdmans, 1961.

Ranger, Terence O. "Missionary Adaptation of African Religious Institutions: The Masasi Case." In *The Historical Study of African Religion with Special Reference to East and Central Africa*, edited by Terence O. Ranger and Isaria N. Kimambo, 221–51. London: Heinemann, 1972.

Redfield, Robert. *Peasant Society and Culture: An Anthropological Approach to Civilization*. Chicago: University of Chicago Press, 1956.

Reiss, Katharina. "Adequacy and Equivalence in Translation." *Bible Translator* 34.3 (July 1983) 301–8.

Reiss, Katharina, and Hans J. Vermeer. *Grundlegung einer allgemeinen Translationstheorie*. Tübingen: Niemeyer, 1984.

———. *Towards a General Theory of Translational Action: Skopos Theory Explained*. London: Routledge, 2014.

Reynolds, Gabriel Said. *The Qur'ān and Its Biblical Subtext*. London: Routledge, 2010.

Rhoads, David. "Biblical Performance Criticism: Performance as Research." *Oral Tradition* 25.1 (2010) 157–98.

Ross, Andrew C. *Blantyre Mission and the Making of Modern Malawi*. Mzuzu, MW: Luviri, 2018.

Ross, Kenneth R. *Mission, Race and Colonialism in Malawi: Alexander Hetherwick of Blantyre*. Edinburgh: Edinburgh University Press, 2023.

Routledge, Robin. "Ḥesed as Obligation: A Re-Examination." *Tyndale Bulletin* 46.1 (1995) 179–96.

Sakenfeld, Katharine Doob. *Faithfulness in Action: Loyalty in Biblical Perspective*. Philadelphia: Fortress, 1985.

———. "Love." In *Anchor Bible Dictionary*, edited by David Noel Freedman, 4:374–80. New York: Doubleday, 1992.

———. *The Meaning of Hesed in the Hebrew Bible*. Missoula, MT: Scholars, 1978.

Saleem, Teyyeb. "The Myth of Theologically 'Neutral' Terms." *Bible Translator* 74.3 (2023) 453–68.

Salt, Henry. *A Voyage to Abyssinia and Travels to the Interior of That Country [. . .]*. London: Rivington, 1814.

Sanderson, George Meredith. *A Dictionary of the Yao Language*. Zomba, MW: Government Printer, 1954.

———. *A Yao Grammar*. London: SPCK, 1922.

Sanneh, Lamin O. *Translating the Message: The Missionary Impact on Culture*. Maryknoll, NY: Orbis, 1989.

Seed Company. "Unleashing the Potential of the Global Church." https://seedcompany.com/about/.

Sheldon, Kathleen Eddy, and Jeanne Marie Penvenne. "Mozambique." In *Encyclopedia Britannica*, last updated Feb. 2, 2025. https://www.britannica.com/place/Mozambique.

Showalter, Catherine J. "Getting What You Ask for: A Study of Sociolinguistic Survey Questionnaires." In *Survey Reference Manual*, edited by Ted G Bergman, 338–60. Dallas: SIL International, 2008.

Simpson, D. P. "Vulgaris." *Cassell's Latin Dictionary*. 5th ed. London: Cassell, 1968.

Somers, Margaret. "Deconstructing and Reconstructing Class Formation Theory: Narrativity, Relational Analysis, and Social Theory." In *Reworking Class*, edited by John R. Hall, 73–105. Ithaca: Cornell University Press, 1997.

———. "Narrativity, Narrative Identity, and Social Action: Rethinking English Working-Class Formation." *Social Science History* 16.4 (1992) 591–630.

Stannus, Hugh Stannus. "The Wayao of Nyasaland." In *Harvard African Studies: Varia Africana III*, edited by EA Hooton and NI Bates, 3:229–372. Cambridge: Harvard University Press, 1922.

Stecconi, Ubaldo. "Five Reasons Why Semiotics Is Good for Translation Studies." In *Doubts and Directions in Translation Studies: Selected Contributions from the EST Congress, Lisbon 2004*, edited by Yves Gambier, et al., 15–26. Amsterdam: John Benjamins, 2007.

Steere, Edward. *Anjili ya Bwana Wetu na Mwokozi Isa Masiya kwa Mattayo [The Gospel of Our Lord and Savior Isa Messiah of Matthew]*. London: British and Foreign Bible Society, 1876.

———. *Collections for a Handbook of the Yao Language*. London: SPCK, 1871.

Stine, Philip C. "An Experiment in Audio Scriptures." *Bible Translator* 31.4 (1980) 419–23.

Stoebe, Hans J. "חֶסֶד." In *Theological Lexicon of the Old Testament*, edited by Ernst Jenni and Claus Westermann, 2:449–64. Peabody: Hendrickson, 1997.

Strauss, Mark L. *40 Questions About Bible Translation*. Grand Rapids: Kregel Academic, 2023.

———. "Bible Translation and the Myth of 'Literal Accuracy.'" *Review and Expositor* 108 (2011) 169–93.

Sundersingh, Julian. *Audio-Based Translation: Communicating Biblical Scriptures to Non-Literate People*. Bangalore: Saiacs & United Bible Societies, 2000.

Suter, W. *Genesis in Chiyao*. Likoma, MW: Universities' Mission to Central Africa, 1906.

Suter, W., and C. Ker. *Genesis–Deuteronomy: Chi-Yao*. Likoma, MW: Universities' Mission to Central Africa, 1913.

Talman, Harley, and John Jay Travis. *Understanding Insider Movements: Disciples of Jesus Within Diverse Religious Communities*. Pasadena: William Carey, 2015.

Tennent, Timothy C. *Invitation to World Missions: A Trinitarian Missiology for the Twenty-First Century*. Grand Rapids: Kregel, 2010.

Thorold, Alan. "Metamorphoses of the Yao Muslims." In *Muslim Identity and Social Change in Sub-Saharan Africa*, edited by Louis Brenner, 79–90. Bloomington: Indiana University Press, 1993.

———. "Yao Conversion to Islam." *Cambridge Journal of Anthropology* 12.2 (1987) 18–28.

———. "The Yao Muslims: Religion and Social Change in Southern Malawi." PhD diss., Cambridge University, 1995.

Toler, Kristofer Martin. "Internalization: A Key Ingredient in Achieving Naturalness in an Oral Translation." MA diss., Dallas International University, 2020.

Turaki, Yusufu. *Engaging Religions and Worldviews in Africa: A Christian Theological Method*. Carlisle, UK: Hippo, 2020.

Ubah, C. N. "The Supreme Being, Divinities and Ancestors in Igbo Traditional Religion: Evidence from Otanchara and Otanzu." *Africa* 52.2 (1982) 90–105.

UN Department of Economic and Social Affairs. *World Statistics Pocketbook: 2016 Edition*. New York: United Nations, 2016. https://unstats.un.org/unsd/publications/pocketbook/files/world-stats-pocketbook-2016.pdf

UN Office of the High Commissioner for Human Rights. "Mkamulano Wa Ilambo Yosope Pa Ufulu Wa Chipago Wa Wandu [Universal Declaration of Human Rights]." Geneva, 2000. https://www.ohchr.org/en/human-rights/universal-declaration/translations/yao.

Venuti, Lawrence. "Theses on Translation: An Organon for the Current Moment." *Quaderns* 28 (2021) 163–73.

Vermeer, Hans J. "Ein Rahmen für eine allgemeine Translationstheorie." *Lebende Sprache* 23 (1978) 99–102.

———. "Skopos and Commission in Translational Action." In *Readings in Translation*, edited by Andrew Chesterman, 173–87. Helsinki: Finn Lectura, 1989.

———. "Skopos and Commission in Translational Action." In *The Translation Studies Reader*, edited by Lawrence Venuti, 227–38. London: Routledge, 2004.

———. "Vom 'richtigen' Übersetzen." *Mitteilungsblatt für Dolmetscher und Übersetzer* 25.4 (1979) 2–8.

Vernant, Jean-Pierre. *The Origins of Greek Thought*. Ithaca: Cornell University Press, 1982.

Vitrano-Wilson, Seth. "Functionalism: Why the New Dominant Paradigm of Bible Translation Makes Syncretism Inevitable." *Journal of Biblical Missiology*, May 17, 2021. https://biblicalmissiology.org/2021/05/17/functionalism-why-the-new-dominant-paradigm-of-bible-translation-makes-syncretism-inevitable/.

Vries, Lourens de. "Bible Translations: Forms and Functions." *Bible Translator* 52.3 (2001) 306–19.

———. Foreword to *Contextual Frames of Reference in Translation: A Coursebook for Bible Translators and Teachers*, by Ernst Wendland, xiii–xiv. Manchester: St. Jerome, 2008.

Waller, Horace, ed. *The Last Journals of David Livingstone, in Central Africa, from 1865 to His Death: Continued by a Narrative of His Last Moments and Sufferings, Obtained from His Faithful Servants Chuma and Susi*, volume 1. London: John Murray, 1874.

Walls, Andrew F. *The Cross-Cultural Process in Christian History: Studies in the Transmission and Appropriation of Faith*. Maryknoll, NY: Orbis, 2002.

Walt, Barend Johannes van der. *Understanding and Rebuilding Africa: From Desperation Today Towards Expectation for Tomorrow*. Potchefstroom: Institute for Contemporary Christianity in Africa, 2003.

Wang, Shumin. "Euphemism Translation from the Perspective of Skopostheorie." *Theory and Practice in Language Studies* 10.9 (2020) 1173–78.

Warren-Rothlin, Andy. "Die Bibel in muslimischer Sprache." In *Yearbook on the Science of Bible Translation 2022*, edited by Tianji Ma. Nürnberg: VTR, forthcoming.

———. "Linguistic Equivalence in Muslim-Idiom Translation." *Bible Translator* 74.3 (2023) 350–65.

Wegner, Paul D. *The Journey from Texts to Translations: The Origin and Development of the Bible*. Grand Rapids: Baker Academic, 2004.

Wendland, Ernst R. "Yahweh – The Case for Chauta." *The Bible Translator* 43.4 (1992) 430–38.

———. *Contextual Frames of Reference in Translation: A Coursebook for Bible Translators and Teachers*. Manchester: St Jerome, 2008.

———. "Duplicating the Dynamics of Oral Discourse in Print." *Notes on Translation* 7.4 (1993) 26–44.

———. "Framing the Frames: A Theoretical Framework for the Cognitive Notion of 'Frames of Reference.'" *Journal of Translation* 6.1 (2010) 27–50.

———. *Orality and the Scriptures: Composition, Translation, and Transmission*. Dallas: SIL International, 2013.

Wilson, John D. "Scripture in an Oral Culture: The Yali of Irian Jaya." PhD diss., University of Edinburgh, 1999. https://www.academia.edu/8807995/Scripture_in_An_Oral_Culture_The_Yali_of_Irian_Jaya.

Wilt, Timothy, ed. *Bible Translation: Frames of Reference*. Abingdon, UK: Routledge, 2014.

Wilt, Timothy, and Ernst R. Wendland. *Scripture Frames and Framing: A Workbook for Bible Translators*. Stellenbosch, SA: Sun, 2008.

Winspear, Frank. "A Short History of the Universities Mission to Central Africa." *The Nyasaland Journal* 9.1 (1956) 11–50.

Wycliffe Bible Translators. "Beliefs." Last updated Mar. 5, 2024. https://www.wycliffe.org/about/our-beliefs.

———. "Why Bible Translation?" Last updated Mar. 5, 2024. https://www.wycliffe.org/about/why. (Link discontinued.)

www.ingramcontent.com/pod-product-compliance
Lightning Source LLC
Chambersburg PA
CBHW060609230426
43670CB00011B/2043